LIVES DIVIDED

Birgitta Gottlieb McGalliard is a retired foreign language teacher, who taught French and German at the college and high school levels as well as English and French at the middle school. While still teaching, she was a frequent workshop leader as well as presenter at North Carolina statewide foreign language meetings. She has also spoken to many students over the years about her family's experiences during and after World War II and shared her story with various community groups. She currently resides in Boone, North Carolina after having spent her growing up years living in various countries including Austria, Sweden, Germany, Canada and the United States because of her father's work as a German diplomat.

Both of Birgitta's parents were avid letter writers and journal keepers and kept copies of all their correspondence. This written archive, recorded in real time, informed and illuminated the memories Birgitta and her sisters shared as she was writing this memoir.

LIVES DIVIDED

My family torn apart by WWII and the Russian Gulag

Birgitta Gottlieb McGalliard

Birgitta G. McGalliard

birgitta1944@bellsouth.net

ISBN-13: 978-1490404233

Acknowledgments

Many years ago a dear friend of mine, Dr. Judith Carlson, with whom I served in the Alpha Gamma Chapter of the Delta Kappa Gamma International Society of Women Educators, encouraged me to set pen to paper and write my story down. Many others joined the chorus of encouragement over the years. Thus a seed was sown, which has now fully blossomed into *Lives Divided.*

I want to thank my friend, Kathy Prairie, in Victoria, British Columbia, who was tireless in her efforts in helping me clarify my point of view as well as other finer points of writing. She was also instrumental in coming up with the final title for my book.

Another person to whom I am very indebted is Dr. Peter Petschauer, Professor Emeritus from Appalachian State University. As I began the revision process, he spent countless hours both reading my manuscript as well as discussing it with me over a delicious cup of coffee in his home. Because of our similar backgrounds, both of us being native German speakers, it made it easier to discuss the finer points of historical and cultural references.

Many thanks also go to Judy Geary, my final editor, who through her enthusiasm, encouragement and helpful suggestions, served as the last stepping stone in making it possible for *Lives Divided* to be published.

Particular thanks also go to:

Joyce Cheek, my sweet sister-in-law,
who has always been more like a true sister to me,
for her helpful suggestions especially regarding
the first chapter

Chrissy, my wonderful daughter-in-law,
who spent lots of time listening to her mother-in-law
and making suggestions on how to make
the language flow better

Billy, my technical genius son,
who answered his mother's call for technical help
with patience and kindness when the computer
did funky things, which happened quite frequently with
his inexperienced mother

Karin Östling, my darling middle sister,
who made many helpful suggestions along the way
and complemented my own memories as we talked about
the life we shared growing up

Ingrid Wegener, my darling older sister,
who supplied me with many of the details of our family's life
before I was even born, helped me remember some of
the details I had forgotten, and told me
stories of long ago

Bill, my wonderful and patient husband,
who put up with my spending countless hours at the computer
over the years working on one edition of my book
after the other and who always encouraged me
not to give up

In Loving Memory
Of
My Parents
Roland and Ruth Gottlieb
Their strong love for each other while living through years of great uncertainty and suffering inspired me.
Their indomitable spirit and steadfastness served as my guiding light.
My admiration for them grew commensurately as our family's story unfolded in
Lives Divided.

Roland Herman Adalbert Gottlieb &
Ruth Ingeborg Lönnqvist
Wedding date: September 7, 1935

Contents

11. I: Beginning School, Borås 1951
21. II: My New Mission, Borås 1951
32. III: First Big Move, Berlin, 1940- 41
41. IV: Move to Sofia, Bulgaria, 1941
47. V: Bombardments, Bulgaria, 1941-42
59. VI: Fleeing Sofia, Bulgaria, 1944
67. VII: Excursion to Wels, Austria, 1944
72. VIII: Place of my Birth, St. Gilgen, 1944
80. IX: Captured, Bulgaria, 1944
89. X: The "White Bus" Journey, November 1945
101. XI: Renewed Hope, Borås, 1950
109. XII: Devastating News, October 1952
117. XIII: Adjusting to New Circumstances, Fall 1952 – Fall 1953
126. XIV: Mollösund, Summer 1953
135. XV: Mollösund Here We Come!, Summer 1953
144. XVI: Changes in the Air, Fall 1953
153. XVII: The First Postcard, January 1954
163. XVIII: Mother's Mission, Germany, 1954
173. XIX: Waiting, Spring 1954
186. XX: Hope Renewed, Fall 1954 – Spring 1955
198. XXI: Patience Rewarded, Summer 1955
214. XXII: Reunion, August 1955
226. XXIII: The Big Day, August 20, 1955
234. XXIV: Interviews, Mollösund, 1955
245. XXV: Fulfilled, 1955—
254. Glossary & Appendix

LIVES DIVIDED

Gustaf Adolfsskolan
in Borås before renovation in the 1930s

CHAPTER I

Beginning School

Borås, 1951

I will never forget the day I began first grade in Sweden just a few days after my seventh birthday. Before that day I never realized that my family was anything but ordinary.

All summer long I eagerly looked forward to returning to Borås from our little cottage in the fishing village Mollösund on Sweden's west coast. I was finally going to be joining my sister Karin in that huge mysterious three-story red brick building, the Gustaf Adolfsskolan. The school was only a short walk from my grandfather's house, where I lived in a small apartment on the third floor with my mother and two sisters.

The only thing I dreaded about starting school was that I had to leave my beloved grandfather and no longer be able to spend my days with him. As things turned out, however, *Morfar* was the one who left me rather than the other way around because he died quite unexpectedly in the middle of the summer while we were still in Mollösund.

After returning to town at the end of August, it was very difficult for me to get used to the idea that *Morfar* was not in his apartment below us anymore and that I could no longer simply run in to see him whenever I wanted to. I was therefore that much more eager to start school. At least my days would now be filled with going to school every day instead.

By the end of my first morning at school, I really wished I had stayed at home. Instead of being the happy day I had anticipated for so long, it turned out to be a nightmare. After telling my new classmates that my father was in *fängelse,* they started to snicker behind their hands, point fingers at me and ask me dumb questions. I felt completely humiliated.

I simply could not understand why they were taunting me like that. How could they possibly think that my father was a criminal just because he was in prison? Mamma had told me many times that the Russians had captured him while he was working as a diplomat in Bulgaria. This happened a few days after I was born in Austria. Surely, that didn't mean that he was a criminal, did it?

Before going to school that morning I was happy as a little lark and very excited. I was finally old enough to leave the house with Mamma instead of simply having to watch her from our open balcony climb on her bicycle for her quarter-hour ride to her job in the center of our town. Swaying our clasped hands back and forth, the two of us happily hummed some familiar melodies as we trotted and skipped the three blocks to school. It didn't bother me in the least that neither one of us could remember the words to the songs. I was just full of happy anticipation.

I was also feeling especially pretty because Mamma had splurged and bought me the prettiest light blue dress with a smocked bodice and a dainty white lace collar, albeit a size too large for me. Being practical and frugal, she said she wanted me to be able to wear it a long time. I didn't mind at all because being the youngest of three girls, I hardly ever got to wear anything but hand-me-downs of hand-me-downs. Mamma never had enough money for such luxuries as a new dress. Instead she relied on the goodness of her friends who gave us their children's outgrown clothes. Wearing a new dress therefore made me feel very special this particular morning.

Before long, Mamma and I arrived at the school where we went up the three flights of stairs to my first grade classroom. We were not alone because other children with their mothers crowded the stairwell, all heading for the same floor.

Full of seven–year-old curiosity, I took the first step into my new classroom. The room was gigantic and filled with lots of desks arranged in straight, neat rows. A piece of paper lay on top of each desk in front of a recessed inkwell with a penholder beside it. While wondering if one of those desks had my name written on it, I let my eyes wander to the front of the room where a black chalkboard covered the entire wall behind the teacher's desk, which sat on a raised platform. Above the chalkboard a long banner showed the capital and small letters of the Swedish alphabet. Oh, how eager and anxious I was to learn how to write those letters and put them together to form words. I was more than ready!

The room was very crowded and noisy. Boys and girls were running around while mothers were talking to each other. Eagerly I scanned the room trying to discover who my new teacher was. This turned out to be a little more difficult than I expected because the room was filled with so many grown-ups. Just as I was about to give up, a young, pretty woman, her blond hair tied up in a bun at the back of her head, turned around and looked straight at me. When she waved and grinned at me, I smiled back at her hoping that she was my new teacher. I liked her already and was confident she would like me as well.

Turning away, I looked around at all the children, wondering if I knew any of them and who might become my best friend. I only recognized two girls and a boy because they lived in my neighborhood, but I was very eager to make new friends.

Before Mamma left with all the other mothers, she pointed to a desk and told me it was mine because the name BIRGITTA GOTTLIEB was printed on that piece of paper I noticed earlier. I wasted no time claiming it, quickly plopping into the chair behind the desk and reverently touching the inkwell before I carefully opened the wooden lid to see what was hidden inside its huge cavern. It was still empty, but I hoped it would soon be full of many exciting new textbooks and notebooks. I felt right at home and cheerfully waved goodbye to Mamma as she left the classroom with all the other mothers.

I was ready to begin school.

When the teacher clapped her hands, a hush fell over the room. After everyone settled down, she welcomed us and said she hoped we would have a wonderful school year. She also told us that her name was Miss Gustafsson. Then she handed out books and admonished us to take good care of them since other children would be using them next year as well. There was a book with lots of numbers in it and another one with many pictures and big words. I was totally enthralled. My very own books! At least for this school year.

Next, the teacher asked us to say our names and tell something about ourselves. She pointed to a girl with pigtails sitting in the first desk in the row closest to the window. "Why don't you begin, Kristina?"

Because my desk was all the way over in the fourth row closer to the door, I knew it would be a while before it was my turn. I didn't mind though because now I could just sit back and listen to what my new classmates had to say.

As one after the other told the class something about themselves, I couldn't for the life of me understand why none of them mentioned where their mothers worked. Instead everyone just talked about what his or her father did. They also talked about how many sisters and brothers they had and where they lived. That was why I decided to follow their example when it was my turn.

As soon as the boy in front of me stopped talking and sat down, I got up from my seat, completely unafraid or nervous. "My name is Birgitta Gottlieb and Pappa is in *fängelse* and I have never even seen him. I have two sisters, Ingrid and Karin and we live in my grandfather's house." The words just came tumbling out in my eagerness to share with my new classmates.

Shocked silence followed my words. Twenty-three sets of seven year-old eyes were staring at me, their owners' mouths wide open. Why was everyone looking so strangely at me? What had I said? Then snickering and pointing fingers at me, they bombarded me with the silliest questions I had ever heard. "What did your pappa do?" "Did he rob a bank or something?" "Why haven't you seen him?" "Did he kill someone?"

Their outburst stunned me. What were they talking about? My pappa hadn't killed anyone. Why did they think Pappa was some sort of criminal because he was in prison? As far as I knew, he had never killed anyone or stolen any money. How could they even think such a thing? Why were they so mean and hateful?

Totally overwhelmed, I just stood there as if frozen to the floor while they continued to pelt me with their stupid questions. I simply could not move.

A minute more or so passed before I finally shouted, "No! No! No!" as I stomped my feet on the floor. "You are wrong. Pappa didn't do anything bad. He is not a thief or a murderer! It was the Russians who took him during the war!"

To my great chagrin I felt hot stinging tears coursing down my cheeks. Sitting down with a thud in my new desk, I wished with all my heart that I had never come to school that morning. I put my head down on my desk because I did not want my mean new classmates to see me crying like a baby. The tears would not stop. Snuffling into my tightly fisted hands, I wondered what I had said that was so bad.

Before long I felt someone squeezing my shoulders and whispering a few comforting words into my ear. Slowly I looked up and saw that it was my new teacher telling me that everything would be all right and that I should try to stop crying. To please her I gave it a valiant effort even though I was still smarting from my classmates' assault.

It was a nightmare except I was very much awake. I wished I could go back home to *Morfar* and never come back to school again.

The rest of the day passed in a blur, the minutes until the final bell sounded ticking by excruciatingly slow. I was unable to pay attention to anything the teacher said. All I could think about was going home and never coming back again. Even recess was no fun because some of my classmates continued to pelt me with questions to which I had no answers. I was sick and tired of it all. My teacher was kind though and tried to comfort me.

What a big disappointment my first day of school turned out to be! It certainly did not resemble the magical day I had envisioned for so long. All my wonderful expectations flew out the window. I did not at all feel like Glittran, which means glitter, *Morfar*'s special nickname for me because he always said I glittered or sparkled like sunshine. Could he see me now, he would quickly realize that his nickname for me did not fit today and ask me why I was so unhappy.

When the bell finally rang announcing the end of the school day, I ran home as fast as my little legs would carry me. My plan was to beg Mamma to let me stay home with *Morfar* from now on. School was no fun after all and I never wanted to go back.

After reaching *Morfar*'s house, I rushed up the first flight of stairs to the second floor where I was going to wait with *Morfar* until my sisters came home. I knew that Mamma wouldn't be home from work until five o'clock.

Just as I was getting ready to open *Morfar's* apartment door, I came to a sudden stop. In my unhappy state of mind I had totally forgotten that *Morfar* didn't live there anymore. A new family with two boys had moved in a week ago. *Morfar* was dead!

"Why did you have to die, *Morfar*? Don't you know how much I need you?" I wailed as I slid down on the floor. Crouching up against the wall beside his closed door, I cried my heart out for the second time in one day. My eyes were already puffy and swollen. I am sure I looked a fright, but I didn't care.

As I sat there with my head on my drawn-up knees, I couldn't help thinking about that awful day in July when we found out that *Morfar* had passed away.

I was just getting ready to go to a birthday party when the mistress of the Mollösund telephone and telegraph office came in person to our cottage to deliver the devastating news from *Moster* Anne-Marie, my mother's oldest sister. Overcome with grief I threw myself on my bed, curled up into a tight ball, and cried my heart out. How could *Morfar* possibly be dead? He had just left us a few days before after paying us a quick surprise visit at our tiny summer cottage. I knew he had a cold when he came, but nobody usually died from that. It was not until I was fully grown that I understood that it was his weakened heart that had killed him rather than the cold.

Sitting now in front of his closed door, I remembered how my friend's father came and picked me up, screaming and kicking all the way over to her house where the birthday party was already in full swing. How could anyone possibly have thought that I would enjoy going to a birthday party when my heart was broken? It could not have been any fun for my friend either having to put

Birgitta and *Morfar*, Christmas, 1950

up with such an unhappy guest. I know it was the worst day in my life—that is until today, my first day of school.

Now, just a few weeks later, here I was sitting in front of what used to be *Morfar*'s apartment, feeling sorry for myself and wondering what to do until the rest of the family came home.

I began to think about all the things *Morfar* and I had always done together when I spent my days with him while Mamma went to work. How often had I not accompanied him to "inspect" a construction site or waited for him in one of the church pews while he practiced with his men's choir? Every day I used to sit beside him at the miniature drawing table he made for me, which was now upstairs in my room instead of beside his much bigger architect's table on the second floor. Now, we would never again snuggle up in his huge bed for a nap or take another trip up north to visit my cousins. He would never again give me an orange as a reward for going to the dentist. Why, oh why did he die? How I missed being together with him.

Suddenly I sprang to my feet. *Morfar* was no longer in his apartment. He was never coming back. Why should I sit here and pretend that he was? It was no use! He had deserted me when I needed him. He had no right to leave me like this! I became angry just thinking about it.

In this angry state of mind, I forced myself to climb the next set of circular stairs to our apartment. But when I reached the top landing, I could go no further. I simply could not face entering our empty home. Instead I plopped down on the stair just below it to wait for everyone else, however long that would be.

Fortunately, it was not too long until I heard my two older sisters, Ingrid and Karin, come rushing up the stairs. Surprised to see me sitting there they came to a sudden stop.

"What in the world is the matter with you, Gittan? Did something bad happen at school today? Are you hurt?" Ingrid demanded to know when she saw how swollen and puffy looking my eyes were.

"The children laughed at me when I told them that pappa was in *fängelse*."

When I began to cry again, Karin and Ingrid hunkered down, one on each side of me and just hugged me. Like two little mother hens they tried to console me. It felt so good not to be alone any more. Together the three of us waited for Mamma to come home.

It could not have been too long after that when we finally heard the outside door open and close below and Mamma starting up the staircase. As she rounded the last set of stairs, I got up and threw myself into her arms. "Mamma, Mamma, all my new classmates were laughing at me and asking me stupid questions about Pappa. They think he is a criminal."

"Why in the world would they think that, Gittan?" she asked as she tried to catch her breath after my hurling myself so unceremoniously at her.

"I don't know, but when I told them that Pappa is in *fängelse,* the children all started laughing at me and asking me if he had killed someone or stolen something. I just don't understand why they would think something like that. Pappa didn't do anything bad like they think, did he?" The words just came rushing out of my mouth. It was such a relief to be able to tell Mamma what had happened.

"Of course not, Gittan. My poor baby, you just used the wrong word. You should have said that Pappa is in *fångenskap*, which is the Swedish word for someone who has been captured as the result of a war. *Fängelse,* you see, is where people have to go after they have committed a crime. These are two different words. Unfortunately you used the wrong one." Mamma sounded very sad.

Years later I wondered whether my first day of school would have turned out differently, if I had just known to use the correct word.

But then again it might not have made any difference at all. As my mother went on to explain, my classmates probably didn't even know that Russia was another country far away and not just another city somewhere in Sweden.

"Your pappa didn't do anything wrong, Gittan. Don't ever think that he did. He was just in the wrong place at the wrong time. It wasn't his fault that the Russians captured him along with all the other diplomats at the German Embassy during the war when they invaded Bulgaria. You know that, don't you? That is why you have nothing to be ashamed of." Another deep sigh escaped her.

Although I felt relieved that Pappa was not in a prison for criminals like the children at school thought he was and that I had just used the wrong word, I was still puzzled why the other children didn't understand about this war that had robbed me of my father. "I know all about it and so why don't they?" I asked Mamma.

"Well, you see, Sweden has not been at war in almost a hundred and fifty years. Therefore your classmates and their families have not experienced what it is like to be at war or to have enemies who take prisoners of war, like the Russians did with your pappa. You were too little yourself when we came here from Austria in 1945 to remember all this. But you have heard us talk about this all your life and that is why you know all about it," Mamma smiled down at me wistfully.

Nodding in agreement, I knew she was right about that. Long ago she had put up a huge map of the world that took up half of our living room wall. We had marked all the places with colorful flag pins that were important to us as a family. There was a pin marking St. Gilgen in Austria where I was born, for instance, and another one showing Sofia, Bulgaria where Father was captured and my sister Karin was born.

Just recently we had stuck a pin into a place called Vorkuta where we believed Pappa was being held prisoner. It was way up at the top of the map in a country called the Soviet Union, far above the Arctic Circle and close to the North Pole. It had to be absolutely frigid there. Just thinking about it made me shiver. Poor Pappa!

"But how in the world am I going to explain this to my new classmates?" I asked.

"Don't worry, Gittan. I will just go with you to school again tomorrow and explain it to your class. What do you think about that?"

I eagerly agreed with this plan. As promised, Mamma went with me to school the next day, and after explaining the difference between being a prisoner and a POW to my class, no one laughed at me anymore or made my life miserable because of it except maybe for one girl. She was the biggest girl in the class, who teased and taunted me throughout our five years together. To be quite fair, it was not always because of my father but also because I was less well off than she. She teased me about my hand-me-down clothes, for example, or about the fact that Mamma could not afford riding or piano lessons.

None of that mattered in the long run, however, considering what happened later that changed everything.

CHAPTER II

My New Mission

Borås, 1951

That first day of school I learned a very important lesson, and it was not how to read, write and do arithmetic, although over time I learned how to do all those things. No, what I learned was that my family was anything but ordinary and I had absolutely nothing to be ashamed of.

In retrospect, I think of that day as the day I began to really grow up. I became very intent on trying to understand what it was about my family that made us different from everyone else around me although it took many years before I was able to put all the pieces together that made up the extraordinary fabric of our life.

Until that day I had been content, taking everything for granted just like all children of that age usually do. I had been perfectly happy living in the present and never worrying or thinking about what went on before as long as I had a mother who loved and spoiled me, sisters who helped take care of me, relatives galore who gave me presents, a cottage on the west coast where I could spend the summers, a bed to sleep in, food in my stomach, goodies to eat, and friends and toys to play with. What more could anyone wish for?

But I knew better after that first day of school. I had no father like the other children in my class, and my mother had to work and couldn't stay at home like my classmates' mothers did. I became envious of them because their mothers were waiting for them when they returned after a day at school while I always came home to an empty house.

As if that wasn't bad enough, I discovered that people you love very much can be there one day and gone the next. One day *Morfar* was visiting, then puff he was gone forever. As long as he was alive, I never really missed not having a father. *Morfar* had occupied that vacant space in my life.

Everything was different after that first day of school. For the first time I wondered about what had actually happened to prevent my father from being with us in Sweden. All I knew was what Mother had told me many times, but words like the Soviet Union, POW, or diplomat, were words without real substance. I had never met a prisoner or been in a war and the Soviet Union was just a place marked with a pin on our big wall map, just like Germany, Austria, and Bulgaria. Whenever Mamma described Pappa as a diplomat, she always sounded very proud, which meant that we should be proud too. But I didn't really understand what any of those words actually meant.

However, from that first day at school, I peppered my mother with lots of questions or listened intently to conversations between Ingrid and her, especially when they were talking about things that happened before we came to Sweden. As young as I was, I really wanted to understand everything. I never got tired of hearing the answers over and over again to questions such as: "Why was Pappa taken? How come Karin was born in Bulgaria and I in Austria? What was it like in Bulgaria? Did you have enough to eat when the bombs fell? Does Pappa know that he has another daughter? Does he know my name? When will those awful Soviets release Pappa? Why didn't he come with us when we came to Sweden? How come Ingrid speaks German and Karin and I don't? How did you meet Pappa? Does he speak Swedish?" I was hungry for the answers.

It also dawned on me that Ingrid, who was eight years older than I, might know the answers to some of these questions. Even to this day, I still query her about those early years, hoping that she will remember some things she has not yet told me. If I am lucky, she gives me detailed descriptions of events or places. But sometimes she also becomes frustrated and simply answers, "That was such a long time ago. How do you expect me to remember that? I was just a little girl."

I also began to pay closer attention when I discovered my mother crying, which I often saw her do. Until now I had always thought that was quite normal. As I learned more about our story, I became much more sensitive to these emotional swings in her. Even though most of the time she tried to hide her fears by acting upbeat and cheerful, I was finally old enough to understand that she had a very good reason to be worried and unhappy.

A week or so after I started first grade, I found Mother crying again. I had been playing outside in the street with my friends from the neighborhood, which is what I usually did after school if the weather was nice. I suddenly realized how late it was and that Mother must be home from the office.

Rushing up the three flights of stairs and through the door to our living room, I shouted, "I am home, Mamma. Where are you?"

I loved it whenever she was home before me and answered with "Here I am!"

This time she didn't answer me even though I could see her sitting right there on the sofa in the living room. Something must be terribly wrong! Her shoulders were hunched, and she was supporting one elbow on her knee, and it looked like she was crying.

Rushing over to her, I threw my skinny arms around her neck and hugged her really hard as I softly whispered into her ear, "Mamma, what is wrong? Are you sick? Can I kiss the hurt away?" which is what she always did whenever I hurt myself.

"No, Gittan, I wish it were that simple, but I am not sick. I am just very sad today." She hugged me back. Her eyes were swollen and her face was still wet from tears, which she tried to wipe away with an already soggy-looking handkerchief.

"But why, Mamma?" I asked.

"Well, you see, today is the seventh of September. Your pappa and I got married exactly sixteen years ago, and I don't even know whether he is alive or not." Once again wet tears rolled down her face as she gazed at the picture frame lying beside her on the sofa. She must have dropped the familiar picture of my father when I surprised her with my hug.

For once I was lost for words, but not for long because I knew I had to try and cheer her up somehow. I could not stand to see her so sad. Then I had a bright idea. Perhaps if she remembered the happy time when she got married, she would stop crying.

"Mamma, why don't you tell me about what it was like when you and Pappa got married, and I don't mean for you to tell me about the Ramnakyrkan, where the wedding took place. I know all about the church and have seen it hundreds of times."

I was exaggerating a little, but I was really quite familiar with it since it was an old church that stood in the park where I often went skating when the nearby lake, Ramnasjön, was frozen over. We also put up a miniature copy of it as part of a snowy winter village scene every Christmas.

Mother picked up Father's picture once again. Nodding her head several times, she was clearly considering how best to answer my question.

"You were a beautiful bride," I prodded, smiling brightly in encouragement as I pointed to their wedding picture hanging on the wall behind us. "You both look so happy. What was it like to get married, Mamma?"

"Where do I begin, Gittan? Yes, I was a very happy bride. My dream was finally coming true. The man I had loved for five years was going to be mine forever." She sighed deeply at those last words.

"Why did it take five years before you got married? That is an awful long time to wait, isn't it? Didn't you know right away that you loved each other?" I asked innocently.

"That is a long story in and of itself. Suffice it to say that your pappa was still a student at the Vienna University of Economics and Business in Austria when I met him in 1930 at the Swedish (Svea) Club. When he proposed to me four days after we met, he warned me that it would take five years before we could get married because he needed to finish his studies and get a job first."

"But why was he studying in Vienna and not in Sweden?" I continued my questioning, really getting into the subject now. I sensed that I was going to hear things I hadn't heard before but had often wondered about. I was right because what Mother told me that evening went a long way towards explaining our extraordinary circumstances and why I was so different from my classmates.

"Your father was Austrian and not Swedish and that is why he was studying at the university in Vienna and not here in Sweden," Mother replied.

I knew that Father was from Austria, of course, but it was still difficult for me to understand how they could have gotten to know each other when they were living in different countries. "Did you study in Vienna as well and that is how you met?"

"No, Gittan, I did not go there to study but went to school right here in Borås, where I grew up in this very house we are now living in," Mother replied patiently.

"But how then did you meet Pappa if he was in Vienna and you were in Sweden?" I persisted. I was determined to get to the bottom of this nagging question.

"Because I went there to visit some of your *mormor*'s friends during Christmas 1929." Seeing that I still seemed somewhat puzzled, Mother went on to explain that she had spent the fall after graduating from high school in 1929 taking care of a very sick little boy in Berlin. "His mother was a childhood friend of your grandmother's." Pointing at me, she went on to say, "He was the same age as you, Gittan. Since it was hard work, my mother thought I needed a small vacation. She wrote to another friend from her school days who had just moved to Vienna because of her husband's job and asked if I could come for a visit."

"But that still doesn't explain how you met Pappa," I countered.

"Yes, I know, it is a little complicated. But let me tell you what happened then. My sister Ingrid, your *moster*, had also visited Vienna recently. She recommended that I go to the Svea Club where university students got together for some fun activities, such as dancing, which she knew I dearly loved to do. And that is where I met your pappa."

"That is a funny name, Svea Club. What does it mean? And how come Pappa was there?" I wasn't giving up easily.

"The club was founded by students who were thankful to have

been invited to Sweden when they were young children right after World War I was over. You see, many people were starving in Austria at that time and since Sweden was not involved in the war, Swedish families wanted to help out by hosting a child from Vienna for the summer. Your pappa was one of those children, and that is how he came to Sweden in the first place. He was only nine years old at the time, just a little older than you. He fell in love with his Swedish family, the Karlssons, who were farmers in Sörmland, and they with him."

Pappa and his two brothers & father, shortly before his father's death in 1919

This was a lengthy explanation, but I was hanging on to Mother's every word because I had not really heard much about these things before. By this time my two older sisters had also joined us on the sofa. I could tell they were just as fascinated as I was even though I am sure Ingrid knew some of this already.

Her comment confirmed my suspicion. "Mamma, tell Karin and Gittan why Pappa came back to Sweden that following Christmas."

"It is true what Ingrid is saying. After your father returned to Vienna in the fall, the Karlssons wrote to his parents begging them to let their son come and visit again during his Christmas holiday. And that is exactly what happened. While he was there, his father died and his adopted family wrote to his mother, suggesting he should stay on a little longer to ease the burden on *Omama*. She reluctantly but thankfully agreed to this plan since it was one mouth less for her to feed. Your *Onkel* Heinz was only seven and *Onkel* Walther eleven years old at that time. Come to think about it, that is about the same ages as you and Karin," Mother answered as she smiled down at

Karin and me.

I could tell Mother was really caught up in her story for her tears had disappeared as she relived the happier past. I was pleased to see her smiling again and decided to continue our trip down memory lane.

"How long did he stay, or did he never go back to his mamma? "

"Of course he went back home but not until after the following summer. After spending so much time in Sweden and attending school during the spring of 1920, he fell in love with everything Swedish and vowed one day to find a Swedish girl to marry. And as you see, he was true to his word for he found me, didn't he?" Another happy smile punctuated her words.

All three of us nodded in agreement. Naturally, we were happy that Pappa had found Mamma and married her.

"Did Pappa only stay in Sweden that spring? And how could he understand what the teacher was saying at school?" Having just started school myself, I was particularly interested in hearing Mother's reply to my last question.

Mamma looked at me quizzically before she answered. "When you spend long enough time in a country, it is easy to learn the language, especially if you are young like your father was. It helped him that he was able to return to Sweden several summers in a row until *Omama* no longer could afford it. Her financial situation was very bad after the stock market crashed in the 1920's, which was followed by a severe depression. She lost everything, including her inheritance from Croatia. But by that time your father was speaking Swedish just like his native German."

"But I thought he lived in Austria. Do they speak German there as well?"

"Of course, Gittan, all Austrians speak German since there is no such thing as an Austrian language," she explained.

Her answer made me feel a little dumb especially because I actually knew that all Austrians speak German. What I didn't understand, however, was why I didn't speak German as well since I was Austrian.

"How come Ingrid speaks German when she wasn't even born in Austria like I was but in Sweden?" I couldn't help that I sounded a little whiny, but this was something that had always bothered me. Whenever Mamma and Ingrid chattered away in German, it made me jealous, perhaps because of the special bond they seemed to have at that moment—which excluded me. I also didn't think it was fair that they had a secret language that nobody else in the family could understand.

"Ingrid lived in Austria when she was your age, Gittan, and went to German-speaking schools even when we lived in Bulgaria. We only spoke Swedish in the family when no outsiders were present, which is why she also spoke it fluently when we came back to Sweden after the war in 1945."

"That still doesn't explain why Karin and I don't speak any German. We lived in Austria as well," I persisted, her answer obviously not having satisfied me.

"Because German is not my native language, it was harder for me to speak it naturally to you when you were a baby. It was also a question of time since I now had to work all day and couldn't stay at home with you. Besides, by then we had already moved to Sweden, and I saw no need to try to keep up both languages. If your pappa were here with us, I am sure you would be speaking German as well. But he isn't. We don't even know whether he will ever come home to us. Oh, how much more difficult and complicated everything is without him!"

Was that frustration or dejection coloring her voice? It was hard to tell because both feelings, under the circumstances, were completely understandable. Seven years had gone by and we still did not know whether Father was dead or alive.

A few minutes passed before anyone could speak again. We were all thinking the same thing, that is, wishing we could know something definite about Father's whereabouts and fate.

"Girls, I am glad we are talking about this. You need to understand how everything came to pass. It is always good to remember the past. At the same time we must not give up hope that your pappa will come home to us again." I could tell Mother was making a valiant effort to sound more optimistic and upbeat than she really was. It cannot have been easy for her.

"Did Pappa always plan to be a diplomat?" This was something else that had puzzled me. "Perhaps if he hadn't been one, the Soviets wouldn't have captured him, and he would be here with us right now instead."

"Yes, Gittan, sometimes I have wondered that myself. The answer to your first question, however, is no. He never really planned on being a diplomat. That kind of happened by chance as so many things in life often do."

"What do you mean, Mamma?" Karin, who had been sitting quietly until now, chimed in.

"Well, it is a little complicated, but I will try to explain it to you." She sounded a little happier to be talking about life the way it used to be before Father was captured by the Soviets, which changed her life so radically. "The summer after we met— the summer of 1930—your father came up from Austria to visit me in Borås. Because I didn't want my parents to know yet that he had come all that way just to see me, we decided to pretend he was there to study the weaving industry for which our town is famous, as you know. My parents soon saw through this scheme, but because they really liked this young man, they were happy to see him stay on to court me." Mother smiled at the memory of her and Father's unsuccessful little ruse.

She went on to describe how Father courted her for the next five years. Luckily for both of them, he was able to spend every semester break in Sweden after the Austrian Consul in Göteborg hired him as his temporary assistant that first summer. Apparently the consul became very fond of him and really appreciated his hard work. This made it possible for my parents to see each other at least four months out of the year while having to stay in touch by mail for the rest of the time.

No wonder a file marked 1930-34 in Father's beautiful handwriting is so thick, I thought, as Mother continued to tell how he ended up becoming a diplomat.

"Then after your pappa graduated in 1934 with his *Diplomkaufmann* degree, he was thrilled when the consul recommended him for a permanent position at the Austrian Embassy in Stockholm. With this appointment we were finally able to get married. Oh, what a joy that was! We were so happy. When Ingrid was born

Ingrid & Pappa, 1938

a year later, life became even more perfect. Life was really smiling at us then," Mother finished with a smile as she squeezed Ingrid's hand.

"But why was he working at the German Legation in Sofia and not at the Austrian one?" Ingrid asked. "I have always wondered about that. I didn't understand it back then because I was too young, but now after studying world history in school, I wonder if it has something to do with Germany's annexation of Austria in 1938?"

"Yes, it does, Ingrid. I am so glad you have been paying attention at school. It has everything to do with what happened back in 1938. After Germany annexed Austria, the Austrian Embassy was dissolved because the country was no longer independent but rather under the rule of Germany. Your father was asked if he would be willing to work for the German Embassy instead. After thinking about it for a while, he agreed to switch, especially if it meant he could remain in Stockholm. By that time your brother Helmut was also born. It seemed the right thing to do at the time."

"What happened after that since Pappa ended up in Sofia instead of staying in Stockholm?" This was fascinating. If I had ever heard this before, I must either not have understood anything or had simply failed to pay as close attention as I was today. But after what happened on my first day at school, I was determined to try to understand why my family seemed so different from everybody else's.

"Well, Gittan, that is another chapter in our lives. But what you must understand, as young as you are, we never have any guarantee that life will always go as we plan or wish. Far from it! What happened to us is certainly proof of that. The long and the short of it is that the *Auswärtiges Amt* or Foreign Office in Berlin had other plans for your father. In 1940, after two years at the Stockholm Embassy, he was transferred to the AA, the abbreviated form for the *Auswärtiges Amt* in Berlin. He was very unhappy about that

decision because he didn't want to leave peaceful Sweden and move to Germany, who was at war by then. That is the reason he tried so hard to come up with an alternative plan. Unfortunately, nothing came of it before it was time for him to leave for Berlin as ordered." At this juncture in her story, Mother sighed wistfully.

I have often wondered how things would have turned out if Father had not agreed to go to Berlin. Would I have been born in Sweden? Would I always have had a father as I grew up? That move definitely played a decisive role in what happened to the Gottlieb family just a few years later.

Seeing how sad and unhappy Mother looked again, my sisters and I jumped to our feet, reached out and took hold of Mamma's hands and pulled her to her feet.

"We are famished, Mamma. It is high time to get supper on the table," my practical sister Ingrid declared.

We hurried off in different directions, with Mother and Ingrid going into the kitchen to fix supper, Karin into the dining room to set the table, and me into my little cubbyhole of a room that used to be a closet before Mother converted it last spring into a small bedroom for me. I was always an expert at making myself scarce when work was to be done, as my sisters are more than willing to testify.

I was still sitting on my bed, trying to digest everything we had talked about, when I heard Ingrid calling us in for supper. Wasting no time because I knew that my all time favorite *falukorv*, a type of Swedish bologna, mashed potatoes and peas were on the menu, I dashed into the dining room, which also doubled as Mother's bedroom.

CHAPTER III

First Big Move

Berlin, 1940-41

Every year on August 31, my birthday, Mother always told me that Father had been captured by the Soviets just a few days after I was born in 1944. Somehow the two events were linked in her mind as they also became in mine.

"Does Pappa know that he has a third daughter?" I asked her every year never tiring of hearing her unchanging answer.

"Yes, Gittan, he does because I sent a telegram to him in Bulgaria from Austria just after you were born. I know he received it because he sent me one a few days later in which he welcomed you into the family and stated that your name should be Birgitta. That was the last time I heard from him."

That answer had satisfied me until I started school. Before that, I never thought to ask her why that was the last time, probably because I knew he had been captured shortly afterwards. With my newfound awareness, however, I realized that there had to be something more behind his capture. I began to suspect the answer lay in what transpired in the years prior to my birth, especially after what Mother told me the day I caught her crying on her sixteenth wedding anniversary.

In writing about the events that took place before I was born or was able to fully understand what happened, I am truly grateful that both my parents were prolific letter writers or had a penchant for recording their thoughts in small notebooks, as was the case with my mother. Over the years they had ample opportunity to write long and detailed letters when separated by great distances from each other. This happened far too frequently to suit either of them. Rather than throwing these letters away, they believed in saving them in marked folders. How these folders escaped destruction through the vagaries of war and several moves from one country to another is a miracle.

After Father disappeared in 1944, Mother continued to save all the letters she received as well as to keep carbon copies of those she sent. These she filed in folders, which she kept in the *secretaire*, a mahogany desk with three deep drawers that stood in the same room where we ate and Mother slept. Because she needed to find out what had happened to Father, she was always appealing to some government official or other. As a result these file folders grew very thick over time. In addition, she kept up a brisk correspondence with all the friends she had made while she was away from Sweden, letters she also saved.

One day, when I noticed her putting a letter she had received from one of these many friends into one of those files, I asked her why she didn't just throw it away.

"I save all these letters so that I can go back and reread them later."

"But Mamma, why would you want to go back and read all those old letters again?" little Miss Curiosity wanted to know.

"In some cases, it makes me happy because many of these letters remind me of what life used to be like when your pappa was still with us. When we were engaged, for instance, he wrote the most wonderful and loving letters from Vienna that are like lollipops for me today. And now that both *Mormor* and *Morfar* are gone, it is as if they are right there beside me whenever I reread the encouraging words they wrote after we left Sweden. The same is true for all our friends with whom I still stay in contact, friends from Austria and Bulgaria and friends who don't live in Borås any longer," Mother concluded as she showed me all the files with different names printed on their side tabs.

Leaning down to get a closer look, I could tell that many of the letters were written in German while others were written in some other foreign language or hard to decipher longhand. This piqued my interest.

From then on when these letters with foreign stamps arrived, I begged Mother to translate them for me. Sometimes she did if they were just short letters. When they ran several pages long, she often refused because she was too tired after working all day. Oh, how I wished I could read German because then I would be able to read them for myself and not have to bother Mother. I was convinced that they held some of the answers to my family's history.

How right I was! These letter files proved to be a veritable goldmine of information. As I delved into them, frayed and yellowed with age, I unearthed many details of what happened before I was fully cognizant of the events that helped shape my life. They also served as a tremendous source of inspiration because they helped me understand and appreciate what my parents must have gone through during those very difficult years.

When World War II began, my parents were still living in blissful happiness in Stockholm. But after Father's unexpected transfer to Berlin, their life immediately became much more complicated. In many ways it was the beginning of all the troubles that followed.

When his transfer orders came in June 1940, he seriously considered other options, but the only one that came to mind was to enter a partnership with his good friend Siggi Hummer, another Austrian living in Stockholm, who ran a travel agency there. Working out the details of such an undertaking took more time than he had, however. As a civil servant in Hitler's Germany, he had no choice but to comply with his transfer order, especially because he also had a wife and two young children who depended on him for their livelihood. His life, as well as that of his family, would more than likely have turned out quite differently had he resigned and stayed in Sweden.

With this move came the first of a number of setbacks. Because he had not yet procured a place to live in Berlin, Father had to leave Mother behind in Sweden but promised it would not be long before he would send for her, perhaps a week or two at the most. In the meantime, she should look for a moving company and start to organize the move, which of course she did.

Unfortunately, he forgot to take into account the severe housing shortage that existed in Berlin, which the numerous bomb raids on the city had caused that spring of 1940. As a result, many people were homeless and waiting to be assigned a place to live. His name was way down on a very long waiting list.

Father was lucky to even find a tiny little room in a boardinghouse that was barely large enough to hold him. It certainly could not hold his whole family, which by now included my four-year old sister Ingrid and my one-year-old brother Helmut. Reluctantly, he wrote to Mother that she would have to remain in Sweden for the time being. He hated to be separated from her for any length of time, but what could he do? The situation was totally out of his control.

Several months passed with Father still no closer to finding a place. The *Auswärtiges Amt*, also known as the AA, was getting increasingly impatient that Mother was still living in Sweden, but no more so than Father. He was told in no uncertain terms that she must join him in Berlin immediately. But where would she and the children stay, he demanded to know, since an apartment wasn't yet available? He never received a helpful answer to that question but just another demand that she must leave Sweden.

Father surmised that one of the reasons for this unreasonable demand was economic. As long as he had to keep the apartment in Stockholm for his family, the AA was forced to pay him a supplement every month as if he were still stationed there. That situation meant additional costs for the AA, which could not be tolerated any longer than absolutely necessary.

Father also speculated that perhaps an even more compelling reason for the AA's unreasonable demand was that Mother happened to be a citizen of a country over which Germany had no control, Sweden being neutral. If he should be transferred to a foreign country as an official representative of Germany, it would be untenable for his wife to remain Swedish, or so the AA claimed. It therefore further demanded he take immediate steps to rectify this situation by applying for German citizenship for his family. Until this question of citizenship was resolved, he was informed, he would not be considered for any foreign postings. Being a relative newcomer to the diplomatic service, he had been unaware of this regulation.

Although Father could understand why Mother was not altogether happy about having to leave peaceful Sweden and become a German citizen, he also knew that she would agree to anything just to be together with him. The current separation was unbearable for both of them. Therefore she gave up her Swedish citizenship and became a citizen of the German Reich along with Ingrid and Helmut, a decision, which would hurt her later.

Father's housing problem was not as easily solved, however. His first solution was to try to find a place, if not directly in Berlin because of the tremendous housing shortage and long waiting list, then somewhere outside the city limits. He thought that at least they would be closer to each other again. It was tearing on both of them to be so far apart. He missed his family and Mother missed Father. If this involved some daily commuting on his part, so be it, he reasoned. Unfortunately, that idea fell through as well because houses or apartments were not available anywhere close by. In fact, the closest he could get was a room in a *Gasthaus* 250 kilometers from Berlin!

After explaining the situation to Mother in a letter that arrived while she was busily packing up their furniture in Stockholm, he wrote that he would ask his mother "if she will house you in Salzburg, but just until I can find something else closer to Berlin. At least that way you will be within the Third Reich and the AA should have no objection to that."

Omama, my grandmother, agreed to this plan although it could not have been easy for her with her weak heart to house three people, two of whom were young children, in her small one bedroom apartment. Father soon realized that this was an unsustainable solution especially because of the huge distance that still separated him from Mother, making frequent visits both time consuming and expensive.

Another month went by before he was finally able to locate a room for them in a *Gasthaus* in Titmoning, Bavaria, only (!) around two hundred kilometers from Berlin. This was still too far away for them to be together other than on some weekends. The only advantage was that they were no longer having to impose on *Omama*, which was much more important to him at that point.

Omama, my father's mother

During the next six months, he continued looking for something closer to Berlin. But with each successive move from one *Gasthaus* to another, he only managed to get his family as close as northern Bavaria, which still made it impossible for him to commute on a daily basis.

Having to pay rent in two places, his room in Berlin and Mother's room in whatever *Gasthaus* she happened to be staying, was taking a heavy toll on their finances. Exacerbating this situation was the added cost for the weekly train fares just to visit. He worried constantly about running short on money, especially now that his salary was so much lower than it was while he was posted to Sweden. Foreign postings always mean a higher salary, even today.

Not everyone was as concerned about this complex situation, as my sister Ingrid proved to me when she told me the following story about what happened one Saturday afternoon when Father came to visit. He came upon her peeping through the open door of the ceramic floor-to-ceiling chimney stove in their room at the inn in Titmoning and asked her what she was doing.

"I told him that I could see through to the next room where some soldiers were staying. Father leaned down and peered into the open chimney stove and looked very surprised when he could clearly see into the other room through another door on the opposite side inside the chimney stove. He warned me to be careful that the soldiers didn't catch me at my little spy game. I just laughed because I knew they just winked at me as they grabbed the mug of water that was warming up inside the stove."

I smiled when Ingrid told me this story and thought how adorable and mischievous she must have been at this most innocent stage of her life.

Father's inability to find accommodations in Berlin continued to exasperate him, but it was by no means the only cause for his dissatisfaction. What also vexed him was that the *Auswärtiges Amt* failed to come through on several promises it had made.

For one thing, when he was transferred so suddenly from the Stockholm Embassy in June 1940, he was under the impression that he was going to be assigned as an assistant to the minister for trade. That was a position that would have suited him perfectly because he had studied both trade and economics at the University of Vienna. Instead he was told to report for duty at the telegram bureau where he would be one of two people in charge. Surprise, surprise!

No one ever explained to his satisfaction the reason for this change in assignment. He was particularly unhappy that he had to work so many long hours, the telegram bureau needing to be manned twenty-four hours a day because of hundreds of highly secret, time sensitive and coded telegrams either received or sent during the week.

One of the most important telegrams that Father encrypted was the one he sent in July 1941 to the German Ambassador in Moscow from the Foreign Minister von Ribbentrop, which was to be delivered to Vyacheslav Molotov, the Soviet Minister of Foreign Affairs. It was supposed to serve as Germany's official declaration of war, thereby breaking the uneasy alliance between Germany and the Soviet Union. When the war finally ended in 1945, the Soviets denied ever having received this official declaration of war and consequently refused to acknowledge having any German POWs, political or otherwise. This refusal on the Soviet Union's part played an enormous role in what happened to my father.

Father's assignment in the telegram bureau also turned out to be quite dangerous because the bureau was never, under any circumstances, including bomb attacks, to be left unattended. Since these seemed to occur very frequently, he often happened to be the one staying behind. He reasoned that had he decided to leave the bureau unattended anyway, the bomb attack would probably be well over by the time he was able to reach AA's bomb shelter located several blocks away. Besides, his office was on the fifth floor, which would require even more time. And so he always stayed.

Consequently, he came very close to being killed on several occasions with one standing out in particular, which he described in one of his letters to Mother:

> *Just as I had done countless other times, I simply crawled into the kneehole of my desk when I heard the now all too familiar sharp shrilled warning siren. Next followed the sound of the droning airplanes and the whistling and hissing bombs falling on the city. This time, however, an explosion sounded really close to me, which made my whole body jump. Carefully poking my head out from beneath my desk, I saw a big gaping hole where once the outside wall of my office had been. The floor was littered with broken glass and papers that had spilled out from the filing cabinets. That was too close for comfort. I never want to be that close again.*

After a year of moving from *Gasthaus* to *Gasthaus*, Father could only see one way out of their difficulty: to request a transfer to somewhere abroad. He was almost desperate enough to accept anything as long as it would take him away from the AA in Berlin, but he was not desperate enough to accept the offered posting to Saigon. The problem was not with Saigon itself, he claimed, for he would have enjoyed being stationed there; the problem was rather with how to get there. The only way was by submarine, which was impossible now that Mother was pregnant with their third child. It was simply too risky, and going by any other means, like an ocean liner, would have been suicidal because of the war raging all around them. Instead, he decided to wait until a more suitable post became available.

A year after Mother left Sweden, including numerous moves, Father finally found accommodations at a farmhouse in the Mark Brandenburg, a district just to the north of Berlin. It was not perfect, but Drahendorf in the Spreewald was only fifty kilometers, or around thirty miles from the city, which meant that he was able to ride his bicycle to a nearby train station, board a train, and come back home every night. That seemed like a viable plan especially because their new accommodation was so much closer than any of their previous ones.

They had barely moved to Drahendorf in the fall of 1941, however, when the Foreign Office finally decided to honor Father's request for a transfer. He gladly accepted the posting to the recently established German Legation in Sofia, Bulgaria, which had come about as a direct result of Bulgaria's joining the Axis powers, as he found out later.

When the war began in 1939, Bulgaria tried at first to remain neutral. But then in 1941 Tsar Boris III joined the Axis in an effort to avoid German occupation of his country. He had the choice of either having his country be occupied or allowing German troops to use it as a base from which to attack Yugoslavia and Greece. The advantage of joining the Axis was that Bulgaria would be allowed to occupy Yugoslavia, Macedonia and parts of Serbia. Thus, Bulgaria yielded to German pressure and declared war on Great Britain and later also on the United States but assiduously avoided declaring war on the Soviet Union.

This was the status when the Gottlieb family boarded a train for Bulgaria where Father was going to take up his post as Consular Secretary by the end of October 1941.

CHAPTER IV

Move to Sofia

Bulgaria, 1941

When we talked about this period in her life, Mother always declared that she was just as impatient as Father to get out of Germany and their confined accommodations at various inns. That was why she was ecstatic when Father told her about his transfer to Bulgaria as she explained to me one evening.

It was a rare treat for me having Mother all to myself. My sisters were still out roaming around with their friends. Snuggling up close to her in the sturdily built huge armchair that Father had designed before they married in 1935, the two of us were enjoying a cozy chat in the living room.

"Although I was very happy that we finally were going to live together as a family again, I was not thrilled when I realized that the AA was not willing to ship our household goods to Bulgaria. Because Berlin was constantly heavily bombarded, I was afraid that the warehouse, where our container was stored, might fall victim and all our belongings would be destroyed. Luckily for us that did not happen!"

I followed Mother's gaze as she looked around our living room now filled with everything she had left behind when the family moved to Bulgaria. If all the tables, chairs, books, carpets and pictures could talk, they would have quite a story to tell, I thought, especially since it took nine years before they were unpacked in Sweden again.

"Why didn't the furniture go with you, Mamma?" I asked.

"The Foreign Office informed us that it was not worth the risk or the cost because your father was still a young man and could easily be drafted into military service at a moment's notice. As things turned out, your father almost did get called up a few years later."

Reflecting upon that situation, I can't help but wonder if Father would have been better off had he become a soldier like his two brothers. After all, they came back just after the war was over.

As Mother and I continued our little *tête à tête,* I was fascinated no end to hear her tell about events that took place before I was born. Her story this evening about the family's move to Sofia and what life was like for them in those years made the people and places that I had never seen or met come alive. I felt as if I were right there.

"Our journey began in the latter half of October 1941," Mother picked up where she left off. "We had to change trains so many times as we crossed through Czechoslovakia, Hungary and Rumania. Under normal circumstances it would have taken two days at the most, but instead it took over a week. Sometimes we even had to spend a night in some little town before our connecting train arrived. We were told that the delay was due to the massive troop movements to the eastern front, which I could see for myself because the trains were always very crowded with soldiers. Believe me, I was completely worn out by the time we arrived in Sofia especially since I was eight months pregnant with your sister Karin."

To show what she meant, she put a sofa pillow under her blouse and then pretended to collapse in her chair, panting as if she were out of breath. "Having two small lively children did not make it any easier," she added, laughing at the memory.

At the mention of Czechoslovakia, Hungary, and Rumania, I quickly inched out of the chair and ran over to our wall map to locate these two countries that were new to me. Following Mother's oral clues of "Go further to the south" or "Now go to the east" or "You are getting warmer," I located them fairly quickly. With a shout of triumph I stuck a flag pin into their respective capitals before cuddling up again beside Mamma.

"By the time we arrived in Sofia, everyone was exhausted," Mother went on. "That didn't deter your father, however, from immediately rushing over to the German Legation after first installing us in a hotel. He needed to let his ambassador know that we had arrived safely and to explain why the trip had taken so much longer than expected."

"Weren't you afraid to be left by yourself in a foreign country, Mamma? I would have been. It sounds scary." A shiver went up my spine at the mere thought.

"Not really, Gittan. I knew your father would soon be back. And he was! I just hated the idea of having to stay in a hotel once more. I hoped it would not be for too long this time, though, because I was sick and tired of it." Mother chuckled, maybe because she realized the irony of her having to stay at a hotel once again when this was one of the main reasons why Father had requested a transfer. "I really wanted to have a place of our own so that I would finally be able to do my own cooking."

Knowing how great Mother's cooking was and how much she loved to try out new dishes, I understood to some degree what she meant. However, not ever having stayed in a hotel myself, I could only imagine how wonderful it would be to be waited on hand and foot, with no table to set or dishes to wash afterwards. What a luxury!

"Did you have to stay long in that hotel or did Pappa find an apartment soon?" I asked.

"Fortunately we didn't have to stay there very long at all because he found a very roomy furnished apartment on the third floor of a six-story building on the Czarista -Joanna Boulevard just a few blocks from the German Legation. I was ready to move in sight unseen."

Just then Ingrid and Karin came sauntering into the living room. I was surprised to see them because I was really caught up in what Mother was telling me that I hadn't heard the door to the hallway open and shut. When they saw the two of us snuggled together, they plopped down on the sofa and demanded to know what we were talking about.

"Mamma was just telling me about your arrival in Sofia. I don't mean you, Karin, because you were still in Mamma's tummy." I snickered into my hands.

Having managed to get Mother telling about their time in Sofia, I was loath to stop just to play a board game, read a book, or listen to the radio program "*Karusellen,*"which is what we normally did on our family night. Instead I begged her to continue. Happily she agreed, especially after my sisters added their pleas to mine.

"When your father returned from the legation that day, I threw myself into his arms after he told me that he had already found an apartment for us. You cannot imagine how giddy with excitement I was at the prospect of having a place of our own. I had felt draggy for days, not only because of the long journey but also because I was carrying you." Mother winked meaningfully at Karin, who smiled back shyly. "I no longer felt the least bit tired and was itching to get back into a kitchen and start cooking again. I promised to prepare your father's favorite dish for our first home cooked meal in over a year."

"I bet his favorite dish is *Wienerschnitzel*, isn't it, because that is also my all-time favorite," I exclaimed and was thrilled when I saw Mother nod in agreement. Even though I already knew this about Father, I never got tired of hearing it confirmed. This tiny shred of connection, tenuous at best to my lost and unknown father, made me feel closer to him somehow.

"I was in my element again. Your pappa soon also found a young girl from the countryside to help me with my shopping at the market since I didn't speak Bulgarian. I believe her name was…"

"Batska," Ingrid finished her sentence. "I really liked her. She liked playing games with Helmut and me."

"That's right, Ingrid. What a good memory you have!"

As Mother continued to tell us about her experiences in Bulgaria, I glanced up at the paintings showing scenes from Sofia that hung on the wall above where we were sitting. They intrigued me because I had never been there but wished I had because then I would have known Father just like Ingrid and Karin did. I always felt a little jealous of them because of that.

A month or two after Karin was born that November, Mother told us how ready and eager she was to invite some of Father's colleagues and their wives for dinner. "It was high time to start entertaining again and get back into the diplomatic social life, which I had enjoyed being part of in Sweden. I really missed the dinner parties we gave and went to in Stockholm."

As I grew older, I was able to witness many times what a wonderful and delightful hostess and tremendous asset my mother always

Family outing, Bulgaria, 1941

was to my father in his work as a diplomat. This was not only due to her cooking skills, which were legendary, but was a direct result of her extra ordinary *joie de vivre* and extroverted nature. She served as the perfect foil for my father who could be very warm and charming in his own Viennese way, but whose natural disposition was much more reserved, serious minded, and contemplative.

"What else did you do besides having people over for dinner?" I asked. "That doesn't sound like much fun to me."

"Well, sometimes we would take a bus into the countryside, where we hiked in the beautiful mountains surrounding Sofia or went for a swim in one of the many lakes, or went for a picnic." Mamma answered.

"I remember the picnic basket," Ingrid filled in the rest of Mother's description, "with delicious small *banitsas,* [flaky cheese and meat-filled pastries] and *kozunaks,* with lots of sugar on top. Sometimes Mamma also made *kåldolmar* [cabbage rolls filled with a meat and rice mixture] that we all like so much." Ingrid's memories of the years spent in Sofia, as young as she was, were always strong and quite vivid, which time did not diminish but only intensified.

"Oh, yes, Ingrid, you are so right! We were happy again. Life was smiling on us. We had three wonderful children. The war also seemed very far away. At least it was not touching Bulgaria yet, which made our lives that much better."

Mother then went on to describe how life soon settled into a routine. "While I stayed home with Helmut and Karin, your father dropped you off at a Bulgarian Catholic convent school, Ingrid, where you were enrolled in kindergarten. I envied how quickly

Mamma with Ingrid, Karin & Helmut
Sofia, Bulgaria, 1942

you learned Bulgarian. This turned out to be a tremendous help to us because you sometimes ended up translating for us. Do you remember that? Do you remember how you even used it to your advantage as well?"

"What do you mean?" Karin asked, intrigued by Mother's statement.

"Let me be the one to tell them, Mamma, because I know exactly what you are talking about. Pappa had fussed at me for something or other I had done—I don't remember what—and sent me to my room as punishment. Anyhow, I was angry with him. When he came to my room a few minutes later and asked me to come back out because he wanted me to translate what an old man at the door was saying, I pretended I didn't understand a word. It wasn't true, of course. I just wanted to pay him back for sending me to my room. Later I was ashamed of myself because I realized that I had probably cost the old man a sale of some paintings. He was the one I punished instead of Pappa."

We all laughed at her story. It was not difficult for us to imagine Ingrid doing just that because she could be quite pig-headed at times.

Noticing Mamma's glance at the clock as it chimed eight, I knew what that meant—bedtime for me, even on a Saturday evening! Reluctantly I got to my feet, knowing fully well that it was no use begging her to allow me to stay up just a little while longer. Mamma was completely intractable on that score, a characteristic she apparently shared with her oldest daughter. No less stubborn, I was just as determined to pick up the thread of this conversation at a later date.

Chapter V

Bombardments

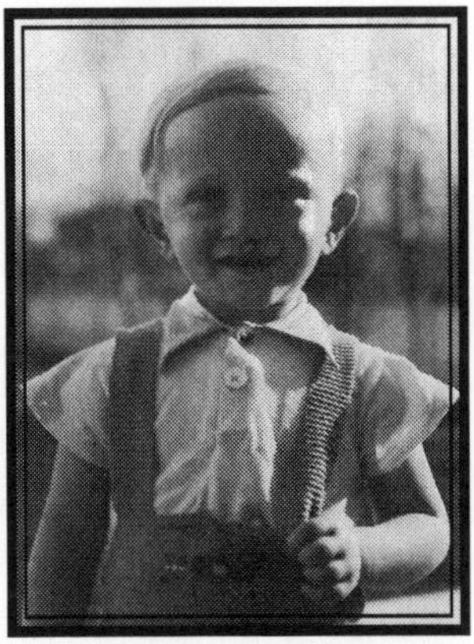

Bulgaria, 1942-44

It was my brother Helmut's birthday, January 11, or would have been, which was probably why Mother was more melancholy than usual.

Although I knew that my brother had died in Sofia and had heard some of the story before of what happened to him, I had never paid as close attention as I was these days. Because of my newfound interest in learning about the "why" behind our family's history, I wanted very much to understand exactly what caused my brother's death.

After supper we all went into the living room where we lit a candle beside Helmut's bust that stood on a shelf that was mounted in a corner in the living room. We always commemorated his birthday in this way. After a few minutes of quiet reflection, I suddenly decided to jump up and look for the cloth covered photo album with all the pictures from my family's years in Bulgaria. Thumbing through it, I soon came upon a picture that showed Helmut's grave.

"Why did Helmut die, Mamma?" I asked a little hesitantly because I hated to intrude on her personal time of grieving for her lost son. But this was something I had wondered about for some time.

Mother sounded so sad when she answered that Helmut had died as a result of a terrible and tragic accident in September 1942. "He was very badly scalded and suffered horribly from third degree burns on his face, neck, and shoulders before he died three days later. He would have turned thirteen today! Not a day passes without my thinking about him and wishing it had never happened."

"What exactly did happen, Mamma?" I asked with trepidation.

"Your brother was curious like all small children often are. When Ingrid and I went into the living room to work on her homework, Helmut stayed behind in the kitchen. I remember saying something about needing to check on the pot on the stove to see if it was boiling, never dreaming for a single moment that he would reach up and get hold of the pot handle to check on it. When he did, the pot tipped over and fell to the floor spilling its boiling water all over him in the process. I will never forget his screams as long as I live."

Tears trickled down her cheeks as she looked sorrowfully at Helmut's bust. "Poor little fellow. He was such a brave little boy with the sunniest smile in spite of all he had been through as a baby."

"What do you mean, Mamma? Was he sickly or something?" I asked.

"Not exactly, but because he was born with a cleft palate and a harelip, he had already undergone so many surgeries. Your father and I were absolutely devastated when he died three days after the accident. I always blamed myself for not being more careful while your father believed that if he hadn't forced us to leave Sweden but had tried harder to find a different job in Stockholm, Helmut would probably still be alive. For one thing, here in Sweden he would have received a proper treatment."

"I don't understand, Mamma?" Karin said. I could tell that she was just as puzzled as I was by Mother's last statement.

"In that case, let me try to explain it to you. You will remember that Europe was at war, but Sweden always remained neutral and was therefore not as touched by it. It was a different story with Bulgaria, not that the war had arrived there as yet, but it was getting closer. In the late afternoon of the accident, a siren sounded warning that Sofia might come under attack, which, incidentally, never happened. However, in those early days the only way the officials there knew how to protect the city was to turn off its entire power supply. By shrouding it in total darkness, the airplanes were less able to target the city properly, they reasoned. To our great misfortune the power was not turned back on for almost twenty-four hours. Without electricity, it was impossible to sterilize the needles for the injections that Helmut needed to stave off the infection from his burns. An equally serious problem was that we could not boil the water he needed to stay hydrated. You see, we always had to boil the water in Sofia before we could drink it. It was sheer agony to see your brother suffer like he did and be absolutely powerless to do anything about it."

Ingrid, Karin & Helmut, 1942

Mother's story made me cry. How he must have suffered! At the same time I became angry that this stupid war had not only robbed me of my father but had also taken my brother from me.

A few minutes passed before Mother spoke again. "To make matters worse, your father became very upset when his colleagues began whispering behind his back. Apparently, it had something to do with what happened during the funeral procession to the cemetery."

"What happened, Mamma?" I cried out.

"When a bouquet of blue and yellow flowers fell off the coffin, I quickly bent down to pick it up and tossed it down on top of the coffin just as it was lowered into the grave, never dreaming that I was drawing attention to the flowers. It was this act that set their tongues wagging."

"Why would they start talking behind his back about something like that? How uncharitable of them!" Ingrid exclaimed. Obviously, she was just as incensed at their callousness as I was.

"Well, it wasn't as simple as all that, Ingrid. As I understood it afterwards, it was not the act of tossing the bouquet *per se* that infuriated his colleagues but rather that the flowers were blue and yellow like the Swedish flag."

"That doesn't make any sense, Mamma. How could the color of the flowers possibly offend anyone?" Karin and I cried out at the same time.

"No, it shouldn't have, but somehow it did. The bouquet was meant to be from *Mormor* and *Morfar* in Sweden, whose flag color is blue and yellow, as you know. I chose those flowers, not even thinking about the color combination, never dreaming that they would cause such a strong reaction. But apparently your father's colleagues took affront, claiming it was treasonous on my part to show such an overt allegiance to Sweden, my former country." She paused a minute, perhaps wondering how much she should try to explain. "Several days later your father began to notice that his colleagues were snubbing him. After hearing the vicious rumors they were spreading about me, he became furious, especially because they were totally unfounded."

"What did Pappa do? Did he tell them off?"

"In an act of pure anger and defiance, he secretly wrote to Berlin requesting to be called up for military duty as soon as possible. He was well aware of his particular status as "uk," short for "*unabkömmlich*," or indispensable, a status accorded to those militarily eligible men who worked in an official government position," Mamma explained.

Nothing came of Father's request until a year later. In early October 1943, he received a letter ordering him to report for military duty in Berlin by November. But he never went. When Beckerle, the German ambassador, received word that he was going to lose his consular secretary, he called Father into his office and asked him if he knew anything about how this could have happened.

"Your father thought it best to keep his mouth shut. His boss was ranting and raving about how he couldn't afford to lose his best assistant and that he would immediately send a telegram to Berlin requesting that this call up notice be rescinded. What could your father say at that point? He simply did not have the heart to tell his ambassador that he was personally responsible. True to his word, a few days later Mr. Beckerle called him into his office to inform him that he would not have to leave Sofia after all."

"Were you happy that Pappa didn't have to join the army after all, Mamma?" I wanted to know as I snuggled closer to her in the chair the two of us were sharing.

"I was because I did not want to leave Bulgaria yet. I thought we were safer there than anywhere else, other than in Sweden, of course. Besides, I did not want your father to become a soldier. Your father, on the other hand, was not at all happy about this outcome because it changed all the plans and preparations he had already made for our leaving Sofia. He was so certain that his request would be honored. While on assignment to Berlin in the fall of 1943, he had taken a lease on an apartment in Wels, a town not too far from Salzburg, which was still under construction at the time. He wanted to be sure I had a safe place to live while he was in the army. He had even promised our apartment in Sofia to a colleague and sold all the food we had bought in preparation for the coming winter." Mother paused, perhaps contemplating what might have been if things had turned out differently.

"Right after this incident the war started to come closer to Bulgaria. Your father became increasingly worried and concerned for our safety when the Allied Forces began to execute bombing raids over Rumanian oil fields just north of Sofia in November1943. This was an attempt to cut the German forces off from their oil supply. Every day the situation was growing more and more dangerous with the attacks coming ever closer to Sofia. Suddenly we were no better off there than we had been in Berlin. I will never forget the three-day, heavy, unrelenting bombardment of Sofia in the early part of January 1944."

Once again Mother stopped, her face clouding over with the remembrance of the events of those days. Her comment about the bomb attacks really caught my attention. It wasn't that I hadn't been captivated by everything she had told us so far because I truly was. But she had never told me anything about these bomb attacks before. This was the first time I heard about them, or maybe it was the first time I really understood what she was talking about.

"What was it like when the bombs came down? That must have been awful! Were you scared or hurt?" These were only the first of many questions on the subject.

"When I heard the wail of the siren warning of an imminent attack, I immediately took you, Karin, and went down into the basement of our building that served as bomb shelter. As I sat in total darkness, I worried about your father, of course, but especially about you, Ingrid, and whether you had made it into a bomb shelter in time. I had given you permission earlier that day to go to your friend's house after school because your teacher had not shown up and you were therefore dismissed early. You wanted to stay for lunch because Püppchen's mom had cooked tomato soup and pancakes, which was your favorite."

"Well, I almost didn't make it to the bomb shelter, Mamma. Do you remember?" Ingrid seemed eager to pick up the story from her.

Turning her attention away from Mother, Karin demanded to know, "How come you almost didn't make it, Ingrid?"

Karin has told me that she always wished she could remember those days just like Ingrid did. But how could she? She was only a little over two years old at the time.

"I remember everything as clearly as if it were yesterday," Ingrid continued. "Püppchen's mother wanted her to run to the pharmacy to get some medicine for their maid because she had hurt her foot. When Püppchen complained that she wasn't feeling very well, I offered to go in her place. After I got to the pharmacy, I realized I had forgotten the money and would have to go back to get it. But then when I was on my way back to the pharmacy for the second time, I heard an awful wailing sound. It scared me half to death."

"What did you do, Ingrid?" I asked.

"I hurried into the shop because I knew it had to be sirens warning that airplanes would soon be dropping bombs from the sky. I had no idea how I was going to get back to Püppchen's house now. I didn't dare go outside again, but the pharmacist shooed me out the door, yelling at me to find the closest bomb shelter. I was shaking all over as I ran outside where total chaos reigned. I could hardly believe how, within just a few short minutes, wild acting carriage horses, standing on their back legs and neighing fiercely, and people running in all directions had transformed the tranquil neighborhood street. Stopping dead in my tracks, I had no idea what I should do or where to turn. All I could think about was that I had to get back to Püppchen's house as quickly as possible. Then, somehow I started running as fast as my trembling legs would carry me and didn't stop until I reached her house where her mother was anxiously waiting outside for me. Quickly she pulled me inside their dark bomb shelter where we joined all the others from their apartment building. For the next hour or so we listened in terror to the heavy booms in the distance, wondering if the next one would bury us. I was ever so relieved when I finally heard the all-clear siren and realized that no bomb had fallen on us this time."

Karin and I were sitting spellbound by Ingrid's vivid description of what she had experienced that long ago day in Sofia. I, for one, was very glad that it wasn't me because I don't know if I would have known what to do like Ingrid did. And to think this happened to her when she was just the same age as I was now!

"How brave you were, Ingrid! What happened next? How did you get back home after that?" Karin and I both asked at once.

"When Pappa finally came and got me, I was so thankful that I cried. As we were making our way back to our apartment, I will never forget the awful sight that met our eyes— bombed out houses, smoldering heaps of debris everywhere, and gigantic holes in the pavement. I had to step really carefully to avoid stumbling and falling down on the broken pavement. I could hardly breathe; the air was thick with smoke. And I was worried sick about Mamma and Karin even though Pappa had assured me that they were safe."

I could tell that Ingrid was visibly shaken in reliving that terrible bomb attack when she was only seven years old. No one said anything for a few minutes while we tried to digest what she had experienced.

"What happened then?" Karin finally broke the silence.

"That was one of the worst days in my life. It was the day when our lives changed forever." Instead of Ingrid, it was Mother who spoke up.

"What do you mean, Mamma?" I asked furrowing my eyebrows inquisitively.

"Well, it was shortly after that attack that we left Sofia. After all we had been through, your pappa's near death experience at the legation, Ingrid's being caught outside a bomb shelter in the midst of it, and Sofia's destruction, your pappa was more determined than ever to get us out of Sofia. If we stayed any longer, we would be in grave danger. Who knew what the next bomb attack might bring?"

"Did you say that Pappa nearly died that day? What happened? How come?" All three of us spoke up in unison. That was the first we had heard about that.

"Yes, I did. Do you want me to tell you what happened?"

"Of course, we do," the three of us answered with one voice.

"All right, girls. Where do I begin?" She paused a moment. "I remember how awful your pappa looked when he came to the bomb shelter after the first attack was over, so shaken and pale. He also had a terrible headache. When he discovered that you weren't at home with me, he left our shelter and frantically went in search of you. Later that night, once we were back in our apartment with its blown out windows and no heat, he finally shared with me what he had been through that day."

In her usual effusive manner that always made me feel as if I were right there experiencing it all, Mother went on to describe Father's near death experience. When he first heard the drone of the airplanes, he tried to make it to the cellar, but before he could get to the door, a nearby heavy explosion shook the building. He felt a searing pain in the back of his head as the impact threw him across the room and into the wall. Luckily, he wasn't bleeding. Feeling dazed, he staggered on unsteady feet to the outside wall of his office to look through the newly shattered window. It shocked him to see the impact of the bomb. Outside, where a bustling square filled with people going about their business should have been, all he beheld was a craterlike hole and hundreds of dead bodies. He realized how lucky he was to be still alive. Had that bomb fallen just a few feet closer, he would have been among those dead.

It made my skin crawl just hearing Mother tell this story second hand. I couldn't help but wonder, and not for the first time, what Father was going through while we were sitting in our comfort-

Ingrid & Helmut with the Lessman children

able apartment, with a fire burning bright and warm in the open fireplace. Was he suffering? Was he starving? Was he cold? Did he even know where we were? Eight years without a word from him had gone by and all we knew from a returning prisoner of war was that he was probably somewhere in the cold Siberian tundra.

We had been sitting quietly for several minutes trying to absorb what Mother had just told us when she broke into our thoughts. She was not finished with her tale yet of what happened that long ago January when Sofia suffered such devastating bomb attacks.

In his mad dash to check on his family, Father had to pass by his colleague Lessman's home. It was a gruesome scene that met his eyes. Nothing was left of the house. What was even worse was seeing the mutilated bodies of Lessman's wife and their newborn baby and two older children lying splayed out in the yard. His poor colleague had lost his whole family that afternoon. Father was terrified that he would be met with an equally grisly scene. He was eternally grateful when such was not the case.

After Father told Mother about the Lessman family, she was very upset and could hardly stop crying. All she could think of, she said, was that it could just as easily have been her lying there instead of Lessman's wife. What a tragedy! Five lives snuffed out before having a real chance at living!

Mother's description made an indelible impression on me. It was difficult to get the picture of that poor baby out of my mind for I realized that it could have been me. After all Mother was already pregnant with me at that time.

Reflecting back on why Mother felt the need to tell us such an awful story, the only reason I can think of is that she wanted us to realize how thankful we should be that the same thing hadn't happened to us. We had all survived World War II while many others had perished. And we were grateful; at least I knew that I was!

After a few more minutes passed in shocked silence, I heard Ingrid say, "I remember playing with those two children, but until tonight I never really understood what happened to them. We left Sofia just a few days later, didn't we? I also remember how I refused to get undressed that night because we had already had to go down into the bomb shelter several more times. When Pappa told me to get undressed for bed, I told him why should I bother. There would probably be another attack anyway."

The story of the Lessman family, along with many others, made me much more aware of what Mother must have gone through in the past and was still going through, for that matter. She had every right to be unhappy, living in such uncertainty about her beloved husband's fate and constantly worrying about him. Her hair was even turning prematurely gray. She had experienced so much, so many tragedies, more than enough to cause anyone to become morose, depressed and unhappy. No wonder it didn't take much for her to start crying. It is surprising that she was ever able to smile or enjoy life during those long years of waiting. Fortunately for us, her naturally sunny and optimistic disposition enabled her to mask her true feelings—most of the time anyway.

Mother was not quite through yet telling about those eventful days in Sofia that totally changed our lives.

"After the first strong wave of strafes hit that day and continued for the next two days, we went out to a camp just outside Sofia, which the legation had designated as an evacuation camp." Mother picked up the thread of the story, her voice sounding stronger and less weepy. "It was really unfit for staying overnight and even less so if we had to stay for several days. It didn't have running water, indoors plumbing or even a kitchen for that matter. How were we supposed to live like that? The worst part was that no one knew for sure how long these bomb attacks would last or whether any apartment buildings would even be left standing when all was said and done."

Because Mother seemed to slow down, her words coming further and further apart and finally coming to a complete stop, I became worried. I really wanted to find out what happened next. I had heard bits and pieces before, of course, but never like this. When she just sat there, staring straight ahead and totally lost in her own thoughts, I nudged her with my shoulder to remind her that we were still there and waiting.

Finally, she noticed. Smiling apologetically, she started talking again. "Late on the third day of the allied air raid attack, your father happened to run into an old acquaintance from his Berlin days, a Herr Schneider, who was the pilot of the airplane assigned to the Foreign Minister von Ribbentrop and his staff. Surprised to see him in the corridor of the legation, he asked Schneider what had brought him to Sofia. He explained that he had just flown Mr. Altenburg, von Ribbentrop's Second in Command, down for a quick conference with Ambassador Beckerle. He then very kindly inquired after us. When your father told him how worried he was about us, Schneider offered to let us fly back with him to Berlin the next morning. He had some extra seats on the plane, but we needed to be at the airport by six o'clock in the morning."

When Father came back out to the evacuation camp that evening, he told Mother about this stroke of good luck. He felt it was the answer to their prayers. Mother hoped he was right but hated to become separated from him again, feeling somehow it would be much worse this time because of the precarious political situation in Bulgaria. The tension between Germany and Bulgaria was escalating, as she tried to explain to us. No one knew how long it would be before the alliance was totally dissolved. What worried her was whether Father would manage to leave Bulgaria before the communist partisan groups took over the country and allied themselves with the Soviet Union.

She begged him to come with her, but he claimed he couldn't because it would be tantamount to desertion. He would be arrested the minute he set foot on German soil. Knowing he was probably right, she reluctantly agreed to leave the next morning without him. He even came prepared with two suitcases crammed full with the clothes she did not have time to pack the night they fled from the bombs in Sofia.

"I wish I could have gone back to our apartment, but there was no time," she finished as she glanced at the clock on the mantle.

I knew what that meant. "A propos time, I see that it is way past your bedtime, Karin and Gittan. We will have to stop for tonight. If you are as exhausted as I feel, you must be very tired indeed. Come here and give me a kiss before you go."

Only on the promise that she would continue to tell us what happened next some other time, I gave her a quick peck on the cheek and a hard hug.

Before I reluctantly headed off to bed, I whispered in her ear, "Mamma, this was so much better than reading a book or playing games."

CHAPTER VI

Fleeing Sofia

Bulgaria 1944

Although lots of snow had fallen outside on a cold February evening in 1952, a warm fire was burning in the open hearth in the corner of our living room. Lit candles everywhere added to our feeling of *Gemütlichkeit* and contentment. Mother had just finished translating a letter from *Omama* in Salzburg, with whom she always stayed in very close touch.

A few weeks had passed, but it was finally the perfect opportunity for Mother to tell us what happened after she and my sisters left Sofia. I was sitting on a big square pillow on the floor in front of Mother with Karin and Ingrid on either side of her, all eager and ready to hear about how we ended up in Austria. As a special treat, Mother had even splurged and bought cinnamon buns at the bakery.

Apparently, Father was not totally happy about sending his family to Berlin, but he couldn't do anything about that because that was where the plane was headed. He was extremely worried how Mother, who didn't know anybody in Berlin, would manage all by herself. Besides, the war was now in its fifth year with all the dangers that entailed. What if the railroads weren't running regularly, and she would have to find some other means of getting from Berlin to Wels, Austria, where hopefully their new apartment would be waiting for her? She said he hated to put her in that situation, but he saw no other way for her and the children to get out of Sofia.

"What also concerned your father was that there was no time to get prior approval from the Foreign Office for us to leave. Under ordinary circumstances that would have been necessary, but time being of essence here, he decided it was well worth the risk of incurring censure. That is how convinced he was that he had to get us out of Sofia. And who knows?" Mother paused, seemingly lost in her thoughts.

My sisters and I immediately started to speculate about what might have happened if Mother had not left when she did.

"If you had stayed, Mamma," I said, "Wouldn't that mean that I might have been born in Sofia just like Karin was? Perhaps we would even be living there now instead of here in Sweden."

"That also means that we would probably be speaking Bulgarian instead of Swedish and going to school there," Karin continued my line of thinking. "I wonder what that would have been like?"

"You are both right," Mother answered, coming out of her reveries, "but I am glad we aren't still in Bulgaria because then we would be living under a Soviet communistic regime since Bulgaria is now behind the iron curtain."

"What do you mean?" "What is that?" "Iron curtain?" the three of us asked all at once.

"Well ..." Mother said. "Let me see how I can I explain it to you?" She paused and thought for a moment. " 'Iron curtain' is an expression used in referring to those eastern European countries that came under the communist rule of Soviet Russia after the war was over in 1945. If I am not mistaken, I believe it was Great Britain's prime minister, Winston Churchill, who first used the term to imply that those countries are not free and self-governing like the western nations are. People living in these Eastern Bloc countries have no choice but to do what their Soviet masters tell them. They don't have a democratically elected government like we do in Sweden, for instance, even though we have a king. They are not free to travel or to move to any western countries like we are. Instead the Soviets rule them with an 'iron fist,' keeping them behind a curtain, so to speak, that feels as if it were made of iron because it is so difficult to cross over into the free world. Many people have died trying to break through." Mother sounded more and more passionate as she spoke.

As young as I was when this particular conversation took place, I decided that I was very glad that she left Bulgaria when she did because I would not have liked living in a country where I was not free. Her explanation of the "iron curtain" and how the Soviets were forcing people to live behind this awful curtain made an unforgettable impression on me. This was further strengthened after we moved to Germany in 1956 where I heard firsthand how people risked their lives trying to escape from behind the iron curtain into the free and democratic west.

I will never forget the story that Heinz Weber, a classmate of mine in Bonn, told the class one day about his family's harrowing escape form East Germany. His father, a border policeman with the *Grenzpolizei* at Marienborn in East Germany assigned to patrol along the *Niemandsland*, was not happy under the totalitarian regime. Because of his intimate knowledge of how the border patrol worked, he was able to carefully plan their escape.

Heinz explained for those of us in the class who didn't understand what this *Niemandsland* was, that it was a wide strip of land where no one was allowed to live. It stretched along the border that separated East Germany from West Germany and was heavily fortified by a three-meter-high barbed wire fence. Every few hundred meters stood very intimidating high watchtowers, equipped with searchlights powerful enough to turn night into day. One night, he and his parents, dressed in dark clothes, managed to evade the strobe lights by crawling across the *Niemandsland,* fearing every step of the way to be caught in the roving lights and be shot. It took them all night to crawl across the five-kilometer stretch of land before they reached freedom.

After hearing his story I was thankful once again that Mother had left Bulgaria when she did. It also brought back memories of the day when Mother was telling my sisters and me about leaving Sofia.

Before she was able to drop off to sleep that last evening on their improvised mattresses at the camp outside Sofia, Father gave her a bundle of *Reichsmark*, which he said should see her through until she was settled in Wels. He also promised her that he would come for a visit as soon as he could. He kept his promise because he arrived just in time for Ingrid's birthday six months later.

"But Mamma, he didn't stay for my birthday, as I recall" Ingrid interjected. "I was terribly disappointed when he left a week earlier than he was supposed to."

"Yes, I know, but he left because he received a telegram from the German Legation demanding his immediate return. He hated to disappoint you, Ingrid, but duty called him back to Sofia. Believe me, I tried to make him stay. I hated to see him go back into danger and leave us again, especially since I was so close to giving birth to you, Gittan." Mother smiled down at me where I sat with my legs curled up beneath me.

June, 1944. This visit a few days before Ingrid's birthday, was the last time the family would see Pappa before his capture by the Russians.

Although I wanted to hear more about that particular event, I was more interested in hearing what happened when they left for Berlin.

"The next morning everything went according to plan at first. We arrived at the airport just shortly before six o'clock. After a tearful good bye and many hugs and kisses, we boarded the minister's plane. My heart felt very heavy when I saw your pappa's beloved face disappear through the small window of the airplane as it gathered momentum lifting off. I remember wondering what would happen to him now that we were gone? How would he fend for himself? Who would fix his food and wash his clothes? I never dreamed that I would only see him one more time after that." Her face furrowed in sorrow.

And who could blame her? She had every right. That happened over eight years ago, and she still didn't know much about what had happened to him.

"Please, Mamma, tell us what it was like to fly? I have never even seen an airplane. Do you think I ever will?"

"Who knows, Gittan, anything is possible." Smiling she turned to Karin. "I remember how excited you were. You were jumping up and down on the seat while Ingrid, always my big helper, tried to get you to sit still."

Ingrid squeezed Mother's hands as thanks for acknowledging her as the big helper. It was true that she helped Mother in many ways, like taking care of Karin and me when we were at our cottage in Mollösund, while Mother had to stay in town to work. She could be awfully bossy at times, though.

"I remember that. Maybe that is when you developed that little wart you had on your chin, Karin. Your face was constantly bobbing up against the window of the plane," Ingrid teased.

"That is not so, is it, Mamma?" Karin protested indignantly and stuck her tongue out at Ingrid; it was true that she had a little wart on her chin that was taken off when she was about five years old. Not that I remembered it, but I had heard about it before.

"Stop it, girls. Do you want me to continue, or not?" Mother asked, impatient at their bickering.

"Ingrid, do you remember the other family that was travelling with us? You seemed to take quite a liking to that boy who was about your age." Mother winked at Ingrid, who was blushing from ear to ear but was nonetheless smiling. "Nothing much has changed since then, has it? You still like to flirt with boys, don't you?"

"Mamma, you are such a tease!" Ingrid laughed.

Mother was right because I had seen her flirting with boys, even holding hands with them. I had never seen her kissing one, though, but wished I had. Even though it was fun seeing her blush like that, I was more interested in having Mother continue her tale about their flight from Bulgaria.

Mother went on to tell how she had barely closed her eyes after taking off from Sofia when she was aroused by a voice whispering into her ear. Sitting up she realized it was none other than Mr. Altenburg himself trying to tell her that he had been ordered to return to Sofia for another urgent conference with Ambassador Beckerle. He wanted to know if she wanted to return with him or get off in Belgrade where the plane had to refuel.

"Where is Belgrade, Mamma?" I interrupted for that name was a new one to me.

"Go to the map, Gittan, locate Austria, and then go south from there until you come to a country called Yugoslavia."

I did as she suggested. With a triumphant shout of "Hurrah, I found it!" I stuck a fresh pin into its capital, which was clearly marked with a small black star on our map.

"I felt disoriented and very confused," Mother continued once I was back on my pillow and was leaning up against her with my arms on her knees. "What was I to do? Go back or try to make it to Austria on my own? As much as I wanted to return to your father, I knew that would defeat the purpose of leaving Bulgaria in the first place. And since I didn't have any reason to go to Berlin anyway other than that the plane was going there, this really simplified matters for me. Now I was able to take a train for Austria directly without having to go all the way to Berlin first. That saved me a lot of money as well."

Looking back on that comment, I realize how typical this statement was for my mother. She was always very practical and tried to save money any way she could, perhaps a tendency that resulted from surviving World War II and later from being forced to support her fatherless children.

"Please go on, Mamma," I begged her. "What an exciting story! What happened next?"

"As soon as we landed," she said as she made a sweeping motion with her pointing finger to include my two sisters and herself, "the three of us took a taxi to the train station. I was hoping that a train would leave for Vienna, if not that night perhaps the next day. We could always stay at a hotel if we had to, I reasoned."

"Did you have to sleep in a hotel?"

"No, I didn't, Gittan, because thank goodness I was able to get tickets for a train leaving that same evening." Turning to Ingrid, Mother asked her whether she remembered what happened the next morning when they arrived in Vienna.

"Vaguely. I think you couldn't find your passport or something? Is that what you mean?"

"Yes, you are partially right. I became very nervous when I discovered that I had Mrs. Waldstein's passport instead of mine. I was afraid the passport inspector wouldn't believe me when I told him that I thought Mr. Altenburg must have made a mistake when he handed our passports back to us at the airport. Thank heavens the man believed me! He must have seen how tired I was from traveling all night with two small children in a train overcrowded with noisy soldiers and took pity on me. But how was I to get my identity papers back? I felt sick about it! I had no way of contacting Mrs. Waldstein. I couldn't even think straight, I was so worn out, which is more than I could say for you two, who had slept like little angels all night."

"Did you ever get it back?" Totally captivated by this tale of the lost passport, I was eager to find out what happened next.

"Yes, I did, Gittan. Luckily, Mrs. Waldstein, unbeknownst to me, did not stay in Belgrade as planned but had taken the same train as I had."

"But how in the world did you find her?"

"The kind official suggested I should try the stationhouse just in case the other lady had turned it in. Following his advice, I was so happy and relieved when I saw Mrs. Waldstein standing at the counter, where she was probably trying to explain her own predicament. Hugging and talking a mile a minute, we exchanged our passports before going our separate ways. I never heard from her again. Finally, with me carrying our two suitcases and you, Ingrid, holding on to Karin, the three of us made our way through the throng of people to the platform where the train to Salzburg was waiting to depart."

"What happened when we arrived in Salzburg, Mamma? Didn't

Omama with Karin 1944

we go directly to *Omama's*?" Ingrid asked.

"Yes, we did! Three hours after leaving Vienna, we walked the short distance from the station to *Omama's* apartment."

"Did *Omama* know you were coming, or did you surprise her?" I asked.

Even though I had no memory of *Omama*, being only eighteen months old when we left Austria, I felt like I knew her because of her letters. Besides, a picture of her sat prominently displayed right beside Father's in our family picture gallery on the bookshelf in the living room. This was Mother's way of keeping the people we loved present in our daily lives even though they were absent in body.

"*Omama* was very happy and even relieved to see us because she was very worried, not having heard from us in several months. That did not surprise me at all. The war was disrupting everything from the postal services to our personal lives." Mother sighed.

Mother then went on to tell us how emotionally and physically drained she was, not only because of the long journey and the bomb attacks over Sofia but also because she was consumed with worry about Father. "I was so happy to see *Omama's* beloved face. For the first time in many days I felt safe again."

It was getting late by this time, but Mother promised she would continue her tale another time.

CHAPTER VII

Excursion to Wels

Austria, 1944

A few days passed before Mother was able to keep her promise to tell us what happened after her sudden arrival at *Omama's* doorstep.

"I quickly realized that I could not continue to impose on your grandmother for very long, Nothing had changed since 1941 when we stayed with her because your father could not find an apartment in Berlin. Her heart was still weak and the apartment too small, especially since your uncle Heinz had just returned from Russia after being wounded in battle."

Unfortunately, the apartment in Wels was not yet ready for occupancy, as Father had hoped, which meant that Mother needed to look for another place to stay. Every morning she pounded the streets of Salzburg, going from one agency to another applying for a place to live and extra ration cards. A month later her hard work finally paid off when she was assigned a room at a *Gasthof* in Doettleinsdorf, a village a few miles outside Salzburg. It was the only place the housing authorities in Salzburg offered her. "Take it or leave it," she was told. On the one hand it was not exactly what she had hoped for, but on the other she realized she could not afford the luxury of being choosy.

On a cold day in February 1944, Mother resolutely set out with Ingrid and Karin, waved goodbye to *Omama*, and boarded a bus for Doettleinsdorf. When they arrived at the inn, the landlady told them that the only available room was actually one over the stable that was part of the inn. Disappointed but not daunted, Mother accepted. As long as it was warm and they had it to themselves, she was determined not to return to *Omama* in defeat. The set of her mouth when telling the story showed just how determined she must have been.

"Things would not have been so bad had the innkeeper's wife been a little kinder to us and not quite so short tempered. But apparently she was frustrated because of having to house ammunitions for the army in her kitchen as well as filling up the inn with refugees like us. This made the poor *Gastwirtin* very irritable. Even though I could understand her frustration, I was not happy when she took it out on me. But when your pappa came for a short visit in June, I was happy again."

Shortly after Father's arrival in Doettleinsdorf, my parents decided to check on the promised apartment in Wels, located an hour from Salzburg. Mother explained that he was anxious to find out when the apartment might be ready, knowing that he had to return to Sofia soon and wanting to see her comfortably settled.

"When we boarded the train for Wels, the day for our little excursion was warm and sunny," Mother began her story of that particular day. "At first we felt like newlyweds without a care in the world. The innkeeper's wife, you see, had promised to look after the two of you, Ingrid and Karin, which was uncharacteristically kind of her. Unfortunately, this feeling was short-lived. Just before the train reached Wels, we heard the dreaded sirens, which could only mean one thing.

"Sure enough! As the train came to a lurching stop, we distinctly heard the dull drone of bombers overhead. A mass confusion ensued with passengers madly scrambling to the exits to take cover in the ditches beside the tracks. With our hands covering our heads, your pappa and I crouched in the ditch, staying close to each other, while listening to the airplanes swoop in."

"Weren't you scared, Mamma?" I couldn't even begin to imagine what that would be like.

"I most certainly was, Gittan, even though it wasn't the first time I experienced such a bombattack. But I don't think that is something anyone ever gets used to. I was praying really hard that the bombs would miss us this time as well. Several minutes of sheer terror passed before we heard them dropping their deadly load on the nearby town of Wels. Several more minutes passed—I don't remember exactly how long— before the all-clear signal sounded.

"Thankful to be still alive, we slowly got up from the ditch and brushed off the dirt and grass from our clothes. We had no idea how many lives had been lost or what damages the bombs had inflicted upon the town. And what about our promised apartment? Could it have survived? Or the warehouse for that matter, where our household container now was stored?" Mother paused to catch her breath.

What a fascinating story! I was absolutely spellbound by it.

"But I thought the container was still in Berlin. So how come it was in Wels?" Ingrid took the words right out of my mouth.

"When we left for Bulgaria, your father arranged for it to be moved to Bavaria first. He felt it would be much safer there than in Berlin, which was being heavily bombarded at the time. Then in 1943 he had it moved to Wels instead because he thought he would soon be enlisted, and we would then be living there, " Mother explained before returning to the main story.

"Since the train could not go any further, what with the railway tracks all torn up a few miles ahead, as the conductor informed us as he went by, we decided to continue on foot. When we reached the town and saw the devastation, we feared the worst. Had our promised apartment been hit? What about the warehouse where our furniture was stored? Not being familiar with the town, it was difficult for us to locate either one at first. Smoldering ruins and broken up streets didn't help any."

"How in the world did you manage to find the warehouse if you didn't even know where it was located? Did you have a map, or something?" practical Ingrid asked.

"No, we had to stop and ask passersby. When we finally reached the warehouse and saw that it had been hit, we didn't dare hope that our container could possibly have survived. But it did!" Mother swept the room with her eyes. The evidence was all around us.

"What happened to the container? Did you just leave it there?" Karin asked.

"No, Karin, before your pappa returned to Sofia, he found a farmer just outside Wels, who was willing to rent an old unused barn to him for a very reasonable monthly fee. And there it stayed until I finally was able to afford having it shipped to Borås."

I looked around in awe at all the furniture, books, pictures and carpets, which now graced our home. I will never forget how we laughed when they finally arrived safely in Borås in 1949, and we unpacked the flour container full of little crawly creepers. Mother had not emptied it when she packed it away in Stockholm in 1940, thinking it would just be a few weeks at the most until she would unpack it in Berlin. Why waste perfectly good flour, my frugal mother reasoned. She never dreamed that it would take nine years instead of just a few weeks.

"We first decided to take out our two bicycles from the container," Mother continued. "We reasoned that we would need them to get back to Doettleinsdorf. It would be a few days at least before the train would be able to run again because of the broken tracks, and we couldn't wait that long. Besides, it would make my life easier to have access to some kind of transportation, your father thought. He was always so practical and logical!"

"What about the apartment building? Did you check on it? Was it still standing?" I asked.

"Unfortunately, it was totally destroyed just like so many other buildings in the town. So senseless! What a horrible waste! When I saw it still smoldering, my heart sank. We would not be moving out from our room above the stable any time soon. At the same time I was thankful we hadn't moved in yet because then we might not have survived."

After hearing about my parents' doomed excursion to Wels, it dawned on me how lucky I was to be alive. Mother, pregnant with me, could easily have been killed during that particular bomb attack. For that matter, I almost did get killed in another bomb attack a few months after I was born.

Here is the story I was told about that. Mother decided to take advantage of the beautiful and warm day by letting me nap in my baby carriage just outside our house in St. Gilgen. With hardly any warning at all, allied bombers swooped in over the village and the lake. As soon as she could, Mother rushed outside, absolutely beside herself by the mere thought that she might have lost another child because of the war. Imagine her relief when she saw that I was unharmed even though a bomb had dropped into the lake not too far from where I lay sleeping.

Whenever we talked about the flight from Sofia and the years in Austria, Mother made me feel really special. She always claimed that although all the worldly possessions she was able to bring with her from Sofia fitted into two small suitcases, her most precious cargo were her two young daughters and the little one she was carrying in her stomach, which of course turned out to be me.

It was only after I became a wife and mother that I was fully able to appreciate and understand what Mother must have gone through. Losing her only son to a horrible accident and having to flee from Sofia in such haste after the terrible bomb attacks began could not have been easy, nor could leaving her husband behind in a country that might soon be at war with Germany. How devastated she must have been when she learned that the Russians had captured him! How resourceful she was in managing to get all four of us back to her homeland Sweden in post war torn up Germany! How hard it must have been to live so many years in uncertainty of not knowing whether he was still alive or when he would finally come home, if he were alive! Only a strong person could have remained so positive and full of hope in spite of feeling lonely and sad. I don't know whether I would have been as brave and strong under similar circumstances. Fortunately I have never been put to that test.

In a newspaper interview in 1955 Mother gave a very succinct description of what her life had been like. She compared the years in wartime and those immediately following to a wild roller coaster ride that kept her going up and down, twisting this way and then that way, with hardly any time in between to catch her breath. Sometimes she was full of hope while at other times she was full of despair, but she never gave up hope completely (*Stockholm Tidning*, October 1955).

CHAPTER VIII

Place of My Birth

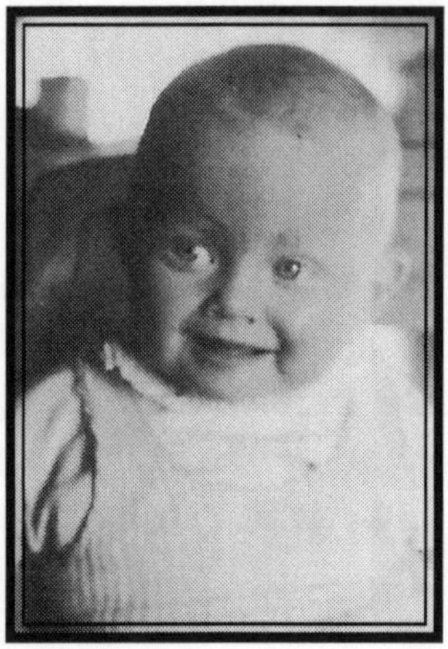

St. Gilgen 1944

I always loved it when Mother talked about the place where I was born. I could usually count on her doing that on or around my birthday because that was when she often went into what I called her "reminiscing mode." Sometimes she even became rather graphic in her description but not before I was old enough to handle some of those kinds of details.

How many times have I not heard her say something like: "Oh, about this time X number of years ago, I was in excruciating pain as you were being born…" Because she repeated a similar statement year after year, I cannot say with exactness when she actually told me everything about St. Gilgen. More than likely my memory is a combination of many such occasions.

It was heavenly relief for Mother when she finally was able to move into the much more spacious living quarters in Lueg, a very small hamlet about a kilometer to the south east of St. Gilgen. The spacious furnished apartment was located on the first floor of a three-storied house built in the typical Alpine style with dark wooden beams criss -crossing the white stucco walls. A series of stone steps led down into the road below where the military had erected a wall of cement and big stones, which would hopefully keep heavy enemy vehicles, such as tanks, from advancing. Just on the other side of the road ran a short railway line that connected Lueg to St. Gilgen. And a few hundred yards beyond the rails, lay a beautiful Alpine lake.

The hotel had been converted into a hospital where I was born.

St. Gilgen, nestled at the foot of the Zwölferhorn Mountain by the Wolfgangsee in the Salzkammergut region not far from Salzburg, is a very quaint and picturesque small town with its typical Alpine architecture of white-washed walls, slanted roof tops and cross-beamed houses with flower boxes brimming with geraniums and many other colorful flowers decorating the curlicue balconies during the summer months. The old City Hall stands in the middle of a square that holds a round fountain around which magnificent flowers grow from spring until fall.

When I saw the village for the first time—and I don't mean when I was born but as a teenager—I fell absolutely in love with it. I felt an immense sense of pride that this was the place of my birth. I remember the occasion well since it was also the first time I was back in Austria after having left it when I was only fifteen months old. We were just returning from a visit with Uncle Walther, Father's oldest brother who lived in Gmunden on the Traunsee; this lake is located a few miles further east and is also part of the breathtakingly beautiful Salzkammergut.

After finding a parking space, we strolled along the beautiful shore of the Wolfgangsee all the way to Lueg where Mother was quick to point out the house in which we had lived. Then turning slightly, she pointed to the window on the second floor of a nearby hotel. The sign out front read *Gasthaus zu Lueg*. "That is where you were born, Gittan."

I was not at all surprised when she went into her usual spiel about what happened at the time. Although I had heard most of it before, somehow this time it was different because we were actually standing in front of the building where I first saw the light of day.

After seeing St. Gilgen, I understood why Mother must have loved living there. It exuded tranquility and charm. The glistening deep blue lake was only a few hundred yards away from the house, but more importantly, the *Gasthaus zu Lueg*, which at that time had been converted into a temporary hospital, was practically next-door to our house.

I laughingly asked Mother whether it had bothered her that the hospital was yet another inn, knowing how she had been forced to move from one inn to another after leaving Sweden in the early years of the war.

"Of course not, Gittan, I was happy that there was a doctor in attendance nearby. What I did not like, however, was that your father would not be there like he had been all the other times when your sisters and brother were born," she paused slightly before continuing to relate another memory of those days. "Your pappa did everything he could to help me even from far way Sofia. When a woman knocked on our door in early July 1944, I was very surprised to hear her address me in Bulgarian and tell me that my husband had sent her to help out in the household. Naturally, I was thrilled to get some help since I was now in my last month of pregnancy and was always feeling tired. She also brought a basket filled with fresh fruit and vegetables and several jars of jam that your father had prepared himself. In one of his shirts he had wrapped his homemade spaghetti, made from the last batch of flour. I cried at the welcome sight of all the wonderful goodies, and when I unearthed his letter, I was completely overcome.

"Unfortunately, Mariska turned out to be of no help whatsoever because she could not stand up for any length of time, her legs always swelling up after a short while. I ended up waiting on her instead of the other way around. When I confronted her about this one day, she reluctantly admitted that the only reason she had taken the job was so that she could get out of Sofia at your father's expense. I was forced to let her go."

The house we lived in
in St. Gilgen

During the rest of the outing to St. Gilgen, Mother kept coming back to what happened in 1944, and I was only too happy to let her.

In spite of the troubles with Mariska, Mother was ecstatic that for the first time in many months she could finally prepare meals in her own kitchen, which had been impossible while living over the barn in Doettleinsdorf. She was tired of having to eat what others had prepared; after all, cooking was one of her great enjoyments. Her new pleasant surroundings also helped her feel more hopeful.

The only thing that was missing in this picture of perfection, as far as Mother was concerned, was my father. If only she could know that he was safe, but she had only heard from him a few times after he was ordered to return to Sofia in June 1944. She fervently hoped that nothing terrible had befallen him.

The news on the radio was not good, and from what Father had told her during his last visit, the situation in Bulgaria was changing very quickly for the worse. It looked as if the country would soon declare war on Germany. One of the main reasons that it had even been an ally of Germany was King Boris III's family connection to both Germany and Italy. He had German blood in him on his mother's side and his wife was an Italian princess.

According to Father, the catalyst for the breakup between the two countries was the unexpected death of King Boris just after he returned from a short visit to Hitler's headquarters in Bavaria in August 1943. The circumstances were very mysterious and even suspicious, or so the rumors had it at the time, for the king had seemed in perfectly good health before he went to confer with Hitler. Bulgarians truly mourned their beloved monarch, who had always done so much for his country.

Because his son, crown prince Simeon, was only six years old, a council of regents was established under the leadership of the new Prime Minister, Dobri Bozhilov. Even though this council was still friendly toward Germany, it was not as positively disposed, as King Boris III had been, at keeping the country's own communists at bay. As a result, a massive guerrilla movement, headed by the underground Bulgarian Communist Party, became very active and strong, especially in the western and southwestern mountains of Bulgaria.

Father had told Mother that he was convinced that the untimely death of King Boris was the reason the Bulgarian communists were able to spread their socialist agenda and propaganda among the people. They were definitely gaining in popularity. All the evidence pointed to many communist partisan groups cropping up everywhere. This did not bode well for the alliance between Germany and Bulgaria because the aim of the partisans was to take control of the government and to ally Bulgaria with Russia instead.

The question, as Father saw it, was: Would they succeed? And if so, when? If he was interpreting and reading the political climate correctly, it really was just a matter of time before the royalist Bulgarian government, fearing the Russian invasion from the north, would surrender its control to the communist partisans in the hopes that the country would escape further destruction. If this happened, he knew that it could only mean one thing: the new Bulgarian communist leadership would declare war on Germany and enter into an alliance with their Soviet comrades. As soon as that happened, all diplomatic relationships with Germany would cease, and everyone still at the German Legation would lose their diplomatic immunity status and become *persona non grata.*

After Father told Mother all this, she entreated him even more strongly than ever to stay in Austria even though she knew it was useless. He reiterated what he had told her before when he forced her to leave Sofia without him in January. He simply would not desert his country. She could not help but admire and love him for his strong sense of devotion for a country that was not even really his. That was just one of the many wonderful qualities she loved about him, she always declared.

On another occasion, probably on one of my birthdays or perhaps a wedding anniversary, she told me about the last letter and telegrams she received from Father. Different occasions often seemed to trigger Mother into lapsing into her "reminiscing mode." She was extremely emotional and sentimental, qualities I especially loved about her.

"It was the end of August when I walked to the mailbox in St. Gilgen in the hopes of finally getting a letter from your pappa. I was absolutely beside myself with happiness when I saw an envelope with his beautiful and beloved handwriting. The only thing that would have topped this was if, by some sort of magic, he could have stuffed himself inside that envelope." She smiled wistfully. "But by this point in my life, I was happy to just hear from him."

I was thrilled to find that particular letter safely tucked away in a folder marked Bimbam-Katerman, 1930-1944. Knowing what I now know, reading it really tugs at my heartstrings.

> *My darling Bimili, Ingili and Katinka,* [some of Father's many nicknames for Mother and my sisters]
>
> *I think longingly and lovingly of you and wish I were there with you in St. Gilgen instead of here in Sofia. After work, I come home to this empty shell of a home that now consists of a tiny room in somebody else's house. No Bimili cooking in the kitchen, no tantalizing smells of food, or shouts of laughter or running small children coming to greet me after a day's hard work at the Legation. How long can I endure this loneliness? It is unbearable! But then I think of you, safely tucked away in St. Gilgen. My courage returns and I tell myself I must be strong. It won't be long now until we will all be together.*
>
> *I want to be strong because I know that our love for one another will hold the fabric of our lives together. Nothing can destroy my will to overcome all difficulties knowing how much we love one another. I want you, my children, to grow*

up to be strong people as well so that you can endure any hardships life will strew along your path.

In the meantime, you will soon have another little brother or sister who will share your lives. Ingili, you are my oldest, and therefore I want you to be strong for your Mutti [endearing form for "Mother" in German] *and help her take care of the littlest one in our family. She will really need all the help you can give her since I won't be able to be there for her.*

And as for you, my darling Bimbam, you must know how much I love you and long to be there with you when our fourth child sees the light of the world. But unfortunately duty to my work holds me here. The political situation is getting worse every day. But hopefully I will be leaving soon along with the rest of the legation personnel. We are all just waiting for the ambassador to give us the signal. Maybe it won't be too long now. Perhaps I will even be there before you get this letter...

Obviously, he did not make it!

Although she heard two more times from him in the form of a telegram, this was the last long letter Mother received. No wonder she saved it and read it over and over as witnessed by its dog-eared look and the many smudges that must have come from her tears.

I also found, hidden away inside one of Mother' s several small black notebooks, a piece of paper on which she had scribbled down her thoughts on the night before I was born. I could not help but cry when I read it. I wondered how many mothers would take the time to write down their feelings just before giving birth to their child? Thank goodness she never threw it away. Here is what she wrote:

August 30, 1944

My little one, you certainly are taking your time entering this world. You were due yesterday, but I can fully understand why you don't want to see the light of day yet. You must feel so safe inside of me, being gently rocked to sleep and able to eat whenever you want. 'Why should I leave my warm and cushy nest?' you may wonder. 'I don't know what kind of a world will greet me when I finally make my entrance? Will there be peace? Will the bombs have stopped falling? What will my life be like? What kind of a world will I grow up in?' I worry all the time whether your father will have a chance to know you? Will he be able to make it in time for your birth? I surely hope so but somehow I doubt it very much. However, sometimes the impossible is quite possible. I just have to remain optimistic about that. I must not ever give up hope. Perhaps as I write this, he is en route to us. I know that is wishful thinking, but one thing I am certain of is that if he could, he would be here when you make your grand entrance.

My sweet darling baby, I have so many questions! Oh, how I wish I knew the answers, but only God knows the answers. You and I will simply have to trust Him to make everything right. I hope and pray that He will.

When the telegram announcing my birth arrived at the German Legation in Sofia, Father happened to be at the Turkish-Bulgarian border in Svilengrad. He was in charge of the exchange of German and Turkish civilians who wanted to return to their respective homelands. According to a friend who told Mother about this later, the legation was considerate enough to forward the telegram to him. Upon his return to Sofia on September 4, he telegraphed the following response:

CONGRATULATIONS AND BEST WISHES FOR YOUR AND BIRGITTA'S HEALTH STOP AM HAPPY TO HAVE THREE GIRLS STOP LOVE ROLAND

On September 7, my parents' ninth anniversary, Father sent yet another telegram to Mother in St. Gilgen.

LOOKING FORWARD TO MANY MORE HAPPY YEARS WITH YOU MY DARLING BIMBAM STOP ROLAND

CHAPTER IX

Captured

Bulgaria, 1944

My mother only knew what happened to Father after Bulgaria declared war on Germany on September 8, 1944 because of the firsthand information she received from their very good friend Erland Uddgren, the Swedish *Chargé d'Affaires* in Sofia. Over the years Erland, and his Hungarian wife Elisabeth, stayed in close contact with Mother, lending her support in many different ways. He even brought her Father's diamond ring that Father had entrusted to him for safekeeping just before he was captured.

If it had not been for Erland, we would never have known anything at all. The only thing the German Foreign Service ever told Mother was that their diplomats in Sofia had been captured and that the AA was doing all it could to obtain their release. Obviously this attempt failed miserably; Father was not heard of again for many years after the Soviets had him in captivity.

The following account is based on what I pieced together from the correspondence between my mother and Erland Uddgren, in whom my father obviously put great trust and confidence.

On the day Father sent that anniversary telegram to Mother, he had just returned from Svilengrad, where he had waited several days in vain for a train to arrive from Istanbul that was supposed to contain German civilians leaving Turkey. He had waited for these kinds of train loads many times before during the past month, but never for three days like this time. Fully convinced that the train was not coming, he therefore decided to call Bulgarian officials in Sofia to see if they would allow him to bring the empty train back to help evacuate German families before it was too late. Although they refused to let him have a locomotive, they permitted him to bring back one passenger car and a kitchen car, but only if these could be attached to a regular passenger train headed for Sofia.

Our last photo of Pappa before he was taken by the Russians

After returning to Sofia with the passenger car, Father filled it to capacity with German citizens, including several minor legation staff members and their families. Sending it on its way to Germany, he hoped the train would make it out of Bulgaria before the borders closed. Those who were still left were going to leave by car to Skopje, located across the mountains in Macedonia. Here they would join up with German troops in the area. The Bulgarian government had guaranteed them a safe passage out, including the use of a police escort. Everything might have worked out if everyone had abided by the plan.

By late afternoon on September 7, several cars stood ready and waiting to leave for Skopje. Since Father had no car of his own, he was supposed to travel in the car with the SA officer and the military attaché. The column of cars, with the Bulgarian police escort in front, was only waiting for Ambassador Beckerle to arrive. The ambassador had left some time earlier to go pack up some of his belongings in Chamkoria, a resort area in the mountains, where he and his wife had had been staying at their villa ever since the evacuation of Sofia earlier in the year.

Naturally, everyone was getting concerned, wondering what could possibly be taking so long. It was totally incomprehensible to Father why Beckerle had not already packed up his belongings long ago, given that he must surely have suspected he would have to leave at a moment's notice. After all, the handwriting had been on the wall for some time. Father had long since shipped the rest of their belongings, packed into four sturdy handmade wooden crates marked with RG for Roland Gottlieb, up the Danube River to Austria.

I remember how I came across these crates in our attic in Borås and asked Mother about them. With tears in her eyes she told me how happy she was when they arrived in St. Gilgen. It was the last thing she received from Father. The two of us gently stroked the big black RG initials and shed a few tears, wondering not for the first or last time, when we would hear from him again.

After waiting longer than they thought was necessary or safe, the two men in Father's car began to whisper with the Bulgarian police officer in charge of the escort. Finally, one of the men approached Father and told him that they were going to leave and not wait for Mr. Beckerle any longer. Since they did not enjoy diplomatic immunity like Father did, they felt that the longer they waited the more dangerous the situation became for them. The Bulgarian policeman concurred with them. Father was welcome to join them, but he declined because he felt it was inappropriate and unwise to leave without the ambassador's sanction. When they consulted with the rest of the embassy staff, waiting in the other cars, everyone agreed with Father and decided to wait for Mr. Beckerle.

As Father explained to his good friend Erland, a few minutes later he found himself standing outside the car with his suitcase in hand and watching the car with the military attaché and the SA officer disappear in the distance. To everyone's amazement and shock the police escort that was supposed to see to their safety disappeared in the distance as well. Without the protection of the escort, they were now totally stranded. Everyone was very concerned and worried how they would make it out of Bulgaria in time.

When Mr. Beckerle finally arrived in his limousine, he was irate after hearing what had happened. None of them would now be able to leave via Skopje. With their police escort gone, it would be extremely dangerous to try to make it through the partisan and bandit infested areas along the road to Skopje. Disappointed, they all went back inside the German Legation to discuss their next move.

At the behest of Ambassador Beckerle, Father then sent a telegram to the Foreign Minister von Ribbentrop explaining what had happened and requesting that an airplane be sent to pick them up instead. The telegrammed answer from the minister was negative. He refused to send the plane but ordered them instead to leave via the as of yet non-occupied Soviet territories to the southeast to avoid capture by the Soviets.

The letter, in which Erland tells Mother about this sequence of events, lauds Father for trying to persuade his colleagues to go by car, taking the more southern route towards Saloniki, Greece, since it was still under German control, rather than taking the train to Turkey. Both Erland and Father feared that the Soviets had already advanced too far into northern Bulgaria and were therefore getting too close to Svilengrad at the Turkish border to make it safe for the German Legation staff to take that route. Unfortunately, his colleagues refused to listen. Instead Father was put in charge of procuring a train to take them to Turkey, a decision that proved disastrous.

An explanation may be in order here about what was happening in Bulgaria at the time. Since Russia had already declared war on Bulgaria on September 5, it had almost immediately occupied the northeastern part of Bulgaria along with its key port cities of Varna and Bourgas on the coast of the Black Sea. The weakened Bulgarian government ordered its army to offer no resistance to the Soviets since it was planning to officially change sides anyway.

On September 8, 1944 Bulgaria declared war on Germany, thus becoming an ally of the Soviet Union. For the German diplomats, holed up and waiting for transportation inside the legation, this meant they were now officially *persona non grata* and would no longer enjoy diplomatic immunity. Any Germans still left in Bulgaria would be considered an enemy and, if caught, would be dealt with as such.

Once the decision was made to leave by train for Turkey, Father immediately contacted his friend, Erland Uddgren, to ask if he would offer the stranded German diplomats his protection and help. He only agreed out of friendship for Father. Officially he could not really do that because Sweden's diplomats had just been appointed to protect the Russian but not the German diplomats.

With Erland's help throughout the ensuing negotiation process, the Bulgarians agreed to have a train waiting for them the next day, September 9.

When the German diplomats arrived at the central station in Sofia in the early morning hours of September 9, Father immediately realized that their number had swelled from twenty-five to forty because members from the Hungarian and Italian embassies and some of their wives had decided to join them.

A mutual friend, Walther Küttner, who was CEO of a Swedish match factory in Sofia, reported to Erland Uddgren what happened next. At Erland's request, Küttner was there to help protect the entire group of foreign diplomats against any possible attacks by Bulgarian soldiers before the train could leave. Just to be on the safe side, Erland also arranged for the Swedish Vice Consul, George Nyström, to accompany the whole contingency of foreign non grata diplomats all the way to Svilengrad.

While they were still standing around waiting for the train, Bulgarian soldiers suddenly swarmed all over them, demanding their guns. Luckily, no one was brave or foolish enough to protest but simply handed over whatever weapons they were carrying. After completing a very thorough body search for hidden weapons, the soldiers finally let them get on the train, which soon started rolling towards Svilengrad.

During the nine hour long train journey, Father explained to his colleagues that in order to be allowed entrance into Turkey they would still need the permission of the Turkish government. Unfortunately their visas had not arrived in time. The other option was to try negotiating with the people in charge to let them enter anyway. He was very hopeful that this might work since he had become well acquainted with these officials, having traveled back and forth between Sofia and Svilengrad and negotiating with them during the past few months.

Soldiers, guarding the station in Svilengrad, however, crushed that idea by quite unexpectedly locking them into their railroad car and refusing to let anyone detrain. Protests fell on deaf ears until Father, after lots of haranguing and wheedling, at last persuaded the officer in charge to let him and the Swedish representative off to discuss their situation with the stationmaster.

The stationmaster, who immediately recognized Father, was more than willing to help him obtain the required travel permit by talking to his Turkish counterpart on the other side of the border. Father, along with the Swedish Vice Consul Nyström, then accompanied the stationmaster over the bridge to the Turkish side of Svilengrad. The Turkish official made a few phone calls but was unsuccessful in obtaining the required permission. Finally, in desperation, Father grabbed the phone and called the chief of police in Edirne, Turkey, a city located only about twenty miles east of Svilengrad. The man, whom Father also knew from his negotiations, promised to come the next day to discuss the matter. That was the best he could do.

Disappointed with the results, Father and Nyström returned to the railroad car where everyone looked expectantly and hopefully at them. As Father reported the outcome of his discussion with the stationmaster and authorities, they could hear the car being locked behind them once again, with soldiers standing guard outside, thus imprisoning all the diplomats.

The next day, the stationmaster sought Father out and whispered to him that the chief of police from Edirne had just arrived with the Orient Express and was waiting for him and Ambassador Beckerle in the basement of one of the buildings close by. The Turkish police officer was quite friendly towards them and offered them his help. He told them that naturally an official permit from Ankara would be required before their train could continue on its journey, which was especially necessary now that all diplomatic relationships had officially broken off between Germany and Turkey. He warned them that this might take some time, perhaps as many as four or five days.

Dejected with this outcome but still trying to put a positive face on it for everyone's sake, Father and the ambassador returned to their railroad car to report what they had learned. All they could do now was wait.

Several days passed and nothing happened. Finally, on September 14, the stationmaster came and informed the weary and anxious diplomats locked in their car that their train would have to return to Sofia immediately. When asked the reason for this change in plans, they were told that the president of Bulgaria had ordered it. Shocked to hear that the president had reneged on his earlier promise, everyone demanded to know what the president's name was. A man named Georgiev, who was known to be a communist, was the response. Muraviev, who had been president for a few weeks, had just been replaced.

This was not good news. There was no telling what would happen to them when they returned to Sofia. A communist regime could only mean one thing: they were doomed. The stationmaster further confirmed this by telling them that the Soviets had taken over the whole country.

Once again the train got on its way, this time towards Sofia, a city everyone had hoped to leave behind. Then on September 15, as the train was nearing the capital, it suddenly came to a halt in Poduene, a suburb of Sofia, where soldiers with machine guns immediately surrounded it.

Through the train window Father could see that Erland Udd gren, standing beside Walter Küttner, was pointing him out to a soldier who proceeded to climb into the train. Still standing outside, Erland was holding up a piece of paper on which he had written in Swedish: "Roland, get off." Father had no choice but to follow the soldier out, wondering what was going to happen now.

In a letter to Mother, Erland describes what followed.

I immediately informed him that he was to come with me to negotiate with the officials in downtown Sofia. Küttner was to stay there and make sure that everyone else was not mistreated in any fashion. Before leaving the station, Roland requested to be allowed to explain the situation to his traveling companions, which he was allowed to do. My chauffeur then drove us in my car that was clearly marked with the Swedish colors on its standard to meet with the foreign minister of Bulgaria. It easily passed through all the controls set up after the takeover by the Bulgarian communists, who were now aided by the Soviets. Roland was very pleased when the newly appointed minister readily agreed to let the stranded diplomats return to Svilengrad and even went so far as to allow them to be accompanied by an official from the ministry as well as a communist party member from the Homeland Office to ensure their safety.

Before returning to the train station, Father asked Erland if he could take him to the Turkish Embassy where he wanted to check on the status of the requested and promised visa from the Turkish authorities. The Turkish ambassador assured my father that he would check with Ankara immediately.

Erland then continues to tell what happened next.

After we were finished, Roland had a brilliant idea. He remembered that I had a key to the safe at the German Bulgarian Bank in which several millions of Bulgarian Levis was stashed. He then told me of his plan of purchasing a truck that could hold everyone. They could cross the Maritsa River and force their way through the Turkish border at a different checkpoint from Svilengrad, thereby avoiding the Dimotica Zone entirely. His plan was a good one, I thought. Since I hated to see him leave without first partaking of a good meal, I suggested we go to my house where I knew Elisabeth would welcome him with open arms.

After getting the money and having lunch with Elisabeth, Father and Erland returned to Poduene station where the Bulgarian official from the Foreign Ministry as well as the representative from the Communist Party were already waiting. Once again the train was on its way back to Svilengrad.

In the same letter Erland expresses his deep sorrow at how miserably the whole escape plan failed. He writes:

All I really know is what Nyström reported to me. You will recall, Ruth, that he is the Swedish Vice Consul here in Sofia. The Svilengrad station was totally closed off and well-guarded by the militia when Roland's train arrived. The train sat there for two more days with nothing happening. Nyström got the distinct impression that the two Bulgarians who had accompanied the train had no earthly idea what was happening or why. He told me that Roland tried several more things to see if they could not somehow get across the border, but those also failed.

Finally the train started moving again but unfortunately not towards Turkey but back to Sofia.

They had not gone very far when it came to a sudden stop. Soldiers in Soviet uniforms climbed aboard and with pointed weapons forced everyone, except for Nyström and the Bulgarian officials, of course, to get off and lie face down on the platform where they were frisked very roughly for any hidden weapons. Their entire luggage was examined as well. A long and extremely uncomfortable night followed with all of the diplomats being forced to lie face down on the platform, with their hands above their heads. Uniformed soldiers with guns surrounded them on all sides standing guard. Resistance was futile. The next morning, September 20, Nyström was told that the captured diplomats were officially declared POWs and were being transported to the Soviet Union.

That was the last information Mother received about what happened to Father. She was now completely on her own, her worst fears becoming reality. Father was lost to us because he had not left Sofia in time.

CHAPTER X

The "White Bus" Journey

November 1945

Mother came home one day carrying a box with four slices of delectable cake from the nearby bakery. This was a luxury that she could seldom afford because money was always in such short supply at our house. It must have been December 6, 1951.

"I want to celebrate this day because it marks the sixth anniversary of our arrival in Sweden," Mother said before turning to Ingrid and asking her if she remembered the white buses.

"Of course I do, Mamma, but Karin and Gittan don't since they were too young," Ingrid answered as she carefully put the delicacies on a plate.

I could hardly take my eyes off the slices of princess cake, my absolute favorite, made of a soft yellow sponge cake with vanilla cream in the middle and covered with a thin sheet of green-colored marzipan.

"Can I have a piece now?" I begged, my mouth watering for the marzipan.

"Not until we have eaten supper," Mamma replied predictably.

During supper, I picked up the subject of the white buses once more. I knew we had come to Sweden on them and that Mamma was always so thankful that we weren't still living in Austria. How many times had I not heard her exclaim when I refused to eat something I did not like, "Eat up, Gittan, you don't know how lucky you are to even have food on your plate. If we were still in Austria you might be going hungry."

This usually shamed me into eating whatever it was I did not like.

"Mamma, why were those buses white instead of red or yellow

like the ones here in Borås?" I asked.

"Because they belonged to the Red Cross Organization, they were painted white with a red cross on the roof to distinguish them from military vehicles," was Mother's quick response. She then went on to explain that those buses had also been used during the last part of the war to rescue many others. "By showing this symbol of the Red Cross on top and on all sides, the rescue mission hoped the Allied Forces would not bomb their buses."

That made a lot of sense to me as a child, enough so that I didn't pursue that particular aspect again until I was an adult and became more interested in discovering the larger story behind those white buses.

From various sources I learned that the original mission of the "White Buses" was to rescue Scandinavian concentration camp victims and transport them home to their respective countries in the early part of 1945. This rescue operation was promoted by the neutral Swedish government and was carried out under the auspices of the Swedish Red Cross under the leadership of its second in command, Folke Bernadotte.

Some say that this help action began because Himmler, who could see that the war was going to end in defeat for Germany, was anxious to stand in good stead with the Western Allied Forces. He therefore was eager to facilitate the release of thousands of Danish and Norwegian concentration camp internees, many of whom had been captured when Germany occupied Denmark and Norway. Among them were both resistance fighters and Jews.

Over 15,000 people were saved with the help of hundreds of volunteers, mostly consisting of personnel on leave from their military duties. They manned many white ambulance buses, a huge contingent of trucks carrying food, fuel, and spare machine parts, rescue and workshop vehicles, several motorbikes and passenger cars. These sorts of volunteers and vehicles made up this "White Bus" relief convoy, as they came to be known. They traveled on torn-up highways through bombed-out Germany until the end of the war. It was exactly in such a convoy that my mother arrived in Sweden with my two sisters and me in December 1945.

Even though we were not concentration victims, my family was included in the help action that took place after the war was over. When the Swedish Red Cross, with the help of the Association of Swedes Abroad, decided to extend the "White Bus" rescue operation to include Swedish women and children wanting to return to their homeland from the war ravaged areas of Europe, Mother definitely fitted into that category.

After finishing our dessert of princess cake, we went into the living room where Karin and I begged Mother and Ingrid to tell us about our journey to Sweden. Neither one of us knew very much about it, having heard only bits and pieces before.

"Do you remember, Mamma, how you came barging into my bedroom in St. Gilgen to tell me what you had heard on the Swedish evening news?" Ingrid now began.

"I most certainly do. It was sometime early in October 1945, when the news came over the radio. I was so excited when the announcer said that the Swedish Red Cross and the Association of Swedes Abroad were once again organizing transportation to Sweden for any Swedish-born persons living in Germany and Austria. Buses would start leaving from Malmö (a city in southern Sweden) right away.

"When he mentioned Salzburg as a pick up point, I could hardly believe my ears. Could it really be true? Had he actually said Salzburg? It was almost too fantastic to be true! But how long would it take before the buses would arrive in Salzburg? I simply had to share the good news with you, Ingrid." Mother's eyes filled with tears at that memory.

Raising her eyebrows quizzically, Ingrid looked at Karin and me. "Can you believe our mother would come barging in like that long after I was asleep?"

Karin and I nodded because when Mamma got excited she might do just about anything out of the ordinary.

"Ingrid was very skeptical and told me in her little adult-like voice that it probably wasn't true and that I must have misunderstood." Mother mimicked Ingrid the way she must have sounded at the time before she smiled tenderly at my oldest sister.

"I could understand why she didn't believe it because earlier in March, before the war was over, the Swedish Red Cross was supposed to help us reach Sweden but failed to come and pick us up, claiming that it was too dangerous with the war still raging across Southern Germany and Upper Austria. But as I told your sister, the situation was different this time because the war was over now! I had to believe it was true for this was the first good news in a very, very long time. My imagination was running wild. The idea that I might see my parents again, my sisters and brothers and all my dear friends was mind-boggling, especially since there had been no communication whatsoever for over half a year. All mail service and telegram bureaus had ceased to function in May, when Germany capitulated. Everything was in shambles. I remember starting to pack the first suitcase immediately. But then the waiting began."

"What do you mean, Mamma? Didn't the buses come?" Karin asked.

"Not immediately! The very next morning I took a bus into Salzburg where I went to the Swedish Consulate to find out when exactly the bus was supposed to arrive. They told me they had no exact date yet but that I should check in with them from time to time. This would be very difficult for me, I responded, especially since I did not have a telephone and lived out in the countryside. Afraid that I might miss my only opportunity to get home to Sweden, I spent the next two weeks taking a bus every day in to Salzburg to check at the consulate. In the last week of October my daily treks paid off. A telegram had just arrived that morning announcing that a bus would arrive on November 8. Absolutely beside myself, I rushed back home to St. Gilgen to finish packing the rest of our belongings."

"Did the truck actually come that day?" I asked.

"No, it didn't." Mother answered. "There we were, about fifteen Swedish-born mothers with our children, waiting for the bus outside the consulate. You should have seen the pile of luggage. We waited all day but no truck came. Since we were all getting hungry, we started delving into our food supply, which was really intended for our journey. Imagine our disappointment when darkness came and still no truck had shown up! We were told that it would probably be the next day before we could leave. After piling all our belongings into the cellar of the consulate, those who did not have a place to stay in Salzburg spent the night in the building close by where the International Red Cross was housed.

"The four us, however, were able to spend the night at *Omama's* apartment. The next day Ingrid and I took turns guarding our luggage but still no truck came. We spent another worrisome night with *Omama*. Then on Saturday, November 10 the consulate finally received a telegram explaining that the bus had broken down right outside Garmisch-Partenkirchen and that a truck instead would arrive to pick us up on Sunday."

"I guess it finally showed up because here we are in Sweden," Karin quipped, grinning broadly.

"That is so true, Karin. By the time it did, every one of us mothers was feeling rather jittery because our food supply was rapidly shrinking. None of us would be able to get any more because we had used up all our ration cards in preparation for the long trip ahead. On Sunday morning we were very relieved when a truck, painted with the Swedish flag on its side, pulled up in front of the consulate. I was overcome with joy when several people, wearing Red Cross armbands, greeted us in Swedish."

I could easily imagine the vivid scene Mother was describing.

"We shed many tears that day. Having to say goodbye to *Omama*, who had been my tower of strength in the last year and a half, was heart breaking. We did not know whether we would ever see each other again." Mamma's eyes misted at the memory of the sad parting.

"Do you think I will ever get to meet her, Mamma? Why doesn't she just come to Sweden and stay with us?" I was thinking how great that would be because then I would have her to cuddle up to now that *Morfar* was dead.

"I have suggested it many times in my letters, but she doesn't want to leave her home, especially since your uncle Walther and his family as well as your uncle Heinz don't live too far away. I can't say that I really blame her. Imagine how hard it would be for her to move to Sweden where she doesn't even speak the language! And then there is the question of her poor health. She hasn't been well for many years now, as you know." Mother sounded very sad.

"What happened after the truck finally came, Mamma?" Karin was obviously trying to get Mother back on track. I was just as eager to hear what happened next.

"Well, let's see now. Where were we? Oh yes! After saying our farewells, we piled into what turned out to be a covered furniture truck. It was a tight squeeze with over thirty people and our entire luggage trying to cram into a small space. But somehow we managed. We were just thankful that we were finally on our way home to Sweden.

"That first day was an eighteen-hour nightmare on uneven and rutted roads! When we finally arrived in Weinheim, a small city outside Heidelberg where the main depot for the Swedish Red Cross was located, it was a heavenly relief to be able to crawl out of the cramped truck and stretch our legs. I can still taste the wonderful sandwiches made with real butter, salami and cheese the Swedish volunteers handed us and the delicious hot porridge." Mother smacked her lips, pretending to eat.

This made me laugh. She looked so funny. Oh, how she loved to act things out! Sometimes I thought that show business had lost an actress when she married my father, not that I am complaining because then I might never have been born.

"Did you have to travel in that same truck the rest of the way to Sweden?" Hunching my shoulders and pulling them close together, I pretended that I was sitting in the cramped quarters of that truck long ago. I wanted to show that I could be just as funny as Mother. My efforts were rewarded when everyone laughed and Mother chucked me under the chin with her fingers.

"Of course not, Gittan. " Mother chuckled. "All that day buses and trucks kept arriving at the depot with more people like us. By the end of the day, one hundred and fifty people, sixty adults and ninety children were assembled in the huge barracks, everyone eager to be on the way to Sweden. The next morning we boarded one of five big white buses with the Swedish flag and the words Schweden-Sweden painted on each side. A huge truck loaded to the brim with luggage, several more trucks containing food supplies, a few motorbike-riding officials, and a black car with our leader also accompanied the buses, all heading north. What a sight we were!" Mother sighed contentedly at this remembered spectacle.

"I was the only one of all the children who actually was able to speak Swedish on our bus." Ingrid said proudly, trying to impress Karin and me. "I also remember how you cooked a thin porridge and how we picnicked on the bus during the day."

"You are right, Ingrid. Each family unit received a package of food supplies, which had to last until we stopped for a hot meal in the evening. And since one of the women on our bus had brought a little camp stove, we were even able to make porridge for the youngest children although it required a little resourcefulness in the shaking bus. While one mother held the little stove on her lap and another held on to the pot, a third one stirred the porridge. In this way the children had hot porridge to eat."

We laughed again at Mother's demonstration of how the ladies had managed to prepare food on their long journey north.

"Our caravan plodded northwards, first stopping in Hamburg where English military personnel examined our papers before allowing us to continue toward the German Danish border at Padborg. On our second day on the road I had the brilliant idea of making a hammock out of a blanket, which I managed to attach to the bus ceiling. This made an excellent place for you to nap, Gittan. It also helped free up my tired arms from holding you all the time."

"Wasn't that dangerous?" I asked. "I could have fallen out and got killed, couldn't I?"

"Not really, although it concerned me at first. But after watching the makeshift hammock swing gently back and forth for a while, I was satisfied that you were safe. You probably slept the best of any of us. While all of us exhausted mothers had to sit upright in our seats, nodding off whenever possible, the children either stretched out on the floor of the bus along the aisles or in between the seats. It was a strenuous journey, to say the least, which became even more so because of the bumpy pot-holed roads and the hard wooden seats."

Mother then went on to tell us how relieved and happy everyone was after finally arriving at the Danish border and being able to get off the buses. Their relief was short-lived, however. "Before the Danish authorities would let any of us enter Denmark, we had to go through a delousing process, a most unpleasant experience, which was very demeaning because it implied we were too filthy and might be lice infested."

At the mention of lice, I started feeling itchy and began to scratch my head; the power of suggestion can be very strong.

"Ha, ha! You had lice and needed to be deloused," I teased Karin. "Let me see if you still have some." I leaned over and tried to rub my fingers through her hair.

Angrily, she pushed my hands away and poked me in the stomach. "Well, you did too, silly, because you were there as well, weren't you? Ha! I bet you really squalled like a stuck pig." Triumphantly she turned to Mother after her smart comeback. "What did they really do to us, Mamma?"

I decided to be quiet and not retaliate; I was more interested in hearing Mother's response.

"It was quite demoralizing to stand together with twenty other women and children, completely naked on the icy cold floor and be hosed down with a mixture of water and some nasty smelling chemical." Mother shivered at the mere memory of it, then pinched her nose with the fingers of one hand while waving the other one in the air as if trying to make the bad odor go away. Once again laughter filled the air.

"What did they do with our clothes?" Karin asked once she stopped laughing.

"The attendants took them away to be sterilized as soon as we entered the bathhouse. Right after that nasty procedure, we scrubbed down with soap and hot water before we were led, still totally naked, to see a doctor. After examining us from head to toe for any infectious diseases or lice, the doctor dismissed us into a big hall where our clothes and other paraphernalia lay waiting for us. Although it was a humiliating process, the delicious meal afterwards, consisting of a hearty Danish soup, delicious sandwiches, and rich fat milk, was well worth it."

"I don't remember all that, Mamma" Karin said wistfully.

"No, of course not, you were only four years old. Right after supper we went straight to a huge dormitory barrack where we got our first good night's sleep in many days on a real bed with a soft mattress, clean sheets, blankets and pillows." Mother sounded dreamy when she described how wonderful it was to lay her weary body down on a comfortable bed.

"Go on, Mamma, tell us what happened the next day," I urged, eager to hear more.

"The next morning, after finishing a wonderful breakfast of oatmeal porridge, milk, freshly baked bread, creamy butter, Danish cheese and meat, everyone in my group of women and children said goodbye to our bus drivers. They were heading south again to pick up another load of refugees while my group was going on by train to Copenhagen and from there on another train to Helsingør to board a ferry that would take us across the Øresund to Helsingborg on the Swedish coast."

Ingrid interrupted Mother with a memory of her own. "When we were on that first train, I remember thinking how strange it was not to see any bombed out houses along the way like we had seen in Austria and Germany. Instead, the towns we passed through were brightly lit, which made everything look so cheerful. I also remember the Swedish choir that welcomed us on the pier in Helsingborg. They were singing Swedish folk melodies. Both Mamma and I cried when we heard them."

"They were happy tears, though," Mother picked up where Ingrid left off. "After finally stepping off the ferry on Swedish soil in Helsingborg, I felt as if I were dreaming. It was hard to believe that I was really back in Sweden. Five long years! It seemed unreal somehow. Then, speaking on behalf of the Swedish Red Cross, a major welcomed us home to Sweden and invited us to coffee and Danish pastries. All the children received candy and chocolate."

"I don't remember that, Mamma. Boy, oh boy, how I wish I had some right now." I smacked my lips, my sweet tooth rearing its head.

"Of course, you can't remember that, you silly goose. You were only fifteen months old." Mother smiled indulgently down at me where I was sitting cross-legged on the carpet in front of her.

According to Mother, our train was then hooked up to a locomotive in Helsingborg as we continued on to Malmö, where the headquarters for the Swedish Red Cross was located. Here we had to undergo a second delousing process, but in Swedish style this time.

Mother claimed there was a huge difference between this one and the one we underwent in Denmark. "The Swedish volunteers did not make me feel inferior but let me keep my dignity. Afterwards we were invited to a wonderful meal served on yellow and blue tablecloths, where small Swedish flags decorated every table. I felt overwhelmed by how friendly, kind, warm, and generous everyone was, especially towards all the children, many of whom had never even been to Sweden before.

"What about me, Mamma? I had been to Sweden before, hadn't I? So why didn't I speak Swedish just like Ingrid did?" Karin sounded a little unhappy.

"Well, that is easy to explain. Although we came for a short visit to *Mormor* and *Morfar* in 1943 when you were only two years old, by the time we returned in 1945, you had forgotten how to speak Swedish. I am sorry to say that I just didn't have the strength to keep up both languages after your pappa was captured by the Soviets. Remember, too, that I also gave birth to your sister Gittan right about that same time. I had a hard time coping with everything."

That answer seemed to have satisfied my sister Karin back then but not today, which she recently brought to my attention again. The situation in which she found herself shortly after our return to Sweden was anything but a pleasant memory for her.

Karin told me that the grownups decided that she should go stay with *Moster* Anne-Marie in Broddarp, a small village not too far from Borås where our aunt and uncle taught school. They argued that it was simply too much for *Mormor* to handle, having three young children suddenly thrust upon her, especially with the baby—me—constantly crying. There was no question about letting Ingrid stay because she had to start school immediately in Borås. And of course I was just a baby and therefore too young to be separated from Mother. What made it even worse for Karin was that she spoke no Swedish and my aunt and uncle spoke no German. This made her feel absolutely isolated and afraid.

She doesn't blame Mother for only trying to make the best of a difficult situation although she questions the wisdom of it. She wonders how come the grown-ups did not realize how traumatized she must have been after being uprooted from Austria and having endured a long and difficult journey with all the changes it entailed. What made matters even worse for her was that she also came down with chickenpox shortly after our arrival in Sweden. Poor Karin! It cannot have been easy for her.

Returning now to that dark December evening long ago, I was eager for Mother to tell us what happened after we arrived in Malmö. I was afraid that she would suddenly realize that it was way past my bedtime. To my immense relief she chose to ignore it this one time.

"Oh dear, I did not realize how late it is. You really must go to bed as soon as I finish," Mother said pointedly, glancing at the clock on the bookcase. "Unfortunately, we could not go on to Borås immediately because we had to be quarantined for fourteen days. The Swedish authorities were not taking any chances on our bringing back some contagious diseases from bombed-out and destroyed German territories. I cannot complain, however, because we spent those two weeks at a beautiful castle, called Örenäs, outside Glumslöv. Of course, we did not stay in the castle itself but in a small four-room cottage where the four of us slept in one of the rooms. We only went to the castle at mealtimes and for physical examinations, x-rays, immunizations, and tests for various infectious diseases. Even the police authorities came to interrogate us, all of which were part of the procedural protocols we had to go through in order to be officially admitted to Sweden."

Mother went on to describe the big day when we were finally allowed to leave. "Oh, how I cried when I saw your *morfar,* who came to meet us in Helsingborg. It was a very emotional moment for both of us as we cried and hugged each other after being apart for so long. Together the five of us then continued on to Borås. What a happy day! I was so thankful to be back home again." Closing her eyes, she clasped her hands in thankfulness to God as a few tears rolled down her cheeks.

I completely understood how she must have felt. Even just mentioning my beloved *morfar* reminded me how much I missed him. Only a few months had passed since his unexpected death.

"Why didn't *Mormor* come to Helsingborg to pick us up?" Karin now spoke up.

"She stayed behind in Borås so that she could have coffee and cake ready for us in the living room on Villagatan 17. When we finally arrived, she welcomed us with open arms. We hugged and kissed, and hugged and kissed some more. I was shocked, however, to see how much both *Mormor* and *Morfar* had aged since I had last seen them. They must have worried a lot about us. And who could blame them? But now it is high time for everyone to get some sleep," Mother said as she got up and shooed us off to bed.

As I went into my small cubbyhole bedroom, I couldn't help but think how much better this story was than any of those written by Astrid Lindgren, whose books I simply adored. After all, we were the main characters in this one, and as far as I was concerned, Pippi Longstocking could not hold a candle to our real life adventure of traveling to Sweden from war torn Europe.

Reflecting back as an adult on those early years, I can only say how tremendously I have come to admire my mother. She faced a very heavy burden trying to create a new life for herself at age thirty-four, with three young fatherless daughters to take care of, with no money and no job and completely dependent on her parents at first for everything, not exactly an enviable position for anyone to be in.

CHAPTER XI

Renewed Hope

Borås, 1950—

To this day I can easily picture Mother sitting at the *secretaire* in our third floor apartment in Borås penning the letters I found carbon copies of neatly preserved in well-marked folders. I also discovered all those she received in reply.

As I began to delve into this period of my life, Mother's correspondence testified to me how tirelessly she worked on Father's behalf. I found letters written to different agencies such as the Swedish Foreign Ministry Department, the Austrian and German Foreign Offices, the International Red Cross, the German Evangelical Help Organization, and the Soviet Embassy in Stockholm. She also contacted many individuals she thought might help her, such as Pastor Lippert, countless returning German POWs, and even Stalin himself.

Soon after our arrival in Sweden, sometime in 1946, Mother tried to contact officials from the Soviet Union to find out what had happened to my father. She wrote a letter to D. Kanonnikov, a representative in the consular division at the Soviet Embassy in Stockholm. He answered that he did not know anything about Father's circumstances but promised he would get back to her as soon as he heard from his government in Moscow. She never heard from him again, which is really not surprising, considering what we know about the Soviet Union today.

Five years later she tried to enlist the help of the Soviet ambassador in Stockholm, Konstantin Rodionov, after she heard from a returning POW that Father was still alive somewhere in Siberia. She asked if the ambassador could help her find out where exactly Father was being held captive. Once again she was met with complete silence.

We were gathered in our living room, busily preparing for yet another Christmas without Father when Mother told us she wanted to give the Soviet Union another chance to do right by us. It happened just a few weeks after Mother had recounted the story of how we came to Sweden.

"You know, Mamma, it will now be our eighth Christmas without Pappa," Ingrid said where she was sitting bent over one of her Christmas projects.

"That is right, Mamma, and this Christmas we won't even have *Morfar* with us since he has gone to heaven" I chimed in. I found it very difficult to get into the Christmas spirit. It just wasn't the same without *Morfar*.

"You are right, Ingrid. And you know what I think we should do?" We all looked at her expectantly. "I am going to write to Marshal Stalin, the leader of the Soviet Union, and simply ask him to send your pappa home to us. What do you think of that idea?"

Nodding, we agreed wholeheartedly that it was a terrific idea. Mother immediately went to her desk and returned half an hour later to read the following letter out loud:

Dear Field Marshal Stalin,

Once again it is Christmas. It will now be the eighth Christmas without my beloved husband and the father of my three girls. They are constantly asking me when their father will be coming home from Russia. They want me to write to you and ask you if you could not possibly send him home to us. And that is just what I am doing. It would please us tremendously and make us all so grateful if you would pardon my husband and send him home to us.

I have heard from another German, who was condemned to twenty years of hard labor, that you were so kind and pardoned him, which made it possible for him to return home to his loved ones in Germany. Won't you please do the same for my husband, Roland Gottlieb, who is in Vorkuta, Siberia? I would forever be in your debt and be very grateful. We would be the happiest little family in the world if this were to happen.

Please excuse me for bothering you with this matter, but you are my last hope in trying to get my husband back home again.

Sincerely,

Ruth Gottlieb

Since Mother had no idea how to get this letter into Stalin's hands, she wrote to the Swedish Embassy in Moscow and asked them to forward it. They responded by saying that it would be best if she contacted the Austrian Embassy instead since she was not a Swedish citizen but an Austrian one. Although this delay aggravated her, she followed their advice. The Austrian Embassy in turn responded that they would try to deliver her plea to Stalin. Nothing must have come of that since Mother never heard from the Soviet Union either directly or indirectly.

These approaches were not the only avenues Mother tried. Right after Father was captured in 1944, she was in contact with officials at the German Foreign Office in Berlin, who assured her that they were trying everything to get him released. Obviously they did not succeed. At the end of the war, that office was dissolved along with all other government offices and was not reinstituted until the western half of Germany became recognized in 1949 as an independent country called the Federal Republic of West Germany.

Once this happened, Mother contacted some of its official agencies again. For one thing, she tried to enlist the government's help in recovering Father's investments in the German stock market and their savings bonds. But her efforts turned out to be fruitless.

The reason she couldn't get any money back, she was informed, was that she had not lived in Germany between 1939 and 1945, the time in question. If she had, she would have been entitled to the restitution of lost funds. This response really upset Mother, and rightfully so, because Father had been posted as a German diplomat to a foreign country during those years. It was therefore not his fault that they had not been living in Germany. She felt the government was just using that as an excuse for not paying out what it owed.

She encountered a similar problem when she tried to enlist the help of the German Embassy in Stockholm regarding financial help that dependents of former German diplomats were entitled to. Here her problem was three-fold: She had not lived in Germany in 1949, she was not a German citizen any longer but Austrian, and she was not in a state of distress because she had an income of 700 Swedish crowns per month, which meant she was not destitute. These were just excuses for not doing right by her and her children, she always claimed.

Another big stumbling block for Mother was the question of our citizenship, which has played a large role throughout our lives. It began with Mother when she was forced to give up her Swedish citizenship after Father was transferred to Berlin in 1941 and to become German just like he, along with all Austrians when Austria was annexed in 1938. When the war was over, all former Austrian citizens automatically became Austrian again, which meant that Mother, because she was married to a native Austrian, also became Austrian along with her dependent daughters.

Because of this citizenship issue, Sweden was unable to offer Mother any direct help in regard to Father. Even though she appealed three times to the Swedish government to return her Swedish citizenship, she was always turned down. Since Father had not officially been declared dead, the government claimed that she was ineligible. However, if she were willing to declare him dead, then she could become Swedish again. Because this would have been tantamount to acknowledging that she had given up hope that Father would ever return home, she refused to take that route.

She wanted desperately to hang on to her belief that he was still alive. I remember quite vividly how she sometimes pretended that she heard Father knocking on the door and exclaim, "Girls, could that be your pappa coming home?" That is how strongly she believed.

Some time in early 1950 Mother met a German pastor who represented a Lutheran Help Organization, whose main purpose was to reunite families all across Germany and to help returning POWs find their loved ones. He came to Borås, one of many Swedish cities he was touring, to solicit help for the many Germans still suffering from lack of food and clothes in post-war Germany. After hearing Pastor Lippert talk about his organization and what it did, she approached him with her own sad tale. He promised to add my father's name to the list that every returning POW was asked to scutinize in case they might know any of the missing people. He told her that was how they had managed to locate many missing Germans still being held prisoner somewhere in the Soviet Union. As a result, his organization was then able to send care packages to them. He assured her that as soon as he heard anything definite about Father's whereabouts he would be in touch with her.

This man gave Mother renewed hope and strength to carry on. Perhaps Pastor Lippert would soon be able to let us know about Father, she told us right after she met him. He was true to his word. In fact, Pastor Lippert turned out to be the only official who was able to help Mother in her constant quest of trying to find out what happened to my father.

In June 1950, he wrote that a recently returned POW had sworn that he had seen Father in a slave labor camp in Vorkuta as recently as February 1950. This was the first concrete news that Father was actually still alive. That was more than she had known before.

A few days later she received a letter from Westphalia, Germany, written in a very hard to read but precise old script German handwriting. It was from a returning POW by the name of Helmut Schmidt.

Dear Mrs. Gottlieb,

I was together with your husband, Roland Gottlieb, in a coal mining camp in Vorkuta, Siberia. He is well and wants you not to worry about him. Roland Gottlieb is my brightest memory of Siberia because he always wanted us to make the best of our situation. He encouraged all of us others to desire the kind of harmony and calmness of faith and spirit that he himself had attained.

Vorkuta is situated just on the border between Europe and Asia about fifty miles from the Arctic Ocean. The winds are as strong as a hurricane and the land is only free of ice for approximately two months out of the year. The tundra is desolate looking and I did not see any green leaves on any trees in all the time that I was there. The only thing that grows is centimeter high grass and a few low growing flowers. Vorkuta is not really fit for human habitation…

He went on to say that even though he had been condemned to twenty years of hard labor, he had been pardoned very suddenly for no apparent reason. He never had been able to figure out how the Soviets reasoned, and that is why there often seemed to be no rhyme or reason behind their actions. He encouraged her strongly, therefore, not to give up hope because the same thing could very easily happen to her husband. The Soviets often did the most unexpected and surprising things, he assured her.

My sisters and I had just come home after spending time with friends, when Mother greeted us with tears washing down her face. She was sitting on the sofa in the living room. Waving a letter she was holding, she blurted out that this man had seen Father in Vorkuta just a few months ago. She was trembling with excitement. We begged her to read the letter out loud, but because she had to translate it from German for Karin and me as she went along, it took a little extra time.

Slowly we began to grasp what the letter was telling us. Father was alive somewhere in a place called Vorkuta! This was exciting news indeed; the first bit of positive news in six years! By the time she finished reading Helmut Schmidt's letter, we were all crying happy tears that our pappa was alive. That is a moment I will never forget.

After we began to calm down, Mother went on to tell us that she had gone to the public library right after reading the letter. "I had to find out exactly where Vorkuta was on the map and what the encyclopedia said about it. When I saw how close it was to the Arctic Ocean, I was horrified to think how your pappa must be suffering in that frigid arctic climate. How can anyone possibly survive way up there in the tundra?" She shivered audibly and shook herself as if the Arctic cold had penetrated every fiber of her body. As we listened to her telling us about this horrible place where Father was held against his will, we too began to shiver.

"Vorkuta is situated on the Vorkuta River in the Republic of Komi about a hundred miles north of the Arctic Circle and only a short distance from the Barents Sea to the north west and the Kara Sea to the north east," Mother read aloud from notes she had made. "The most northern tip of the Ural Mountains, which separates it from the vast land of Siberia, lies directly to the east of it. The landscape is very uninviting and uninspiring because of the surrounding bleak and forbidding tundra. The average temperature in the winter runs between -30° C and -40° C which can become much worse when terrible storms known as purgas come in from the Arctic Ocean." By the time she finished reciting these stark facts, Mother sounded drained and distraught.

"Poor Pappa!" we cried out together. "And here we thought Sweden is cold in winter when our temperature is -10° C."

"Here are some more bleak facts, children," Mother said, as she continued her recitation. "Because of the close proximity to the Arctic Ocean with its resultant cold temperatures, Vorkuta is more or less blanketed in snow ten months out of the year. Even during the two short summer months, when the thermometer might occasionally climb to 20° C, the ground remains more or less frozen with the surface barely thawing out somewhat."

We were feeling more gloomy than elated after listening to these cold, hard facts about the place where our beloved pappa was forced to live. In an effort to shake us loose from this gloom and doom, Mother, in her typical effervescent way, suggested that we should find Vorkuta on our big wall map and mark it with a flag pin.

Ingrid, the tallest of the three of us, found Vorkuta first. Pointing to it, she exclaimed triumphantly, "There it is! Can you see it?"

Since I was so much smaller than both my sisters, they lifted me up to the wall map where all three of us put our three pins simultaneously into a tiny little speck at the top of the map marked Vorkuta.

Afterwards the four of us huddled together below the map and thought about our father in that terrible place and prayed he would soon be released from what must be a living hell. This intense moment of shared despair and yet hopefulness is something that has stayed with me. We were united as never before.

Mother's response to Helmut Schmidt was among the letters I found years later. It was full of questions. She wanted to know if the prisoners had enough to eat, whether Father was healthy, if his clothes were sufficient to keep him from freezing, if he had talked about his family, if he had any possibility to write, and what was the reason Mr. Schmidt had been released, and how long had he been in Vorkuta. Could he still laugh? Mother wrote:

> *Please excuse me if my questions sound simple and perhaps somewhat silly, but we have suffered for so many years without knowing anything at all. You have given me the first ray of hope, a lifeline, if you like. I plan to fight like a lioness until my husband returns home to me. My strength and courage have been rejuvenated thanks to you…*

We all noticed a change in Mother after that first letter from Helmut Schmidt. Even as young as I was at the time, I could tell that she seemed more optimistic and laughed more easily. Her mood was infectious and upbeat. She would suddenly start singing in her not so good soprano voice and grab me by my hands and twirl me around. She also bought extra goodies from the bakery on the Saturday after we received that letter in celebration of the wonderful news.

At least we now knew where Father was and that he was alive. She exchanged several more letters with Helmut Schmidt over the next year, but eventually there was nothing more he could add. He always ended his letters by entreating her not to give up hope.

CHAPTER XII

Devastating News

October 1952

For two years after receiving that first letter from Helmut Schmidt, we lived with the renewed hope that we would see Father again—maybe soon. Thanks to Pastor Lippert's intervention, Mother also heard from several other returning POWs, who further substantiated Schmidt's claim. Every one of them had been together with Father at some point or other and entreated her not to give up hope that he would be released soon.

Then in the fall of 1952 all our hopes were crushed.

We had just finished supper when Mother finally decided to open the mail containing several interesting looking letters. She saved the one from Uncle Walther for last, wanting to take time reading and translating it to us.

"Dear Ruth, fate would have it that you will never see Roland again. I am so unhappy to be the bearer of such bad tidings, but..." Mother gasped and screamed, tossing the letter down as if it were burning her hand. Then she slumped over the table.

My sisters and I stared at Mother in shock. What did Uncle Walther mean? Was Father dead? Then as if electrified, we all jumped up from our chairs, colliding as we crowded around Mother like little scared chickens.

I was terrified. All life seemed to have drained out of her. She was not moving. She just lay there.

Finally, she pushed herself upright. "It can't be true. It simply can't be true! Roland is not dead!!!" Repeating these sentences over and over again, she rocked back and forth.

The three of us looked helplessly at each other. We had only heard part of the letter, and it seemed to say that Father was dead, but we were not sure whether we had heard correctly.

Then Ingrid, as the oldest and the most sensible one, took over. She talked softly to Mother, trying to calm her down. Succeeding at last, she cajoled Mother into reading the rest of the letter. She convinced her that we needed to find out exactly what it said.

With trembling fingers Mother forced herself to pick up Uncle Walther's letter again and continue reading the catastrophic news.

> *... A German prisoner of war, a Mr. Meyer, has just recently returned from Siberia and after seeing Roland's name on the list of missing persons told officials here that he was together with Roland in the early part of 1950 when Roland had been very sick with pneumonia and dysentery. Unfortunately, he never recovered from his illness, and Meyer, together with some friends, helped dig his grave in the tundra where he now lies buried. Before I was willing to tell you that Roland has died in Siberia, I asked that Meyer attest to this in front of a judge in a German court of law. Meyer complied with this request and as a result Roland has now officially been declared dead. I have enclosed the document testifying to this effect...*

Surely, it wasn't true! Father simply could not be dead! Hadn't all those men Mother had corresponded with been together with him as recently as a year ago? But how could the official looking document from the German Red Cross in Munich that Uncle Walther had included in his letter be lying? Still not wanting to believe its message, we reread Uncle Walter's letter several times and pored over the accompanying official document, in the hopes the message would change. It never did!

FATHER WAS DEAD!!!

I was devastated. I had been very unhappy when *Morfar* died, but this was much, much worse. At least then I still believed that my father might one day come home, but now that hope was shattered. My father was dead and now I would never have a chance to meet him, and there was nothing I could do about it. I felt robbed.

Although my memory of those first few days remains somewhat hazy, I seem to recall that Mother didn't go to work. I do not know for sure, however, whether my sisters and I went to school. I do remember us crying a lot and eating very little. I can just imagine how swollen and red our eyes must have been from all the tears we shed those first few days.

We did not have a funeral service like the one we had when *Morfar* died. If we had, it might have helped us get closure, made it easier somehow to accept that Father was gone. But since we had no body to bury, no physical proof that he was dead, Mother probably thought a regular funeral service would not be appropriate.

What we did instead was light a candle beside Father's picture where we wept and hugged and tried to comfort each other.

Friends expressed their sympathy in many ways especially after the following death announcement appeared in our local *Borås Tidning.*

First Now
We have received the message that
My beloved husband and
Our dear father
Roland Gottlieb
Has died in a Russian prison camp
In March 1950
Borås, October 9, 1952
Rut
Ingrid, Karin, Birgitta

The telephone rang a lot over the next few days. Friends and family dropped by to express their sympathy. Many sent flowers that surrounded Father's picture, while letters, telegrams and cards filled a silver tray close by. These treasured expressions of condolence reminded me of how great and far-flung my parents' circle of friends and relatives was. I discovered that many had come from all over Europe, but particularly from Austria and Germany. In retrospect, it is comforting to realize what wonderful support Mother received during this difficult period in her life.

Our home felt like a morgue during the first few weeks; it was deathly quiet. No one felt like laughing or smiling. When the four of us were at home we ate, slept and talked in hushed tones. An eerie feeling prevailed as if a heavy and ominous cloud was hanging over us.

Even though I was only eight at the time, I remember how hurt

I was that I would never now get to know my father, the father whom I had idealized and idolized in my mind. In my imagination he was the perfect man and father, someone who was going to be really proud of me when he finally met me. Now that was never going to happen.

I was jealous of my two sisters because they both had known Father, especially Ingrid who knew what he really looked like and how he smelled. I was less envious of Karin because she was only two and a half when she last saw him. She claimed she had no clear memory of him but wished she did.

And yet, as the photographs in our family album testified, Father had held both of them on his lap, laughed with them, read to them, taken them on outings, and celebrated birthdays with them. To my great sorrow there were none of him and me, and now there never would be. That hurt! In fact, there were only about ten pictures of me as a baby but loads of both Ingrid and Karin. I understood why, of course, since Father was usually the one taking the pictures but was gone when I was born. Nevertheless, this didn't diminish the hurt.

More than ever, I wondered if he had known about me and what I looked like since he had never seen me. Mother always tried to reassure me when I voiced such thoughts by saying something like, "Your pappa loves you and probably wonders what you look like and whom you take after." That usually comforted me, thinking I would find out when he finally came home.

I felt cheated. I was angry with the Russians who had robbed me of my father. Because of them, I would never have a chance to know him, to be loved and cherished by him. I was a very unhappy little girl.

We were all different now, but none more so than Mother. The spring in her step was absent and her usual *joie de vivre* was gone. I didn't see her laugh or smile for the longest time, nor did she bring home any goodies for our Saturday evening fun or harass us about our homework. She just seemed to be barely alive although she went back to work just a few days later because she had to.

Today I understand more fully. The tiny, fragile vestige of hope that had been holding Mother upright for so many years and had kept her going had flown out the window. Her hope that Father would come knocking on the door one day and say "Here I am," as she had imagined a thousand times over the past eight years, was dead.

Over the next few months, I often came across her muttering under her breath. She probably thought I did not hear her, but I did, and it upset me to see my darling mamma so distraught. I felt helpless because there was nothing I, or anybody else for that matter, could say or do. We were all dealing with the loss in our own way.

I recall hearing her say things like: "Why, oh why, Roland, did you do this to us?" or "Why didn't you get well again?" or "Why didn't you fight the sickness?" or "Now, you will never see us again and the children will never know you?" or "You will never hold me in your arms, love me and kiss me and tell me how much you love me," or "I will never see your wonderful and warm smile again or get lost in your brown eyes so full of love."

When I returned to school, my classmates seemed uncaring and unconcerned except for my best friend, Ulla Nilsson. All my other classmates treated me as if nothing had happened. I decided therefore to go along with that and pretend that things were as they always had been. I simply bottled the hurt up inside me instead.

Perhaps this stemmed from my sense of self- preservation. I did not want to give Ann-Margaret, the class bully, a chance to say more hurtful things to me like she had been doing ever since that first day of school when she thought my father was a criminal. She had never quite understood, or perhaps she had refused to understand, the difference between that and being a POW. But whenever she said something hurtful to me, Ulla was always very quick to spring to my defense and tell Ann-Margaret to leave me alone or else. I never knew what the "else" meant because, to my knowledge, Ulla never followed through on her threat.

At the time I could not understand my classmates' indifference to what I was going through. As an adult it is clear to me. Children live in the present; they are only concerned with what happens to them and not to others. None of my classmates had lost their father, and so perhaps they could not commiserate. It seemed they were not in the least bit concerned about me.

My friend Ulla was the exception. Even though she still had her father just like everyone else in the class, she was just a better, truer and more compassionate friend. During those first few weeks, she often asked me to come home with her after school. Her mother, who was a stay-at-home mom, gave us an egg yolk each. Using a fork, we whipped it together with lots of sugar in a glass until it was white and foamy. This required lots of energy, but in the end it was well worth the effort because it tasted delicious. I wonder if Ulla's mother realized how much it helped me to whip out the anger and frustration I felt at having been robbed and cheated of a chance to know my father?

Even though Father's physical body could not be put to rest in a grave either in Borås or in Vienna, Mother decided that his name should be inscribed on the family tombstone in the city of his birth. Uncle Walther agreed with her and arranged for it to be done.

What I did not know, but heard about much later, was that my uncle never told *Omama* of her son's death in Siberia. He felt that if she knew, it might be the last straw for her and kill her. She had already been in and out of the hospital after suffering several heart attacks. In his judgment, she was not strong enough to handle such devastating news. Because she was so feeble and still living in Salzburg, there was little likelihood of her seeing his name on the tombstone in Vienna anyway, he reasoned.

In spite of her grief, Mother wanted to get a firsthand account from Siegfried Meyer, the man who claimed that he had buried Father. She wrote to him, begging him to tell what he knew about Father and his last days.

Sometime in early November 1952, she received a four-page letter from this Meyer. He wrote how he had met Father on the transit from the Moscow prison to Vorkuta in 1949 and how they had become good friends. He went on to describe the harsh conditions that the prisoners were subjected to and how Father, as a result of prolonged malnutrition, had suffered from a bad case of dysentery and pneumonia upon his arrival in Vorkuta.

> *...Roland managed to get assigned to an infirmary as an orderly where I saw him from time to time when I had to bring wood to the infirmary where he worked. I was as-*

signed to the timber-cutting brigade. We always managed to exchange a few words even though it was strictly forbidden to do so. One day, I believe it was in the early part of 1950, I heard when I looked in at the infirmary that he had died that morning. The Russian orderlies would not let me see his body but told me that he was in a wooden casket waiting to be buried. Some of my friends, who also knew Roland, helped me later that day to hack into the frozen tundra so that we could dig a grave for him. We were all going to miss him. He had been such a pillar of strength to the rest of us, doing what he could to shore up our confidence and hopes that all was not yet lost. That day I felt like someone had thrust a knife into my own heart, that is how bereft I felt. A good man had died who didn't deserve to die. Shortly thereafter I was transferred to another camp...

He concluded his letter by offering her his deepest sympathy and regrets at being the bearer of such sad news and wished all the best for her and her children.

I don't really understand why Mother chose to inflict fresh pain upon herself, but maybe she felt the need to hear directly from this man how Father had died and not just second hand through Uncle Walther. Perhaps too, she thought she needed to know all the details in order to be able to accept that Father was really dead.

From its crushed and crumpled look in the folder, where this letter was kept along with all the other letters from returning POWs, I can only surmise that Mother must have been very upset after reading it.

Först nu har underrättelse
ingått att
Min älskade make,
vår käre far

Roland Gottlieb

avlidit i rysk fångenskap
i mars 1950.

Borås den 9 okt. 1952.

RUT

Ingrid, Karin, Birgitta

CHAPTER XIII

Adjusting to New Circumstances

Fall 1952- Fall 1953

With the passing of time, we returned to our normal every-day activities. Thus, on the thirteenth of December, when everyone in Sweden celebrates the St. Lucia Day, my sisters and I, dressed in long white gowns tied with sashes around the waist and Ingrid wearing a crown of live candles on her head, entered Mother's room singing the special St. Lucia song. We crowded in around Mother's bed and offered her newly baked saffron buns and hot coffee from a tray Ingrid was carrying. Naturally, we ate some buns too before we rushed off to school.

I have often wondered why Protestant Sweden celebrates this Catholic saint when she wasn't even Swedish but Italian. Some say the legend of Lucia came to Sweden during the eleventh century, when missionaries, trying to Christianize this most northern heathen country, told the story of the young martyred maiden from Syracuse in Italy, who lived in the third century A.D. The story goes that after her Christian mother was miraculously cured of an illness, Lucia went into the catacombs where followers of Christ were hiding. She wanted to express her gratitude to God by bringing them food and drink. To help light her way in the darkness of the catacombs, Lucia is supposed to have put a crown of candles on her head, thus leaving her hands free to distribute her gifts. When her pagan suitor discovered what she was doing, he denounced her, which caused Lucia to be imprisoned and tortured. Neither boiling water nor burning pitch had the power to hurt her before she was finally blinded and slain with a sword.

This legend must have caught the imagination of the Swedes. From the seventeenth century on white–clad maidens, the customary dress at the time of Lucia, wearing a crown of burning candles and offering food to the poor, began to appear all over Sweden on what was believed to be the longest and therefore the darkest day of the year, December 13. In those days, Sweden was still following the Julian calendar that differed by several days from the Gregorian one. After switching from the former to the latter calendar, Sweden continued to mark December 13 as St. Lucia's Day.

St. Lucia doesn't only appear in the homes, but she also comes to schools and community functions. I will never forget how disappointed I was when I was not chosen to represent St. Lucia in my class in December 1952. Somehow I thought that I deserved to be chosen as St. Lucia because I had just lost my father, but my classmates were probably too young to understand that and voted for the tallest girl in the class instead. Although I felt hurt, I eventually got over it but obviously never forgot it.

St. Lucia's Day also serves as the official kick-off to the Christmas season in Sweden. In spite of the prevailing somber mood this particular Christmas, the heavenly smells of ginger, cinnamon, and cardamom soon began to fill our home in preparation for *julafton*, Christmas Eve. I loved shaping the dough of the traditional Swedish *Havreflarn*, *Ökensandkakor* and *Pepparkakor* into cookies, or what remained of the dough after I finished licking the bowl and eating some of it. To this day, these oatmeal lace cookies, desert sand cookies, and gingersnaps always fill my cookie tins at Christmastime. They have become my present day family's favorites as well.

When *julafton* came, we celebrated it like always although it felt different somehow this year. The joy of anticipation was absent. Last Christmas we still had high hopes that Father might soon come home. That hope was now completely gone.

Otherwise, the morning began as usual with visits from Mother's friends, followed by the arrival of our aunt Anne-Marie and her family later in the afternoon. After finishing *doppet i grytan*, the traditional Swedish *smörgåsbord*, consisting of meatballs, ham, beef tongue, red cabbage, boiled potatoes, herring, *lutfisk*, Janson's Temptation, cheese and bread, the whole family went to the special Christmas Eve candle light service in the Gustaf Adolfs kyrkan. Then before returning home to light the live candles on

Our class was chosen to represent the St. Lucia festival for the school with the tallest girl for the staring role.

our Christmas tree and receive our *julklappar,* we walked down to the cemetery to light a candle on my grandparents' grave.

Right after Christmas, we had the first big snowfall of the year. Several inches fell in just one day. Because we were still on Christmas break, I played outside from morning until dark, only occasionally going inside to warm up with a cup of hot cocoa.

Some days I went sledding with my friends, which was a lot of fun. What made it even better was that, for some reason I never quite understood, our particular street, Kvarngatan, was off limits to all motorists after a really heavy snow. This meant that we could fly heedlessly down the hilly street on our toboggans at breakneck speed. No cars were going to get in our way.

On other days, I went cross-country skiing with my friends on the paths through the nearby *Annelundsskogen*, a forest just a block from where we lived. Or we built snowmen that we decorated with carrots for the nose, twigs for the arms, a toboggan on top of the

Me, with my friend Tina, standing on my right side

head and pebbles for the eyes and mouth. Since lots of children lived in my neighborhood, it did not take long before funny looking snowmen decorated every front yard. They were a sight to behold when the temperature went above freezing, and all the snowmen began to melt and look misshapen and lopsided.Just before school started again in January 1953, another big snow fell on our town. There was so much snow that Birgitta and Lena, two girls who lived down the street from me, and I decided to build an igloo in my front yard. We rolled huge snowballs and put them close together to form a wall but left a small hole every so often to allow light to enter. It took us several days to finish our masterwork. It was hard work rolling all those balls and sticking them together to form the hut.

Late one afternoon we were suddenly attacked while we were innocently playing "house" in our little igloo. We were pretending to drink hot cocoa sitting on some old rag rugs Mother let me borrow to cover up the snow-covered floor. We lit a few candle stubs, which made it ever so cozy and warm. Suddenly icy snowballs came sailing through our small window, with one hitting me smack dab in the middle of the face. Because it was hard as a rock, it really hurt and made me cry at first, but then I got mad.

We realized immediately who was attacking us. It was that mean pesky Kjellstrand boy and his friends, who had also built an igloo in the yard next door. As we went home that night, we swore we would be ready for them. The next afternoon other children taking sides decided to join in what turned out to be a really messy snowball war.

In early 1953, Mother came home one evening and told us that the Swedish government was willing to reinstate her Swedish citizenship and to allow her children to become Swedish as well.

"How come, Mamma?" Ingrid asked. "Why suddenly now when the government didn't allow it before?"

"When I applied before, I was still married to an Austrian citizen, which was the reason they gave for denying my application. Now that your pappa is officially declared dead, the Swedish government will apparently allow it. What do you think, girls? Should we accept?" Mother looked questioningly at each one of us in turn.

We could tell she was conflicted and only wanted our reassurance that it was okay under the present circumstances to become Swedish. We told her to go ahead and apply. It took several more weeks before our official citizenship papers arrived in the mail. When they did, we were both sad and happy, sad because it was confirmation that Father was never going to be coming home and happy because it meant that we now really belonged in the country where we were living and growing up.

Many years later during a cozy mother-daughter chat, I decided to take up the subject of what she went through right after we were told that Father had died in Siberia.

"You must have suffered terribly! All those years of waiting and longing and hoping! How did you bear it? I remember that you didn't laugh very much anymore, but other than that, I guess I was too self- absorbed, as most children are, to realize just how difficult it was for you to carry on a normal life. I know it would be for me if Bill suddenly disappeared and left me alone with our son." I smiled down at my newborn baby boy cradled in my arms.

She responded by telling me that her friends had tried to invite her for dinner or to go to the theatre, and how she had refused at first because she was far too unhappy and depressed. She didn't want to subject her friends to her dark mood. After a few months, however, she finally succumbed and decided to accept their invitations. She realized that was the only way she was going to snap out of the deep depression that engulfed her.

That reminded me that sometime that spring of 1953 Mother actually started to go out again. I didn't like it very much because I had gotten used to Mamma's being home in the evenings. I was afraid to be alone. Unfortunately for me, my sisters' bedroom was located off of the landing outside our enclosed apartment while my little cubbyhole bedroom, which used to be a closet under the eaves, was beside our dining room on the other side of the hallway that separated it from the living room and the entrance to our apartment. In other words, my room seemed to be very far from that of my sisters.

Although it helped some that Mother always left the light on in the hallway, I was still petrified that a boogey man would jump out from under my bed. Ever since seeing a movie in which two soldiers hid under their captain's bed and as a joke decided to pull the wife's legs as she sat down on it, I imagined that someone was hiding under my bed and might pull my legs as well. What made it worse was that the light switch in my room was at the door on the opposite side from my bed. Therefore after turning off the light, I had to take a giant leap into my bed to avoid anyone pulling on my legs.

Whenever I mention this to my sisters, they claim that it didn't happen too often that I was alone because Ingrid was usually sitting at the dining room table doing her homework. But it must have happened often enough for me to have such a vivid memory of being afraid on those nights when Mother went out.

I will never forget the party Mother threw for *Valborgsmässoafton*, or Walpurgisnight, on April 30, 1953. And I doubt anyone who attended ever forgot it either. This was her way of returning the favor of her friends' many invitations.

Walpurgis night is a holiday in Sweden that celebrates the end of the long winter days and the coming of spring with lots of merriment, eating traditional foods and enjoying the warmth from a bonfire. Although officially spring arrives a month earlier, it takes a little longer to truly arrive in this northern country because of its close proximity to the polar circle.

I don't really know why Mother chose this particular holiday to give her first party. Perhaps she did it because her winter had seemed extra long and dark or maybe because she was ready to climb out of that darkness that had physically and mentally held her in its grip for so long. Whatever her reason, it turned out to be quite a memorable occasion.

How to prepare all the special dishes and make sure that everyone had a good time was the easy part for Mother. But how to have a bonfire in a third floor apartment was a different matter altogether. That was her big challenge. How she managed to have one, or at least one that resembled a bonfire, just goes to show how creative my darling mother always was.

A couple of days before the big event she asked my sisters and me to stop by the carpenter's shop located just opposite Ingrid's school and ask him to give us as much saw dust and wood shavings we could possibly carry in big brown paper bags.

"What in the world are you going to do with all that saw dust?" All three of us were very curious about this highly unusual request.

"I plan to pour sawdust into empty tin cans and douse it with kerosene. We will line these torchlike cans up along our balcony railing and then, just before the guests arrive, you girls will light them up. Everyone will think we have a bonfire up here on the third floor. Won't that be marvelous?" She clapped her hands in sheer anticipation of the surprised looks on her friends' faces.

We gasped and stared at Mother. Was she really going to do that? Our imagination ran wild at the idea of having real live torches on our balcony. Practical Ingrid then demanded to know if that wasn't too dangerous, but Mother shook her head. She insisted that because our balcony was made of stone, was pretty large and had no ceiling above it, it couldn't possibly catch on fire. We hoped she was right.

"We will need to watch the tin cans carefully, though, and make sure that none fall down into the street or on the balcony floor. Once all the guests have arrived, I put you in charge, Ingrid of making sure that the torches are properly snuffed out." Mother laughed, the kind of laughter I had not heard in a long time.

Finally the day for the party arrived. I could hardly wait to see what Mother's unique brand of bonfire would look like. After lighting up all the cans, I eagerly rushed down the three flights of stairs and into the road. I couldn't believe my eyes. Big tongues of fire seemed to be leaping up into the sky, illuminating our whole third floor. It was a fantastic sight to behold!

That night was probably the beginning of Mother's new social

Our house in Borås. The third floor balcony held the "bonfire."

life as a widow. Around that time she also began a literary club with many of her old classmates agreeing to take turns to host their meetings. The club met every a month to discuss various Scandinavian literary works and world literature under the leadership of their former literature teacher. I overheard her one evening laughingly tell Ingrid that she had had a schoolgirl crush on the man. When I asked Mother what she meant by that she just grinned and told me I would find out soon enough when I was older. I always hated that kind of answer.

I sometimes wonder if Mother liked learning about the characters in literature because they often had problems to overcome just like she did. Perhaps she felt it would help her if she focused on their problems rather than on her own. But then again, she always had a flair for the dramatics, which is why she was such a wonderful storyteller.

I will never forget one of our Saturday family fun nights when she introduced Homer's *Odyssey* to us. Before she began reading it aloud, she explained that she saw herself in the heroine, Penelope, and me in the son, Telemachus.

As the story unfolded, it was not difficult to understand why Mother identified with Penelope. After Ulysses left for war and did not return home for many years, many young men tried to persuade Penelope that her husband was gone forever and she should marry one of them. But she refused to give up hope that Ulysses would return one day. Telemachus, their son, was only a baby when his father left. Finally after twenty years, Ulysses returned home to his faithful wife and waiting son. That story stirred my imagination and for the longest time I secretly thought of myself as Telemachus.

When spring, that is to say May, finally arrived in 1953, I eagerly went out to look for the first wild flowers. I didn't have too far to go to find open meadows and forests carpeted with the springtime *vitsippor*, a small white wood anemone, lilies of the valley, and bell shaped bluebell flowers. Before long, my teacher's desk was totally covered with small jars filled with an assortment of wonderful smelling flower bouquets that her eager students competed in bringing to her.

It was also some time during that spring, I overheard a conversation between my mother and Aunt Birgit, who lived in the apartment below us, the same one that *Morfar* had lived in before he died. They had no idea that I was eavesdropping at the top of the third floor landing.

"Ruth, you really need to go out more and meet some men," I heard Aunt Birgit say.

"I think it is too soon," I heard Mother reply.

"What nonsense, Ruth. Roland has been gone for nine years now."

"True, but I have only been officially a widow for less than a year, and besides, how am I supposed to meet these men? All the good ones are already married, like your Gösta, while the ones who aren't are either widowed or no good. And who in their right mind would want to marry a woman with three half-grown daughters? I will never find anyone as wonderful as Roland anyway." Mother sighed.

"You will, Ruth, you just have to give it time. I will talk to some of our friends and see if they know someone they could introduce you to. You deserve some happiness after all these years. You have been alone far too long," Aunt Birgit replied.

When I heard Mother coming upstairs, I scurried quickly into the living room. I did not want her to catch me eavesdropping. At the time I did not understand the significance of what I had overheard, but later that fall it dawned on me what Aunt Birgit must have meant.

As summertime approached, I could hardly wait for school to be out because it meant going to our beloved cottage in Mollösund on the west coast.

Chapter XIV

Mollösund

Summer 1953

In summertime many Swedes, who live in the city and can afford it, prefer to spend happy and carefree days in small rustic cottages in the countryside or out by the sea. Even though we were far from well off, Mother managed to buy just such a cottage in the quaint little fishing village of Mollösund.

My roots run deep in this village. Both my maternal grandparents, *Morfar* and *Mormor*, were born and grew up in Mollösund. After leaving home to become an architect, *Morfar* returned a few years later to marry *Mormor*, his childhood sweetheart. Although *Morfar*'s parents only came in the late eighteen hundreds when his father was appointed schoolteacher, *Mormor's* ancestors had lived there since the fifteen hundreds or earlier. Therefore, it is not too surprising that no matter where my family is in the world today this fishing village continues to be the one place we often think of as "back home."

I absolutely adore Mollösund. When you view it from afar the colors that stand out are white, red and mustard yellow. A tightly-knit warren of red roofed white wooden houses and red doll-like summer cottages seem to sit on top of each other while a myriad of red colored and white trimmed *sjöbodar* or boathouses, and yellow colored *magasiner* or warehouses perch at the edge of the water.

Located on the southernmost tip of Orust, Sweden's third largest island, Mollösund sports a teeming harbor usually full of all kinds of boats from big yachts to smaller sailboats or cutters, to small rowboats or fishing boats. Many can also be found moored to the wooden docks jutting out from the boathouses all along the shoreline. As always with the ocean, the water is at high or low tide, or moving between the constant ebb and flow causing the boats to undulate against the wharfs. Unless the sea is very calm, the ripples create a very pleasing clucking sound.

Mollösund distinguishes itself in other ways as well. The salty air, mixed with the smell of codfish drying on long racks on the barren cliffs, permeates the air in summer, giving it a distinctive and very hard to miss odor. Its one and only cobblee-stoned street is extremely narrow, which presents a real challenge when two cars happen to meet. The red windmill, a very distinctive landmark, sits on top of a cliff that rises in the background and can therefore be seen from all directions, from both land and sea. As soon as I catch sight of it, I know that I have arrived in Mollösund. These sights and smells always fill me with a sense of wonder and nostalgia.

Going to Mollösund when I was a child, we usually had to take a bus, or if we were lucky we went by car, which had to be ferried across the two sounds that separated Orust and its neighboring island Tjörn from the mainland. Another much more enjoyable way to get there was to take the steamboat from Göteborg, a large harbor city to the south. Today, several long bridges connect Mollösund to the mainland, which makes ferry boats obsolete.

We felt very fortunate that Mother was able to buy the cutest little cottage here that lay just beyond where the road ran out. Because it is, or rather was back then, the last house in the village on the southernmost tip of both Mollösund as well as Orust, Mother baptized it "Kap Horn" after its namesake, Cape Horn, on the southernmost tip of South America. In time, this name became synonymous for us with Mollösund. Anytime we speak about going or being there, we often use the name for our cottage, or as is the case today, for the big house that now stands where the cottage once stood.

A grainy black and white photograph sparks my memory of the first time I saw the cottage that became Kap Horn. What I have

Me, at four, among Mamma's friends on the trip where she found *Kap Horn*

been told about it is that Mother and I went to Mollösund for a few days in the spring of 1948 while Karin and Ingrid were still in school. The photograph of me standing together with some of Mother's friends helps my vague recollection of staying at Mollösund's *Värdshus*, an imposing and very old white house right in the harbor which belonged to my great-grandparents before it was sold after they died. Ever since then, it has served as Mollösund's one and only inn.

I am not certain why Mother decided to go to Mollösund at that point in her life, especially since both her grandparents had already passed away. I can only surmise that she must have had a few days before beginning a permanent job at the Borås Chamber of Commerce as the business affairs manager. Perhaps this was her first opportunity to see her grandparents' home again after being gone from Sweden for eight years.

Surely she needed a break. The worry and uncertainty of what was then four years without a word from my father must have worn her out. She also lost her mother a few months earlier and was still in deep mourning. Mother always told me how close she was to *Mormor* but especially so after returning home with three young children in tow from war-torn Austria.

Where should she therefore have gone but to the one place in the world that reminded her of her childhood and youth, a time of innocence, a time when she was happy frolicking around with her many cousins and friends, and later as she grew up, going dancing and wondering whether she should date Ragnar or Roland. By returning to Mollösund, she probably hoped to recapture this much happier period in her life when she had no worries to speak of.

While the two of us were there, she happened to hear about this rustic one-bedroom cottage that a local fisherman, Ragnar Bengtström, who had grown up in the big house a few hundred yards behind it, wanted to sell. He had built it as a summer cottage, but now it had become too small for his growing family.

Upon seeing it, Mother knew that she simply had to buy it. The only question was how she was going to accomplish this on her small salary from the Chamber of Commerce. She had absolutely no savings because of barely having earned enough at her previous jobs as a temporary receptionist in a doctor's office or part time typing teacher at the business school. In fact, in order to make it, she was already working hard at night slaving away at homemade crafts she then tried to sell.

The earnest money required to hold the cottage must have seemed like a small fortune to Mother, as did the loan she needed to purchase it. For her to contemplate buying Kap Horn was daring and risky, even "foolhardy," as her older sister Anne-Marie was always eager to point out. In her weaker moments, Mother agreed with her.

Fortunately, she had many good friends, much better off than she was, who were willing to help her out. They offered to loan her the earnest money and even went so far as to underwrite the loan of 3000 Swedish crowns, a very small sum in today's currency, but an almost insurmountable one in 1948. With her friends' generous help, she was thus able to buy the cottage. Mother always claimed that this was the best purchase she ever made, and the family agrees wholeheartedly.

Now, in addition to working eight hours at the office, Mother labored twice as hard at her craft projects. Her hands never seemed to be idle and her creativity knew no bounds. Her goal was to repay her friends as soon as possible and to make the mortgage payments on time. She hoped that our cottage was well worth all her hard work.

I remember one project in particular, the *Evaspegeln*, because she made thousands of them. It consisted of a small round hand held mirror, no more than five inches in diameter, which she dressed up with assorted pretty fabrics before selling them to cosmetic stores and to people whom she knew. In time the item became very popular with women all over Sweden. I have no clue how she came up with this idea, but thanks in part to its success, Kap Horn became ours in due time.

The *Evaspegeln* was by no means her only handicraft, although it certainly was her most profitable one. Because she loved to entertain and cook, everything she created had something to do with setting an elegant dinner table, like the miniature matchboxes she dressed up in a unique way for hostesses to place at each guest's place setting. This was during a time when smoking was an accepted way to finish off a good meal.

I have often wondered if keeping busy was not also a form of therapy for my mother. In the beginning it probably helped take her mind off her worries about what was happening to Father or wondering whether he was still alive. But once she knew that he was gone, perhaps it helped ease her sadness, tempered by her frustration and anger towards the Soviets for not having released Father. Or she may simply have realized that her handcrafts were needed to ensure that the cottage would be completely ours one day.

We all fell in love with our quaint yellow-painted cottage where it sat on the bare cliffs just a stone's throw from the water's edge that first summer, which must have been the summer of 1949. The best part about Kap Horn, and which everyone who saw it always envied, was its magnificent and unrestricted view of the many little islands and skerries of the Skagerack. From the roofed-over, but otherwise open and very narrow veranda, where we ate in good weather, we could observe a constantly moving scene of fishing boats and big and small pleasure boats, sailing, motoring

or steaming across the sometimes choppy and at other times calm waters. To us, it was paradise on earth.

Kap Horn was so tiny it could almost be mistaken for a doll's house. The bedroom barely held two very narrow beds and a small closet on either side of the door-less entrance. By putting collapsible beds underneath the two upright ones during daytime, we had enough beds for all four of us although when we pulled them out at night, we hardly had any room to move around. That didn't matter in the least because it was all part of the mystique and fun of roughing it in summertime. Besides, we were hardly ever in the room other than to sleep and occasionally to eat, if the weather was bad.

The cottage also lacked all modern conveniences such as electricity and indoor plumbing. This did not diminish any of its charm. On the contrary! This rustic way of living stood in sharp contrast to our otherwise very ordinary life in the city, which made it much more fun and interesting. We cooked on a two-eyed kerosene burner and fetched water from a community well, located on the other side of the windmill and over the hill. Because we had to carry the heavy water buckets so far, we quickly learned to be very sparing with our water supply. After washing the dishes in a dishpan or taking short baths in a round metal pan that sat on a stand, we simply tossed the dirty water into the bushes right outside the house, which made them thrive. Even after the kitchen was modernized to some degree in 1952, we had to continue dumping the dirty water outside because the water only emptied into a pail sitting directly underneath the newly installed stainless sink. Woe to us if we forgot and the pail overflowed!

No electricity also meant no refrigerator. Instead we made daily treks down to the one and only grocery store in the village for perishables, such as butter, cheese, eggs and meat. All other kinds of food we kept in a cupboard above our improvised sink.

I didn't mind shopping every day because I was fascinated by the old-fashioned mercantile store where the walls were covered from top to bottom with drawers and shelves full of interesting looking merchandise and where you had to stand in line to be waited on. In fact, it looked much like the old Mast General Store in Valle Cruces in the Appalachian Mountains of North Carolina, which is not too far from where I live today.

Because Mollösund was a fishing village, we naturally had easy daily access to fresh and inexpensive fish, such as flounder, cod, herring, and mackerel. We were also very fortunate in having a neighbor who was a sea pilot as well as a fisherman. His yellow *sjöbod*, or boathouse, where he worked on all his fishnets and kept his small single engine fishing boat in tiptop shape, sat just below our cottage. Uncle Wilhelm, as we called him, although he was no relation at all, would often share some of his freshly caught fish from his early morning outings. We couldn't get it much fresher than that. To this day, I am quite partial to any kind of fish because of spending summers in a place where fishing was a way of life.

No electric power also meant no electric lights. But since the sun hardly set in the summer time, Sweden being so close to the Polar Circle, we hardly missed it at all. Having to go to bed already at eight o'clock at night, on the other hand, when the sun was still high in the sky, presented a serious problem for me. I begged Mother to let me stay up later, but to no avail and rightfully so, or I might never have gone to bed at all. To make this a nonnegotiable question, she simply installed dark blue blinds on the windows. What a clever mother!

No indoor plumbing also meant that we had no indoor toilet. Instead we used a *dass,* which was a pintsized wooden outhouse sitting in the shelter of a rockwall a few yards below and off to the side of our cottage. Usually I kept the door open because this helped keep the foul odor, which emanated from the bucket below the hinged woooden seat, from becoming too overpowering. Besides, I enjoyed watching people going by in their sail and motorboats. Hoping they would see me, I hollored and waved to them as they went by. It didn't embarrass me in the least that they could see me sitting on my "throne," doing my business. It simply made me giggle.

Since nobody in Mollösund had either sewage or plumbing back then, the community provided a dump truck, which stopped at the end of our road twice a week around four or five o'clock in the morning. Half a dozen neighbors, including us, patiently lined up to dump the stinking contents of the pails into the truck. Depending on the prevailing wind and weather, the smell could be overwhelming, but pinching our nostrils helped some. Ingrid likes to claim that she was the only one who ever carried out this odious task, but I remember distinctly doing it as well, once I was old enough to help.

Me, standing above the dasset

After *Morfar* died in 1951, Mother decided to use her small inheritance to modernize our little summer cottage. Returning in June 1952, I discovered to my pleasant surprise that our veranda was no longer open but enclosed by three big picture windows on the front and an entrance door to the side. It had even doubled in size. A newly installed bed sofa on the veranda helped make our bedroom less crowded, and a dining table allowed us to eat out there rather than crowding into the crammed kitchen. On stormy days it also felt so much safer to be able to view the lightshow from behind the safety of the big windows.

Another great improvement was the addition of a small wooden porch with steps leading down to the newly created gray-slated terrace sitting just below the house. Here we could sunbathe in complete privacy and entertain friends. We jokingly referred to it as the *ryggskottsterassen*, or the

Cottage with addition

"backpain terrace" after Mother hurt her back dragging those heavy slates to create this perfect shelter from the high west coast winds. Unfortunately, her back was never the same after that, but she could not afford to hire someone to do it because of spending so much money on all other improvements.

Without a doubt, being able to spend summers in Mollösund at our beloved cottage Kap Horn was infinitely better than staying in town. It was the highlight of the year for us.

CHAPTER XV

Mollösund, Here We Come!

Summer 1953

As the summer of 1953 approached, it was difficult to contain my excitement at the prospect of going to Mollösund once again, our fifth summer in a row. Unfortunately, Mother had to work but promised to join us for the Midsummer celebrations a few weeks later. She admonished Karin and me to mind Ingrid in the meantime, whom she left in complete charge.

I was ecstatic when Mother decided to let us take the *ångbåten* directly from Göteborg to Mollösund. Although we still had to take a train from Borås to Göteborg, we wouldn't have to transfer to another train to take us to Stenungsund, a small town on the mainland further to the north, where we usually caught the bus to Mollösund. This was such a tedious and time-consuming process, not only because of three different transfers but also because of the long queue the bus had to wait in before being ferried across the two sounds separating Tjörn and Orust from the mainland. Sometimes these lines could stretch on for miles because of people flocking to these two islands for a bit of fun and sun during summer. Taking the steamboat from Göteborg instead meant we would get to our cottage so much more quickly and easily.

Finally, the day for our departure arrived, dawning sunny and bright after an almost sleepless night. After an hour-and-a-half-long ride by train from Borås, we arrived at the station in Göteborg and walked to the harbor where the steamboat *Bohuslän* was moored. Luckily it wasn't too far, loaded down as we were with several suitcases each. As soon as I caught sight of the Bohuslän, I made a mad dash for the gangplank, with my sisters following closely behind.

Rushing to the open front deck and leaning over the railing, I eagerly watched the crew preparing for our departure on the pier below. Slowly they loosened the big heavy ropes that tied the boat to very thick wooden logs all along the quay. Next came the footbridges, which had to be taken up before the boat could leave.

Trembling with excitement, I listened for the ship to blow its horn signaling we were ready to cast off. There it was! Three short blasts and we were finally on our way to Mollösund. Slowly but surely the boat steamed north, the captain skillfully weaving in and out between the many skerries along the way. Every so often it stopped to let passengers off in one of the many fishing villages that dotted this island landscape of Bohuslän, one of Sweden's provinces. As always it was jam-packed with people, chattering excitedly. Many were going to their cottages or vacation places just like we were.

Two hours later, I punched Karin in the ribs when I spotted two very important landmarks. "There, there they are! You see the windmill and our Kap Horn?" I shouted in order to be heard above all the noise aboard.

Seeing the big reddish brown mill on top of the hill and our tiny cottage not too far below it, where it sat apart from all the other red and white buildings dotting the shoreline, always gave me this weird ticklish sensation in my stomach, a feeling of happy expectation. To this day, I feel the same way whenever I return to Mollösund.

As soon as the *Bohuslän* docked and the gangplank went down, I was ready to get off. I was halfway down when I heard Ingrid yell, "Stop, Gittan, come back here! You forgot

your suitcases! I am not going to carry them for you."

I stopped dead in my tracks, which caused the people behind me to stumble. Turning around, I looked sheepishly at my older sister and backed up the gangplank to retrieve my two suitcases.

Ingrid, looking sternly at me, told me in no uncertain terms that I was to stay with Karin on the pier and watch our luggage while she went to fetch the hand lorry Melker Johansson usually let us borrow. He was Mollösund's local dairyman, who kindly lent us his milk lorry to lug our suitcases to our cottage whenever we arrived.

Surrounded by our pick and pack, Karin and I waited impatiently for Ingrid's return. When she finally showed up fifteen minutes later, we quickly loaded the lorry. Pulling it behind us, we wound our way through the harbor and the cobblestoned village street, past rustic white or yellow colored clapboard houses and the cutest little fairytale looking cottages. When the cobblestones ended, a long unpaved hilly road took over, which stopped abruptly in front of our neighbor's house, just a few hundred yards before we reached our cottage.

As soon as I saw the Berg's gate to their front yard, I dropped my hold on the lorry. Dashing through the yard and jumping across several crevices and over the barren cliffs, I was determined to be the first one to reach our heavenly summer retreat.

"Gittan, come back here and help us with the luggage," Ingrid called out impatiently after my retreating body.

"Okay! Okay! I am coming, but first I have to use the outhouse." This was one of my usual ploys to get out of doing any kind of work, as everyone in the family well knew. But this time it was actually true for I really needed to relieve myself. And down I went to the little *dasset*, threw the door open, sat down with a deep sigh of relief and breathed in the fresh, salty air. With the bucket underneath the seat in the outhouse still quite empty, its usual offensive smell was absent. Thank heavens! It had not had time to putrefy the air... yet!

Every summer when we arrived, we followed the same ritual to get the cottage ready for summer living. First, we had to open up all the windows to let the stale air out. Then, we took all the cushions from the sofa and the chairs, the blankets from the beds, and the rag carpets from the floor, draping them either over the railing or spreading them out on the cliffs. Before putting everything back where it belonged, we also had to sweep the floors. All this was hard work, especially for a nine-year-old eager to go and play.

I tried to object when Ingrid ordered me to make up the beds. I would much rather have gone to the grocery store to pick up a few staples like she told Karin to do. Both Karin and I grumbled and growled even though we understood that these boring and tedious tasks had to be done before we could enjoy ourselves. While we reluctantly followed Ingrid's orders, she went to fetch water from the well located over the hill and behind the windmill, by far the most arduous task of all. This "opening up the cottage" phase every summer was my least favorite part.

After that first day, a long summer of carefree living could at last begin in earnest with all its many varied activities. I loved nothing better than to swim in the deep and cold waters of the Skagerack. Even though I knew the water was still frigid this early in June, with the temperature barely reaching 60°F, I decided to jump into the deep waters right below our cottage. After the first shock wore off, my body quickly adjusted to the cold water as I splashed around. Although it never would get as warm as an indoor swimming pool, it warmed up tolerably as the summer went on.

A really strong memory from my first summer in Mollösund as a five year old was learning how to swim. Somebody, I don't know who, had the bright idea of tying a rope around my waist and telling me to jump into the deep cold water. Because several adults were standing by ready to jump in after me if they had to, I was not in the least bit afraid and quickly jumped in feet first. Feeling secure because of the rope tied around my waist, I started flapping my arms and splashing. This experiment was repeated over and over until I learned how to keep my head above the water and no longer needed this helpline. This must have eased Mother's worries about me possibly drowning.

Just as in summers past, I enrolled in the swim classes the community offered its residents in Katteviken during the summer months. This was a publically accessed swimming hole with trampolines, which lay at the northern end of Mollösund. This particular summer my intention was to earn the bronze badge as outlined by the Swedish Red Cross, which would require a lot of practice on my part. I never lost my love for swimming and even became a swimming instructor as a teenager.

But first things first; I needed to find out if my summertime playmates had arrived yet. Setting off bright and early the morning after our arrival, I quickly left the cottage to see if Mia Gustafsson from Uppsala and her cousin Birran Alm from Stockholm were already here. Mia's family owned a big white house trimmed in green halfway down into the village. From their front door you stepped directly onto the cobblestoned street. Because Birran's family always rented a place that changed from summer to summer, I was not sure where I would find her this year, which was why I went to look for Mia first.

After knocking on Mia's green door, I heard quick footsteps come running and was thrilled when my friend opened it.

"When is Birran coming?" I asked after we finished hugging each other and catching up after being apart a whole year.

"She will be here tomorrow," Mia informed me. "She will be staying at the Bergström's house this summer." I was excited to hear that she would only be two houses over from my cottage.

From then on, until I had to leave to stay with relatives, the two of us, along with Birran once she arrived from Stockholm, went everywhere together. On pretty days we climbed up among the rocks and fished for crabs and sea stars using homemade fishing lines. Or we went swimming, stretching out afterwards on the rocks to sunbathe and tickle each other's backs with long straws of grass. When it rained or stormed, we played in Mia's attic, where she had a trapeze swinging from the rafters. Or we sprawled out on my veranda floor playing Canasta, Rummy, or Monopoly. If it rained too hard and we could not make it to each other's houses, I cross-stitched a sampler that never seemed to get finished or read a book.

Sometimes we got mad at each other and were not on speaking terms for a few days. Usually the two of them ganged up on me, which made me angry and go off in a huff to pout. They teased me about living in a small provincial town and speaking a broad dialect. They thought they were so much better than I was because they lived in the capital or in a university town, where the spoken language was much more refined or classier sounding. Or they lorded it over me that they were so much better off than I was because Birran's father was a pharmacist and Mia's was a director of some big company. As with most children, we did not stay mad at each other for too long but quickly made up and forgot our squabbles.

Whenever we were at odds, I played with the two sisters, Ann-Marie and Britta Berg instead, who lived directly behind our cottage and were almost the same age as I. Their father was a house painter, who lived and worked in Mollösund year round while their mother worked in the fishery factory. I sometimes envied them being able to live in Mollösund year round, but Mia and Birran made fun of them because they spoke with a strong dialect, which was not as "fine" as theirs. That was probably the reason why they never included these two girls in our play.

As promised, Mother arrived the following week just in time to celebrate Midsummer's Eve. Both villagers and summer residents joined in the fun of dressing the Midsummer pole with birch branches and wreaths made of wild flowers, which was then raised up and securely tied in a hole in the middle of the *dansbryggan*, or dancing bridge, located right off the pier where the steamboats docked. Throughout the summer this is where both young and old gathered for dancing on Saturday nights, sometimes even to live bands.

Next to Christmas and St. Lucia, Midsummer's Eve was my favorite festival; it celebrates the summer solstice, the longest day of the year. Young girls typically gather wild flowers, which are then woven into a wreath and worn like a crown. Wearing my freshly made flower wreath, I joined hands with other children as we circled around the Midsummer pole, singing and acting out traditional songs. I especially loved playing Sleeping Beauty, who wakes up after a hundred years and is rescued by Prince Charming.

Unfortunately, we were not able to spend our whole summer holiday in Mollösund because Mother was renting out the cottage for the month of July in order to help make the mortgage payments. In spite of its lack of modern conveniences and its miniature size, our cottage was always in high demand because Mollösund was such a popular summer resort.

When July arrived, we were unhappy about leaving and not being able to return until August when Mother would join us for her annual vacation. Fortunately, however, we did not have to go back to Borås like Mother did because she had managed to make other arrangements for the three of us just as in summers past.

This year Ingrid was going to attend a camp for the Swedish *Unghögern*, or Swedish Young Conservatives, where she would take part in various civic programs and lectures. Politics really interested her. After camp, she was going to stay with *Moster* Ingrid, Mother's older sister, who was a shipyard's nurse in Stockholm.

Karin was going to Mother's favorite cousin Alf Moldén, who had a summer house in Kullavik, a small seaside resort to the south of Göteborg. Mother felt that she could be of some help to her cousin and his wife by looking after their three small children in return for her room and board. Karin didn't mind as long as she could also go swimming, lie in the sun, and have fun. It is strange how she has always seemed to crave the sun the most of the three of us.

I, on the other hand, was off to two different places. First I was going to Lysekil, another fishing village further up the coast from Mollösund, where *Moster* Anne-Marie had her summer home. During the rest of the year she was an elementary school teacher in Borås. I loved being in Lysekil even though my only playmate was my aunt. My cousin Björn was nine years older than I and had absolutely no interest in playing with his little cousin. One of my fondest memories from those days is of climbing up the huge cherry tree in their front yard and picking off the sweet ripe cherries that *Moster* later turned into cherry jam, at least those that did not find their way into my stomach first.

I was always a little bit afraid, or perhaps I should say in awe, of my uncle, *Morbror* Gösta, who was a secondary school teacher. He always struck me as a very unyielding and humorless man, who had published some poems and was always busy writing on something or other. His room on the second floor of their house was strictly off limits, not only to me, but also to his own family; he did not like having his things disturbed whatsoever.

My aunt was very good to me, though, and spoiled me in many different ways, perhaps because she had always longed to have a little girl of her own. I was her little pet even at home in Borås during the rest of the year. If spoiling me meant I could eat as many sweets and baked goodies as I wanted, I was not going to object. My family still blames *Moster* Anne-Marie for my developing such a liking for sweets. When they saw me again later that summer, they were horrified when they saw what a little butterball I had turned into. Looking at pictures from that summer, however, I think they were exaggerating. I don't look a bit fat!

Then for the last two weeks of the summer, I visited Mother's older brother, *Morbror* Carl Arne, who taught driving school in Munkedal, a small town not too far from Mollösund although it was not close to the shore. I actually had more fun there because of my three girl cousins, all within my age range. We got into a lot of trouble and mischief because of our roughhouse playing. I remember several occasions when I was afraid that *Morbror* Carl-Arne was going to spank me just like he did my cousin Margareta, who was the ringleader in all our adventures. Perhaps I escaped such a fate simply because I was his sister's child and not because I was such a perfect little angel.

When August arrived, everyone returned to Mollösund, with Mother coming from Borås and the three of us from our sundry places. For the rest of the summer, we basked in the sunshine, went swimming every day, drank juice and ate biscuits to fortify us after splashing around in the water—all except for Ingrid that is.

This August Ingrid decided to earn some pocket money by working in the local fishery. Although Karin and I were still too young to work there, we followed suit in later summers when we both also learned how to clean herring or put flat wooden sticks into codfish, which were skinned, salted and hung up to dry on long racks on the rocks. It was this process which gave Mollösund its very distinctive odor. The dried fish, known as *lutfisk* in Swedish, was later soaked in a solution of lye to make it edible for Christmas dinner, when it was boiled and served with an egg sauce and potatoes. It was absolutely delicious and a must at a traditional Swedish Christmas feast. Unfortunately, this process is no longer done in Mollösund because of modernization to the point of its extinction. I really miss that smell, in particular, whenever I return to Mollösund these days.

Another pastime was going to the cinema in a big tent, erected in the middle of the big ball field at the entrance to Mollösund. What was even more fun was trying to sneak in for free by crawling under the edge of the tent. If my friends and I were caught in the act, all we had to do was pay the entrance fee. Oh, how we giggled and snickered when we managed to get in for free!

When reminiscing years later about our wonderful summers in Mollösund, Ingrid reminded me that a big ship with lots of young and handsome sailors had lain moored in the harbor during the whole month of August in 1953. She told me how she had been especially keen on one of the sailors, which I happened to remember as well because of how silly I thought she was to carry on so about boys. When I asked her what had become of him, she didn't know because he had just been a passing fancy and someone to go out with.

What I didn't pay much attention to as a youngster, but which Ingrid also told me about as an adult, was that a Swedish marine ship was there that summer to sweep the waters for mines left over from World War II and to make sure they were defused and harmless. I do remember how one such mine washed up on the rocks below our cottage, which we later secured on the cliff with metal pins and even painted silver to prevent the salty wind and water eating it up with rust.

Before we knew it, August passed, and we had to leave Mollösund to return to the humdrum of another school year in Borås, completely unaware of the big changes that lay ahead.

CHAPTER XVI

Changes in the Air

Fall 1953

Starting a new school year was always exciting, but it was even more so this year because Mother promised to let me invite a few friends for my birthday just before school started. My first real birthday party!

When August 31st arrived, I lay in my bed eagerly listening for the sounds of footsteps and hushed voices in the hallway that would announce Mother and my sisters getting ready to come into my room. When I heard them singing *Ja, må hon leva,...* our Swedish birthday song, I sat up, rubbed my eyes and pretended I had been asleep. That was part of the game we always played on our birthdays.

Mother then placed the "birthday" tray on my lap with my favorite breakfast on it. As usual, fresh flowers surrounded my plate while a burning candle added its warm glow to the festive occasion. After devouring my delicious cinnamon roll, a boiled egg and a glass of cocoa, I opened presents. From Ingrid I got a book and from Karin a pencil case. Mother gave me a whole Swedish *krona*—a small fortune—with which I could buy a whole lot of candy, if I wanted to.

As soon as Mother left for work, my sisters helped me get ready for the party later that afternoon. By the time one o'clock rolled around, I was ready to receive my guests. After playing games, drinking *saft*, and eating a yummy cake that Mother had managed to bake the night before, it was time to open presents once again. I felt like a princess opening up so many gifts in one day, more than I had ever received before. I was in seventh heaven!

When school began a few days later, I was surprised to discover

Our class. 1954 - 55

that there were no boys in my new third grade classroom. It remained that way for the next three years. The boys' classroom was even in a different building although we shared the schoolyard during recess. We were thankful not to have to put up with those pesky, loud boys in the classroom any longer. It was enough that they continued their merciless teasing, pinching, and pulling our pigtails out in the schoolyard when the teachers weren't looking.

The only boy I missed being together with in class was Christer Lidén, but because his parents and my mother were close friends, we were able to see each other outside of school. I always thought he was so cute with his big blue eyes and curly hair, but what I liked most about him was that he was my big defender at recess, always looking out for me like my brother Helmut might have done, had he lived.

For the next three years, my teacher was Mrs. Eriksson-Grenhult, whom I remember with very mixed feelings. In looking back on her methodology and pedagogy, I must admit that she was probably ahead of her time. I feel privileged to have had her for a teacher even though I always had a feeling that she never liked me.

Reflecting on this situation as an adult, I believe it may have had something to do with my being born in Austria during the war, which made me German by birth. Many Swedes did not like Germans in those days because of what happened during the war. Perhaps she was one of those who disliked Germans and transferred those feelings on to me. All I know for sure is that I always worked especially hard trying to please her, but somehow it never seemed to be quite enough.

In spite of that, I do have some fond memories of my teacher. She was very keen on physical activities, always taking my class on long hikes or little outings in the afternoons after spending all morning inside. Naturally, none of us complained. It was infinitely more exciting and fun to be outside than cooped up all day in a stuffy classroom.

Of course these outdoor activities depended very much on the weather and the season. During that first fall in Mrs. Grenhult's classroom, I remember going on hikes into the hillsides that surrounded Borås, sometimes just to gather as many leaves from different kinds of trees as we could possibly find or to locate things in nature or something the teacher had hidden beforehand. A scavenger hunt of this latter type usually meant that we set off in groups of two, spaced several minutes apart, and followed clues using a compass. The team who found everything in the shortest amount of time was the winner. This often happened to be my best friend Ulla and me.

The one time we didn't win is the one I especially remember. The two of us were doing really well until I happened to stumble on a root in the forest. Falling headlong on the path, I hit my right shin on a very sharp and pointed stone, which made a big gash. Boy, oh boy, did that hurt like fury! When I looked down and saw all that blood, I thought I was dying.

Even though I was the one hurting, Ulla cried just as hard because she was scared and didn't know what to do at first. Then she took off running in the direction of our teacher. A few minutes later she returned with Mrs. Grenhult in tow, who patched me up with the help of a first aid kit. I probably really needed stitches, but no one thought of that.

School friends on a ski trip with our teacher's little girl. Ulla Nilsson is on the right in front.

For the next few days I limped along while my leg continued to hurt and throb. Needless to say, Ulla and I did not come in first. Losing wouldn't have upset me as much if my archenemy Ann-Margaret and her partner hadn't won first place. What made things even worse was that she lorded it over us and taunted me, claiming it was my fault for being so clumsy that we lost. That was like rubbing salt into my wound.

Other outside activities included skiing in the hills above Borås or skating on the Ramnasjön in winter or going swimming in the public pool in spring. I cannot say with certainty how often we engaged in these activities, but they occurred often enough for me to associate them with being in Mrs. Grenhult's class.

More important for my sisters and me was that we started noticing that Mother was making frequent trips to Stockholm on weekends, always taking the afternoon train on Saturday and returning home on Sunday evening. This was something she had never done before.

At first she claimed that she was trying to find more stores to market her homemade mirrors, and we believed her. But then she began telling us that she wanted to visit her sister Ingrid in Stockholm. That was more difficult to understand because *Moster* Ingrid was usually the one who visited us in Borås, never the other way around.

What was going on here? This was so out of character for our mother.

When we asked her, she just shrugged and told us laughingly not to worry our pretty little heads about it. She seemed to be doing that a lot this fall, laughing, that is, which made her seem happier than she had been in a long time.

It was not until late October or early November, just a year after we were notified that Father was dead, that she dropped the bombshell on us. We had just finished supper and were getting ready to enjoy some games because it was Saturday evening and Mother was at home for once. She handed each of us a bag filled with loose candy, which was not that unusual, but what she said as she gave them to us took us completely by surprise.

"How would you feel if I were to get married again?"

We were absolutely flabbergasted. We just sat there and stared at her with our mouths wide open. My hand was already halfway into my bag of goodies when I dropped the bag in my shock, spilling its delicious contents out on the floor. Quickly I bent down to retrieve it while sneaking a look at Mother's face to see if she was joking. She wasn't! Although she looked rather serious, I could see a little smile slowly lighting up her face as she continued to explain what she meant.

"I know this comes as a surprise to you, but I hope you will understand. This doesn't mean that I will ever forget your pappa. I will always love him. But he is gone forever." She sighed as I had often heard her do whenever we talked about Father. Then she continued resolutely. "But now I have met this man, whose name is Torsten. Last weekend, when I was up in Stockholm, he asked me to marry him. How do you feel about that?" She looked at all three of us in turn trying to gauge our reaction to her announcement. She must have realized that this would come as a shock.

If the cat got our tongues at first that was no longer the case by the time she finished talking. We began to hurl questions at her in rapid-fire succession with each one of us trying to be heard over the other, questions such as "Who is he? How old is he? When and how did you meet him? What is he like? Will we like him? Is this why you have been gone so much this fall?"

Mother threw up her hands in mock despair at this barrage coming at her from three different directions. Calmly and purposefully she then began to relate how it had all come about. "You know, girls, that all my friends here in Borås have been playing match makers ever since we found out last year that your father had died in Siberia. They all felt that I deserved some happiness after so many years of waiting for him. They were eager for me to meet someone with whom I could be happy again."

We nodded that we understood what she was trying to tell us, but we did not say anything. We were anxious for Mamma to continue.

"At first I was reluctant because I felt it was too soon, but then this summer, while you were all gone, I met Torsten from Stockholm at a dinner party. While he was on business here in town that whole week, he asked me out several evenings. I really enjoyed being together with him. Because I liked him and he liked me, I decided to visit him in Stockholm whenever he could not come to Borås. That is of course why I was gone so often in the past few months. We wanted to get to know each other better to see if we wanted to share our futures."

All we could do was stare at her in wide-eyed amazement. Our mother was dating? It felt really weird. That wasn't the normal way of things, was it? Wasn't she too old for that?

"Torsten is just a few years older than I am," she then continued. "His wife died several years ago, leaving him alone with two boys, one just a little older than you, Ingrid, and another one a year older than you, Karin. They are both very nice and well brought up boys. I think you will like them. During my last visit, they told me they were really looking forward to meeting the three of you."

"What does this Torsten do for a living?" my practical sister Ingrid now wanted to know, completely ignoring the last part of what Mother had said.

"He is an engineer and has a big apartment in central Stockholm. If everything goes well, as both of us hope it will, we may all be moving to Stockholm very soon, perhaps as early as next spring." Mother finished with a flurry, as if there were nothing unusual about what she was telling us.

But we knew better. Slowly it began to dawn on us that if Mother married this Torsten, our lives would change completely. For one thing, we would have a stepfather and two stepbrothers and for another, we would have to leave our friends and start over in a new school in a new city.

Suddenly, I remembered what I had overheard several months

earlier when Aunt Birgit, in the apartment below us, and Mother had been discussing this very possibility. Now I finally understood what they had been talking about. However, I was not altogether sure I liked it.

"Why can't he move to Borås instead?" I asked anxiously, seeing my familiar world crumbling around me.

"Because Torsten works in Stockholm, and I would be more than happy to quit my job here. You know as well as I do that I would love nothing better than to be able to stay at home again and never have to go out to work. The three of you will simply be going to school in the capital instead. Won't that be exciting? Just think, you will also get two brothers into the bargain," Mother replied, smiling reassuringly down at little anxious me.

"But Mamma, will there be room enough for all of us?" Karin asked. She hadn't said much so far, always the quieter and more reserved of us three sisters.

"Uncle Torsten, as you will call him from now on, has a very large apartment with plenty of room for everyone," Mother reassured Karin. "But let us not get ahead of ourselves. Enough of this for tonight, but I promise I will let you know how things develop between Torsten and me. I have not said yes yet, but we have agreed that I will give him a definite answer after Christmas."

Then turning to me, she told me to go ahead and set up the Monopoly game we were planning to play that evening. I could tell that neither Ingrid nor Karin was too happy about ending the conversation about this surprising revelation, but they decided to go along. For the present, the discussion was over.

On the following Monday, I was eager to tell my classmates about moving to Stockholm. All puffed up with self-importance, I pranced about the schoolyard, bragging to everyone willing to listen about this exciting change in my life.

My status in class changed overnight. Suddenly I became somebody of importance. Nothing like this had ever happened to any of them. My moment of glory did not last very long, however, because they soon got tired of hearing about it all the time. At least Ann-Margaret stopped being so mean to me while my popularity lasted. My news soon became old, and I was right back where I started—that is until a few months later.

In the month that followed, we saw even less of Mother during weekends. I was actually beginning to look forward to the possibility of having a pappa just like everyone else in my class. What was even better, though, was the prospect of moving to Stockholm. Living in the capital was big stuff to me, probably because I always envied how my summer friend Birran spoke. Her speech wasn't countrified like mine because she was living in the capital and not in a small provincial town like I did.

Christmas neared once again with all the preparations it entailed. The mood around the house was one of exuberance and happiness, so very different from last year's feelings of sadness and sorrow.

By this time we had met Uncle Torsten several times when he came to visit Mother in Borås. I liked him well enough and tried hard to be friendly and open with him. Karin, on the other hand, was very reserved, as was Ingrid, which was perhaps understandable. We had not had a chance to meet his sons yet. But we would meet them as soon as spring came, Mother promised, and before she married Torsten.

When he came to visit Mother just before Christmas, he even brought us some presents. While Karin remembers receiving a deck of cards, Ingrid has absolutely no recollection of what he gave her, probably because it made no deep impression on her.

I, on the other hand, have a very strong memory of the gift he gave me. It was a book filled with lots of black and white photos of the four Swedish royal princesses and the young crown prince Carl Gustaf playing in their summer palace Solliden on the island of Öland. I remember it so well because I used to fantasize about being Carl Gustaf's older sister. After all, didn't I have the same name as one of the princesses who was one of his actual older sisters?

As soon as Christmas was over, Mother informed us that she was planning to spend New Year's Eve with Uncle Torsten in Stockholm. That didn't come as a big surprise. It was a perfect time for Mother to go. She would have a few more days off than usual because that year New Year's Eve fell on a Thursday.

Her workday ended at noon that day, which meant she was able to take the afternoon train to Stockholm and arrive in time to ring in the New Year with Uncle Torsten. She asked Ingrid to bring the mail down to her at the station because she didn't have time to go home before she had to catch the train.

One of the letters in that mail changed everything although my sisters and I remained ignorant until eleven days into January.

CHAPTER XVII

The First Postcard

January 1954

On New Year's Day our downstairs neighbor informed us that Mother's boss had insisted she return immediately from Stockholm in order to go on a business trip to Germany. We thought this was a rather strange and unusual request. She had never gone on any such trips before. But what was even stranger was that she did not even say goodbye to us before leaving even though she must have stopped by our apartment to collect her passport. But knowing how demanding and unyielding her boss was, we accepted the explanation.

When she continued to be absent for the next ten days, we were still not overly concerned that anything out of the ordinary had happened. We had absolutely no inkling that our world was about to be turned upside down once again.

When I returned from school that long ago January afternoon in 1954, I was pleasantly surprised to find Mother sitting in the living room. But instead of greeting me in her usual exuberant way, she just sat there and said nothing at all for the first few minutes after giving me a quick hug and kiss.

Why didn't she say something? She had been gone so long without any good explanation. Because this was so unlike her, I was afraid that something awful must have happened. Perhaps she has received some bad news and doesn't know how to tell me, I thought. But never, not for a single moment, did I imagine she would say what she said when she finally spoke.

"Gittan, your father is still alive!" Mother blurted out.

Her words caught me totally off guard. What was she saying? Had I heard her right? Father was alive? How could that be? How could he possibly be alive?

Dumbfounded, I stared at her in utter disbelief. Then the shock set in. I had difficulties breathing and swallowing. My heart was pounding so hard against the inside of my ribs that I thought it was about to burst. Then I started to shake and tremble.

I shook my head as if coming out of a trance and found my voice again. "Is it true, Mamma? Is Pappa really alive? He is not dead?" My voice sounded weird, very high pitched and squeaky. Had Mamma really said what I thought she said? I wanted to believe that I had heard her right and that this was not some figment of my imagination. But how could it be true?

"It is true, Gittan, your pappa is alive. I know this is hard for you to believe. It must come as a big shock to you just as it did for me. When I first read Pastor Lippert's letter on my way up to Stockholm, I couldn't believe it either, but then I received further proof of it." Her voice shook slightly, and her lips trembled as she held up a strange looking post card that I had not noticed until then.

Before Mother had a chance to show me what she was clutching in her hand, my two sisters also came home, squealing for joy when they discovered her sitting there with me, the post card temporarily forgotten. Once Mother told them what she had just told me, they were equally shocked at this fantastic but unreal news. Our father, who had died in 1950, was now supposed to be alive! How could this possibly be true? Was this some kind of cruel joke?

Poor Mother! We sounded like a bunch of magpies when we bombarded her with a bunch of questions. The one that came through the loudest was: What was this proof she was talking about?

Picking up the card she had dropped in the excitement of all the welcome home hugs, she waved it in the air, jubilantly singing out her answer. "This here is the proof, girls. Your pappa wrote it just a few months ago from Vorkuta. It is definitely his handwriting. I would recognize it anywhere, anytime." Smiling broadly, she reluctantly relinquished the precious card to her eldest daughter, who was trying to grab it from her hand.

Ingrid examined it carefully with me trying to peer over her shoulder. After what seemed like an eternity, she turned to Mother and said in her most serious and very grown-up voice, "Yes, I agree with you, Mamma. Pappa definitely wrote this card. I, too, recognize his handwriting."

In the meantime, Karin and I were impatiently waiting to have a closer look at the odd-looking postcard. Grudgingly, Ingrid handed the card to Karin next, who proceeded to take her own sweet time studying it. It was simply killing me having to wait so long for my turn. It was so unfair, I kept grumbling. Finally, I simply snatched it unceremoniously from Karin's hands. She squealed in protest, but I didn't care as I began to scrutinize the card.

The first thing I noticed was that the card didn't have a picture on the front like other postcards. Instead there were some strange looking symbols that I later learned were Cyrillic letters used in the Russian language. The only words I recognized were Mother's name and an address. Strangely enough it wasn't our address but that of her friends in Varberg. I wondered why that was, of course, but didn't find out the reason until much later. Right then it was much more important that we had finally heard from our father. The card was also twice the size of a normal one, but he had only written on half of it.

"Why did Pappa not use the whole card?" I wondered aloud.

"The bottom half is intended for me to use in writing back to him." Mother sounded very happy and excited.

"Please, Mamma, tell us what Papa has written!" Karin and I demanded, as I reluctantly handed the card back to Mother.

Slowly, Mother began to read it in German first just like Father had written it, knowing that Ingrid could understand it perfectly well. Then she translated it into Swedish for Karin and me.

The card was dated December 6, 1953, just a little over a month before.

My darlings!

May this card find you, my darling Bimili and our daughters Ingrid, Karin and Birgitta in perfect health. Please don't worry too much about me. I am in good health. Even though the worry about you pains me greatly, thinking of you also gives me an unending strength not to give up hope. Please write me and tell me honestly how everyone is, you, Omama,

your parents, your sisters and brothers and my brothers. Please let me know how and where you live. May this card reach you in time for Christmas and give you hope for the New Year. In constant faithfulness and love I send you kisses and hugs from your K'mann-Vati
Roland

After Mother finished translating it, I sat quietly for a few moments, still trying to digest the fact that Pappa was alive and that he had written to us after he was supoosed to be dead even though we believed that he had died in 1950. What made me especially happy was that he mentioned me by name. It warmed my heart to find out for sure that he knew I existed.

Browned with age but otherwise well preserved, this first card from Father, telling us in his own handwriting that he was well, is safely tucked away in a plastic jacket along with all the other thirteen cards that came later.

A few more minutes passed as we sat huddled together trying to assimilate what Pappa had written. It was wonderful beyond belief to know that he was alive. Perhaps he would soon be able to come home! When I said my prayers that evening, and from then on, I always asked God to bring my pappa safely home so that I could finally get to know him.

The rest of the evening passed in a blur. And so did the next few days, even the next few weeks and months for that matter. Our life was in a constant uproar and turmoil as a result of receiving this first sign of life from Father in nine years!

For reasons I could not understand then, the news of Father's postcard and Mother's trip to Germany caused quite a stir of excitement not only in Borås but throughout Sweden. Somehow the press found out what had happened. Probably because Father had been officially declared dead, it made the news of his postcard that much more sensational and unique.

Articles and photographs soon began to appear in Swedish newspapers, not always on a daily basis but definitely on a weekly one. There were constant comings and goings of reporters and photographers in our home. Everyone wanted to interview Mother and take pictures of us, but in particular of me, because I was the little girl who had never seen her pappa, which apparently was a very strange occurrence in the eyes of the Swedish people.

One such occasion stands out in my memory. A photographer arrived late one evening. Even though I was supposed to be in bed already, I had snuck into the corridor that separated my bedroom from the rest of the apartment, curious to find out who our late evening visitor was. I overheard him asking Mother's permission to take a picture of me. Hoping Mamma would agree, I quickly jumped back into my bed, pretending to be asleep. When she "woke" me up to ask if I wanted to have my picture taken, I hopped out of bed, pulled my best dress over my pajamas, and ran into the living room to pose for the photographer. This photo appeared later in the weekly magazine *Året Runt*-Vårat Hem, which means Year Round-Our Home, where our story was told in a series of articles over a period of four or five months. The full-page picture shows me holding a framed photograph of my father with the caption:

Birgitta has never seen her father but she has his portrait. It is her dearest possession.

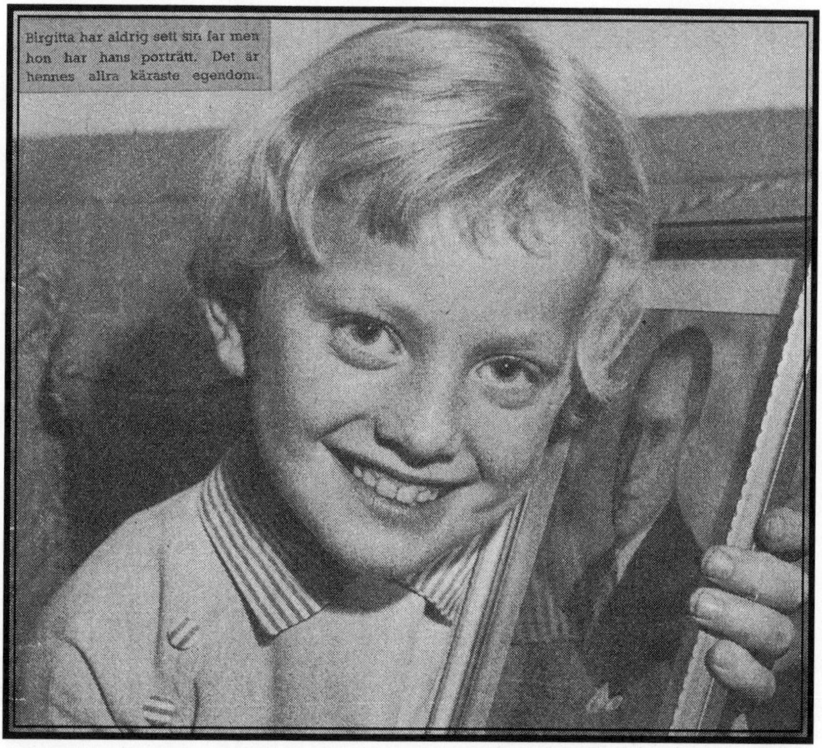

We still have all the clippings from those days, yellow and brittle with age and quite worn on the edges. Here are a few of the headlines from the front pages of some of these newspapers:

A Borås Family Receives Happy News

The Husband is alive in a Russian Prison Camp

Borås Tidning, **January 16, 1954**

***

The Husband of a Borås Woman Declared Dead in Russia in 1950

Now he is Alive, says a comrade!

Göteborgs Tidningen, **January 15, 1954**

***

"The Love for you and the children has given me strength during all these years"

BORÅS WIFE GETS A WONDERFUL MESSAGE

The Husband who has been declared dead lives in a Soviet Prison Camp

Västgöta Demokraten, **January 15,1954**

***

A Letter from a Russian Prison Camp: Father is Alive

A Borås woman with 3 Daughters exuberant

Expressen, **January 15,1954**

***

Siberian Prisoner Lends Strength to all in the Camp

A mother went secretly to Hamburg-but now children know Father is alive

Stockholms-Tidningen, **January 17,1954**

***

In an article in *Dagens Nyheter*, dated Saturday, January 16, 1954, Mother summed up her feelings with the following words:

Since my husband was captured in September 1944, I have often felt as if I have been riding on an undulating sea, sometimes riding high on the crest of hope just to plunge into valleys of despair. This is another such crest of hope, but now I am afraid to put my trust in it for fear of

having my hopes dashed once more. That is why I will hardly dare allow myself to believe in a happy ending this time until my husband actually comes home again and I can see him standing alive before me. If he ever returns home, nothing will ever rob me of my belief that there is a just and loving God and that justice still prevails…

Reporters weren't of course the only ones dropping by at all odd hours. Well-meaning and concerned relatives and friends did as well. I never knew we had so many of them. Everyone wanted to hear directly from Mother what he or she had read about in the newspapers and magazines. Sometimes we could have as many as two or three visitors in one evening. At first we enjoyed the hullabaloo, but then we started getting tired of never having Mamma to ourselves any longer.

It was not until I was fully grown that I understood the uniqueness of our situation. Receiving a postcard from a father who was supposed to be dead was definitely not an every-day occurrence in Sweden. Had we lived anywhere else in Europe, this might not have been the case. Sweden was an anomaly because unlike other European countries, it had not been torn apart by the Second World War, having remained neutral throughout it, just like Switzerland. As a result Swedish husbands, fathers, brothers and sons had not died or been taken prisoners of war. The only exception to this is the case of Raoul Wallenberg, the Swedish diplomat who disappeared in Budapest in 1944 after being captured by the Soviets and who has never been heard or seen since.

Suddenly I found myself becoming very popular at school once again. All my classmates were vying for my attention and wanting to be my best friend. During recess, they begged me to tell them all about Father. I was more than willing to comply, loving every minute of being center stage. Even mean Ann-Margaret changed her tune for a little while; at least until the newness of it began to wear off.

A few days after Mother's return home, I remember overhearing someone—I think it must have been a reporter—asking Mother how come the card had been sent in care of her friends, the Montalvos, and not directly to us in Borås. I had been curious about this myself, which accounts for why I listened very intensely to her response. I remember it well for the question of how Father knew where to get in touch with her never fails to come up in conversations about those days.

My answer is the same as Mother's always was. Father couldn't possibly know where we were or whether we had even survived the war. Nor could he know for sure whether his mother was still living because her heart had given her so much trouble when he had last seen her in 1944. Even though he knew where Mother's parents lived in Sweden, he couldn't be sure they were alive either. He therefore chose to send the card in care of their friends, Sie and Tage Montalvo, realizing that their factory in a small town in Sweden would more than likely still be standing because Sweden had not taken part in the war. He must have reasoned that if we were still alive, these friends would know where to find us. And he was right!

For me the next few months crept by far too slowly. I wanted Father to come home right away and couldn't understand why those Soviets were still keeping him. Didn't they understand that a father belonged at home with his family? I felt anxious about everything, which showed in my schoolwork. My grades started slipping because I was not as attentive as I had been heretofore.

It must have been the same for Karin but with much worse results because she failed to get promoted at the end of that school year. Instead of spending time helping us with our schoolwork, Mother was preoccupied with writing to lots of people or giving interviews to reporters when she came home from work. It is understandable that she was less focused on us. All her energy was spent on trying to find out more about Father and how to get him home.

In the beginning our thoughts centered on speculations about when we would get another postcard from Father. When no more cards arrived, we became very fearful that something had happened to prevent him from writing again. Perhaps he was very ill or had even died. We just did not know, and the not knowing was driving us mad with worry, which manifested itself in how poorly both Karin and I were doing at school.

It was not until much later that we found out why we didn't hear from Father again for so long. It turned out that we weren't even supposed to have received that first postcard. It only arrived as a result of an act of pure human kindness.

What we didn't know was that Father was transferred from his regular camp to the *Schweigelager* or a silent camp because of the Vorkuta Uprising in the summer of 1953. Although he did not actually participate in a hand-to-hand battle with the guards, he was perceived as one of the intellectual leaders behind the uprising, which earned his transfer to this silent camp. As a result he did not have the opportunity to write home like everyone else after the uprising was put down and restrictions were eased somewhat, which included prisoners being allowed to write home.

One day in October 1953 a young female doctor in the silent camp apparently took pity on Father. She was in Vorkuta against her own wishes, having been exiled from the Ukraine as so many others were on trumped up charges. She asked Father, who was working as an assistant in the camp infirmary, if he had heard anything from his family. When he told her that he had never been allowed to write and had no idea whether his family had even survived the war or where they were, she told him to meet her at a certain fence post along the perimeter after their shift was over. She promised she would try to get him one of the official cards with which he could contact his family. As if that wasn't dangerous enough, she also promised to smuggle his written card out of the camp. If she were caught she could be severely punished. She didn't dare repeat this dangerous act as long as Father remained in that camp, which explains why we didn't hear anything from him again for over a year.

We will always be thankful to this courageous young woman. Had it not been for her, we would never have received that first post card in January 1954.

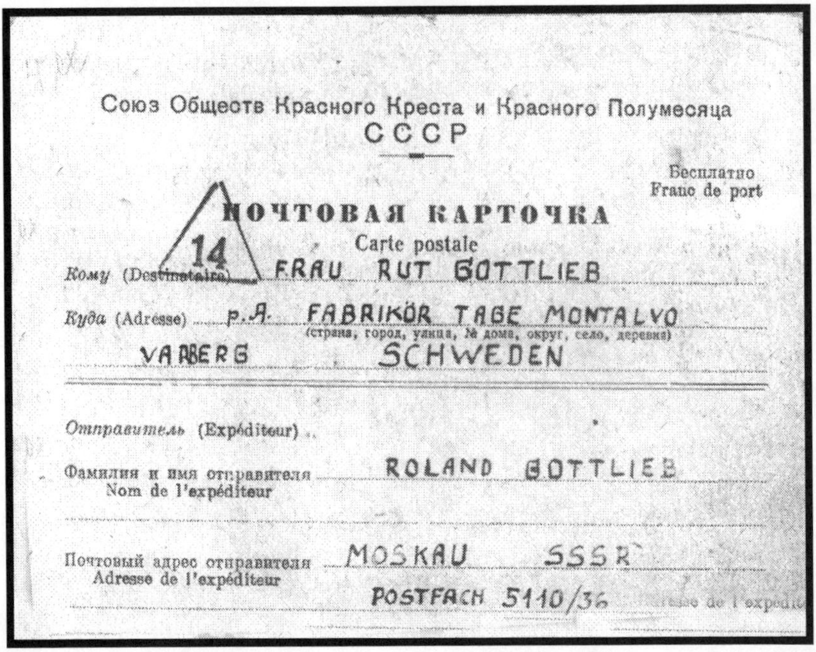

Союз Обществ Красного Креста и Красного Полумесяца
СССР

Бесплатно
Franc de port

ПОЧТОВАЯ КАРТОЧКА
Carte postale

14

Кому (Destinataire) FRAU RUT GOTTLIEB

Куда (Adresse) p.A. FABRIKÖR TAGE MONTALVO
(страна, город, улица, № дома, округ, село, деревня)

VARBERG SCHWEDEN

Отправитель (Expéditeur)

Фамилия и имя отправителя
Nom de l'expéditeur ROLAND GOTTLIEB

Почтовый адрес отправителя
Adresse de l'expéditeur MOSKAU SSSR

POSTFACH 5110/36

The first post card - dated December 6, 1953

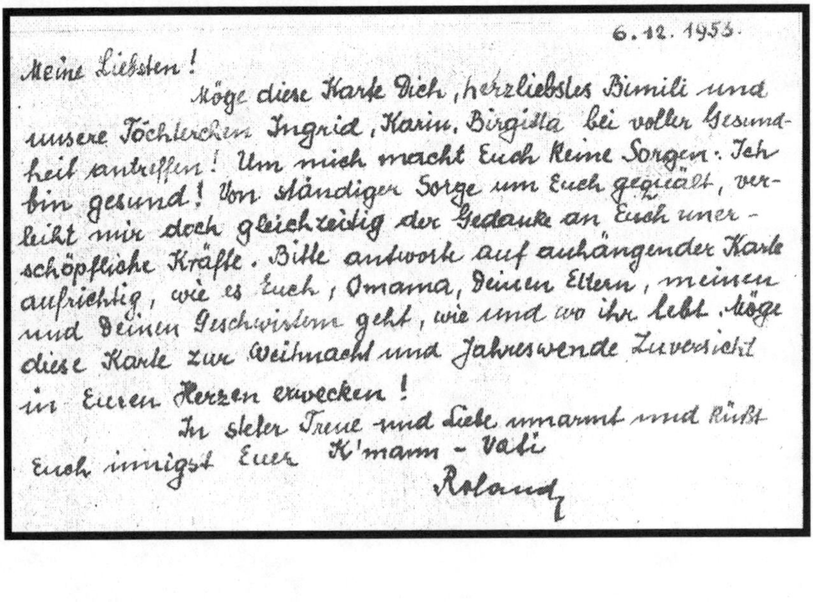

6.12.1953.

Meine Liebsten!
Möge diese Karte Dich, herzliebstes Bimili und
unsere Töchterchen Ingrid, Karin, Birgitta bei voller Gesundheit antreffen! Um mich macht Euch keine Sorgen. Ich
bin gesund! Von ständiger Sorge um Euch gequält, verleiht mir doch gleichzeitig der Gedanke an Euch unerschöpfliche Kräfte. Bitte antwortet auf anhängender Karte
aufrichtig, wie es Euch, Omama, Deinen Eltern, meinen
und Deinen Geschwistern geht, wie und wo ihr lebt. Möge
diese Karte zur Weihnacht und Jahreswende Zuversicht
in Euren Herzen erwecken!
In steter Treue und Liebe umarmt und küßt
Euch innigst Euer K'mann - Vati
Roland

CHAPTER XVIII

Mother's Mission

Germany, 1954

When no more news arrived for several months, the hullabaloo that had so upset our daily routine began to diminish. Slowly we returned to a facsimile of normalcy.

Late one Saturday evening at the end of February 1954, the four of us finally had some time to be alone together. No reporters were at the door clamoring for Mother's attention. Nor were we expecting any relatives or friends to drop by. Hopefully, it was just going to be the four of us for a change.

As was our custom, we gathered around the sofa table in the living room where an inviting fire was blazing in the open hearth in the corner of the room. Candles were brightly illuminating a photograph of Father, prominently displayed on the hutch beside the sofa. A platter filled with pastries and cookies stood tantalizingly waiting for us to enjoy an evening of cozy togetherness.

Munching on the goodies, we were happy to finally have Mother to ourselves. We wanted to hear firsthand all that had happened after she left Borås on that fateful New Year's Eve. Until then, we had only heard bits and pieces as she talked to reporters and friends or what we had read in newspapers and magazines. We were especially interested in hearing all those minor details that were major ones to us.

"After waving good-bye to you, Ingrid," Mother began her tale, "I decided to read the newspaper before opening up the mail that you brought down to the station. When I finally began to thumb through it, a letter with a German stamp immediately caught my attention."

We knew of course already that the letter was from Pastor Lippert, the man in charge of the Friedland Repatriation Camp in Germany. It was also thanks to him that Mother had first found out where Father was. But after hearing that he had died in Siberia in 1950, Mother never expected to hear from the pastor again.

"After reading the first few lines, I dropped the letter like a hot potato and cried out as if it had burned me." To demonstrate in her typical theatrical fashion, she dropped the letter she was holding in her hands and blew on her fingers as if she had burned them. "Unable to move or pick it up from where it had dropped, I just sat there staring at it unbelievingly." Putting her reaction into words, she sat there quietly for a few minutes staring down at the letter before finally picking it up to read it aloud to us.

> *Dear Mrs. Gottlieb!*
>
> *Your husband is alive after all! Yesterday over 200 Germans arrived at our transit camp in Friedland from the Soviet Union. Among them were several civil servants from the German Legation in Sofia, who claim to have been with your husband in Vorkuta as late as June of this year. Mr. Mohrmann, for instance, says that Roland is fine and only has to do relatively light work. You can write to him yourself, if you wish. His address is below. There are many other men as well who have seen or been together with your husband just a few months ago. One in particular is a Mr. Franz Nordt. Unfortunately, I do not have his address at this point but I will get it for you soon, if..."*

Here Mother stopped suddenly, probably just like she had done the first time she read it as her next words proved.

"By the time I got that far, I had to stop. I was trembling all over and wanted to scream. I felt numb. I couldn't understand how that could possibly be so. Your father was dead, wasn't he? Could this be a mistake? Is this some kind of cruel joke? No, a pastor wouldn't joke about this, I thought. Was it really possible that these men might have seen my Roland as late as last summer? But how could I believe it? I felt absolutely helpless. I had no idea what I was going to do. How could I find out if this was true after all? Who could possibly help me and advise me what to do next?

In my desperation I cried out to God asking Him to please help me, to show me the way."

Mother clasped her hands in prayer and lifted them up to heaven. Her face looked stricken, clearly showing the anguish she must have felt at the time. Her words and actions spoke volumes of how rattled and confused she must have been after reading that letter the first time. All of us were still having a hard time believing it could be true. It still seemed so unreal.

We sat quietly, expectantly staring at Mother in hopes she would continue to tell us what happened next. And of course she did. "There I was all alone in the train holding a piece of paper that took me totally by surprise. It was as if my mind had short-circuited and my body had quit functioning. I was shaking inside, and my hands were trembling when I finally forced myself to pick up the letter again. I knew I had to find out what else the pastor was trying to tell me. But it seemed as if the words "your husband is alive" were the only ones I could see. They kept repeating themselves in my mind, moving in time with the clickity-clack sound of the wheels of the train all the way up to Stockholm. I don't remember how long it was before I was calm enough to continue reading the rest of the letter, which confirmed further that your father must be alive. It also dawned on me that I would have to inform Torsten about my altered circumstances and that we no longer could get married."

She then told us how Uncle Torsten had been able to tell immediately that something was wrong when she stepped off the train. "I must have looked awful with my face all splotched from crying; I was a total wreck and quite wrung out from the gamut of emotions. Even though he asked me what was wrong, I didn't think the train station with so many people milling about was the right place to break such news to him. I waited instead until we were sitting down in a nearby restaurant. Besides, I had to eat anyway, didn't I?" She laughed, which brought a smile to our faces because it was such a typical mamma comment.

"After reading the letter from Pastor Lippert, poor Torsten understood what I was unable to express in words. Of course, it was a big shock to him as well. But he was very kind and understanding and told me that he was happy for me and that he realized how this changed everything. After discussing back and forth what I should do, we agreed that I should return home on the next train and prepare to go to Germany immediately. We both felt I needed to talk personally to these men who had seen your father."

"But Mamma, you didn't come back here! I never saw you. How come? What did you do? And where did you go?" I wanted to know.

"I did take the train back to Borås that same night, or rather early morning, but instead of going directly home, I called Dagmar from the train station. I asked her to make sure that you girls would be out of the apartment that morning so that I could get my passport and a few more clothes without your seeing me."

Dagmar was our downstairs neighbor, whose two oldest daughters were the same age as Ingrid and whose youngest one was eight or nine years younger than I. In fact, I often earned an extra 25 *öre* by taking Lillan out in her perambulator to help Aunt Dagmar out.

"Oh, so that is why Aunt Dagmar gave us money to go see a movie. I thought that was very nice and generous of her, even a bit unusual. Why didn't you just tell us you were back home?" Karin sounded a little troubled that Mother had not let us know she was back home and had even gone so far as to avoid seeing us.

"Yes, why didn't you, Mamma? You could have told me what you were planning to do." Ingrid also sounded a little hurt, perhaps because Mother had not even confided in her.

"Maybe I should have, but I didn't want you to be disappointed in case things didn't turn out so well. I simply did not want to raise your hopes if it wasn't true," Mamma responded. "Besides I could not trust myself to hold it all together. I was emotionally and physically exhausted. I did not sleep a wink on the train coming back to Borås. I just could not risk facing you in that condition for fear of completely losing control. Then you would have demanded to know what was wrong, which is what I was trying to avoid at all cost."

"So, that's why you didn't tell us, Mamma." I was satisfied with Mother's explanation of why she kept us in the dark.

"I am glad, Gittan, that you understand. I hope you will forgive me. I had this strong sense of urgency to go to Germany immediately. I just had to speak with those POWs in person who claimed to have seen your father because it would be far quicker than trying to contact them by mail first. I needed immediate answers."

Mother went on to explain that she had called *Moster* Ingrid before taking the night train to Borås, especially since she was supposed to have stayed at *Moster*'s apartment over the New Year's Eve weekend. After arriving in Borås, she also called her boss, Mr. Grenfors, and told him that she needed a few extra days of vacation because she had urgent personal business to take care of in Germany. It took some convincing on her part because he was not the easiest or most understanding boss.

"So, that is why Aunt Dagmar told us it was Mr. Grenfors' idea for you to go on a business trip to Germany! It was really hard for me to believe that he could have been that mean and demand that you go on a business trip over a holiday," Ingrid declared indignantly.

"Don't blame Aunt Dagmar. It wasn't her fault. I told her to tell you that. It was the only excuse I could think of at the time," Mother tried to mollify Ingrid. "I was the one who asked her to give you some money for the cinema because I needed to be able to go into our apartment without running into you. When Dagmar saw how tired I was, she persuaded me to spend the night with them before taking the train to Hamburg on Saturday morning."

"But how did you know where to get in touch with those POWs?" practical Ingrid asked. "Did the pastor give you some addresses in his letter?"

"No, not immediately anyway, not until Tuesday when I received Franz Nordt's address from him. You see, as soon as I arrived in Hamburg, I went to the headquarters of the Lutheran Help Organization where Pastor Lippert worked. Unfortunately, he was not there but at the Friedland Repatriation Camp. After telling them what I wanted to do, they told me they would contact the pastor immediately, and as soon as they had the information, they would call me at the hotel where I was staying."

Years later I read the following entry in Mother's little black diary that she made on Tuesday evening before meeting this Franz Nordt.

Tuesday, January 5, 1954. I am so happy tonight. Roland is alive and is healthy! Tomorrow I am going to meet a man who was together with him for more than three years. May our wonderful and awesome God be merciful to Roland and let him come home to have many happy years together with his family. I have three healthy and wonderful girls waiting for him. His home still stands untouched in spite of the fact that the furniture was kept in storage in several different places in Germany and Austria for so many years. Roland, everything you hold dear is still there waiting for you!

Mother went on to tell us how she took the train to Hanover on Wednesday morning and called Franz Nordt from the train station because she did not want to drop in on him unexpectedly. After he greeted her with open arms, her first impression of him was that he seemed extremely frail and tired but was very warm hearted. He told her how happy he was to meet the wife of his best friend, Roland. He felt like he knew her from everything his friend had told him about her.

"What happened after that, Mamma?" The three of us were eager to hear every little detail.

"Franz was very kind. I asked him if it was true that he had seen your father in June 1953. He was quite adamant that he had. Still not quite convinced, I wanted to know if he could tell me something that would prove to me, without a shadow of a doubt, that he really knew him. He then told me what your pappa's nickname was for me—Bimbam or Bimili—and what mine was for him—Katermann or K'mann. He also knew where we had met, where and when we got married, and your names and birthdays. He even knew all about how and when Helmut died as well as many details about Pappa's childhood in Vienna and his visit to Sweden as a young boy. There was no way Franz could have known all those details if he had not been together with your father. After that I was 100% certain that he did not die in 1950 after all." Tears trickled down Mother's face as she bowed her head and stopped talking.

My sisters and I sat quietly by her side, taking hold of her hands and squeezing them really hard, all of us overcome by this unquestionable proof that Father was not dead. A few minutes passed without anybody saying anything. Although we were anxious to hear more, we didn't want to press Mother too hard, trusting that

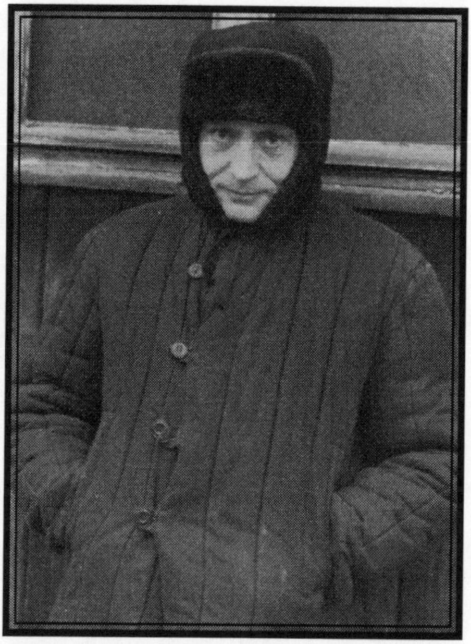

Father in the outfit he wore in the camp

she would continue as soon as she was able to.

I understood her tears only too well for I was still reeling from the shock myself after getting the news that the father I had thought lost forever to me was still alive. Was it any wonder that whenever anybody, reporters, friends or family, asked Mother about him, she never could hold back her tears?

"I spent the next two days together with Franz," Mother finally continued. "I posed hundreds of questions about your father and what life was like for him in Siberia. I simply could not hear enough, was always thirsty for more, hanging on every drop of information. It was as if I had been wandering in the dessert without a drop of water for a very long time, nine long years to be exact! He reassured me that your father was one of the fortunate ones because when he last saw him in June 1953, he was working as a laboratory assistant in the infirmary at the camp in the 40th coalmine shaft in Vorkuta. This was by far one of the more desirable jobs a prisoner could have, he claimed. As a result your father was in good health and in good spirits, always very positive in his outlook, helpful and encouraging to the rest of his fellow POWs. Before I left, I asked Franz one final question that had been nagging me."

We looked quizzically at her. What question could that possibly be?

Bravely Mother enlightened us. "I wanted to know whether your father had ever worried about whether I might have remarried. I was very relieved when Franz told me that they had only talked about it once. He explained that since they were never allowed to write, all of them understood that their loved ones might believe they were long since dead. If that were the case, your father had told Franz that he would just want to make sure that his children were doing well and that he would then quickly go on his way. When I heard that, I went to pieces." Mother wiped another tear from the corner of her eyes.

Retrospectively, I can understand why Father's statement troubled her so much. After all she had been on the verge of remarrying. What a terrible mistake that would have been! What if she had not received Pastor Lippert's letter in time? What would have happened then? Unthinkable!

Before returning home, Mother also met with several other men at the Friedland Repatriation Camp, who had also been together with Father in Vorkuta as recently as a few months ago. Every one of these former POWs reiterated and confirmed what Franz Nordt had already told her, some of them even giving her further details about Father. Without exception these men spoke of Father in the most glowing terms, telling Mother what a wonderful example and role model he was for all the prisoners in the camp, and how they admired his intellect, his leadership, his indomitable spirit, and his good advice. He was always encouraging his fellow prisoners not to give up hope because the day would come when they would be set free again. Dictators or political systems could not last forever, Roland had always assured them, they told Mother. The truth of that was borne out when Stalin died in 1953, which had caused another wave of POWs to be released. For all they knew, Roland could already be in transit to some southern camp before being released just like they had been.

When Mother left Friedland a week later, she was full of hope and quite convinced that Father was alive. This is how she described her feelings to a local newspaper:

> **For almost ten years, but especially after finding out that Roland was dead, I worked so hard at coming to peace with my situation and resigning myself to the fate that life had dealt me. Now that hard worked-for peace simply vanished in the blink of an eye. I am full of energy and feel completely rejuvenated and strong again. I am ready to fight like a lioness for my husband's return.**

Mother was not finished yet telling what else happened on her way back home. After leaving Germany, she had to change trains in Helsingborg for Borås. Using her last few remaining coins, her wallet seriously having been depleted traipsing around Germany for over a week and staying in hotels, she made a short long-distance call to Varberg, where Sie Montalvo, her best friend from her high school days, lived. She begged her to come down to the station so they could talk when the train made a quick stop because she wanted to share her marvelous news with Sie in person rather than over the telephone.

When the train rolled into the station in Varberg, Mother was very happy to see both Sie and her husband Tage, who owned a factory in Varberg, waiting for her. "Imagine my surprise, however, when they handed me a bouquet of yellow roses and a photographer snapped a picture of us. My first thought was that they had remembered that this would have been Helmut's fifteenth birthday, had he lived. When they shook their heads and said that wasn't it at all, I rushed on to tell them that I had just found out that your father was alive. But then when they handed me the postcard from your father, I understood the real reason for the flowers and the photographer.

"You can imagine how I began to tremble and feel weak in my knees when I saw your father's handwriting on that card. I could hardly believe that I was actually holding the first communication from him in my hands. I must be dreaming, I thought. I didn't have time to read it because the train whistle blew, which meant I had to climb onboard again. I barely heard Sie exclaim over all the noise that the card had arrived that very morning." Here Mother paused, probably thinking back on that amazing and wonderful moment of getting this further proof and real evidence that Father was still alive.

"Once I was back on the train, I sat down to read your father's card. After I finished reading it, I could no longer contain my joy. I jumped to my feet and began to dance around like a madwoman and shouted at the top of my lungs, 'My husband is alive! My husband is alive!' Everyone on the train probably thought I had taken leave of my senses." She smiled at the memory of the surprised looks on her fellow passenger's faces. She went on to explain how everyone had laughed and clapped after she shared with them the reason for her happiness and joy.

It was in this state of affairs that she returned home to us on January 11, 1954. No wonder we thought she was acting strange that day!

CHAPTER XIX

Waiting

Spring 1954

After receiving that first post card from Father, we looked forward to hearing from him soon again. But as February passed into March, April, May, June, July, August, and September with no further word, the mood at home fluctuated between hope and deep despair.

This period in our life was almost as difficult as the previous ten years had been when we didn't have anything concrete to pin our hopes on. As month after month went by with no more direct news from Father, despair began to take over. Why didn't he write again? Surely, we reasoned, he must have received Mother's reply card by now that would have told him where we were. We worried that it was just a fluke that we had received that first card, or what was worse, that he might have died since he wrote it and that was why we didn't hear anything more from him.

Whenever we heard indirectly about him, however, through letters Mother received from other returning POWs, we became hopeful again. They assured her that it wouldn't be long before Father would also be coming home because the political climate in the Soviet Union was changing rapidly, especially now that Stalin was dead. Perhaps he was even in a transit camp and that was the reason we hadn't heard from him.

Instead of only looking for more cards from Father, we also began hoping for a message indicating that he was actually on his way home. That was the only way we knew how to cope.

During the next few months I developed a new habit. Rather than playing outside after school, I rushed home to check what the mailman might have dropped through the slot in our front door. Eagerly I shuffled through all the many letters and cards, always wishing that one of them might be from Father, and if not from him, then at least from some Soviet official announcing that he was on his way home. But none came!

What I often found instead were letters addressed to Mother, sometimes from complete strangers who had read about us in one of the many Swedish newspapers. These were far less interesting than the ones coming from Germany or Austria that often contained newspaper clippings listing hundreds of names of returning POWs or articles discussing those countries' negotiations with the Soviet Union for the release of their POWs. Anxiously, I scanned the lists looking for my father's name but was always disappointed when I never saw Roland Gottlieb on any of them. Why, oh, why couldn't my father be one of those lucky ones listed?

After the first few months, the hullabaloo and excitement over Father's first contact with us began to lessen considerably, especially when no more news came from him. Our life returned to what appeared on the surface to be normal. In actuality, Mother began a frenzied correspondence with several of those returning POWs she met when she went to the Friedland Camp in January, leaving my sisters and me in the dark about why she suddenly went to Germany instead of spending time with Uncle Torsten in Stockholm. I can still see Mother typing busily away on her typewriter.

"Why are you writing to all those people, Mamma?" As usual I was sitting at the dining room table trying to do my homework. I was easily distracted these days.

"I want to hear what life was like for them in Vorkuta," she replied while she continued typing away on her machine.

"But why, Mamma?"

"Because in that way I can get a better picture of what your pappa's life is like." She stopped typing for a minute and looked straight at me before continuing. "I know they must have lots more to tell me than we had time for while I was in Friedland. I was in such a hurry then to get home and tell you the wonderful news."

On the one hand, while our only ray of hope during these difficult months came from the letters Mother received from Germany, they also raised our worries about Father as we learned more and more about his life in the Soviet Union. It must be unbearable! We worried about his health and whether he had enough warm clothes to keep from freezing in the winter or enough food to keep from starving to death.

Even though Mother always shared the general gist of the content of those letters, it was not until many years later that I actually read them for myself, including those that Mother wrote in response. Thank goodness for carbon paper!

Some of these letters came from Father's former colleagues at the German Legation in Sofia, who had just recently returned home from the Soviet Union. But there were also letters from people he met in his Moscow prison or in Siberia, and whose names and addresses Pastor Lippert forwarded after Mother's return to Sweden in January.

Günter Müller was one of these men. In a letter dated March 1954, he wrote that he had met Father in the fall of 1951 through a mutual friend by the name of Florian Swoboda, who was from Vienna just like Father. They became very good friends. Müller admired my father very much because "he was so intelligent and knowledgeable, always cheering everyone up and giving us courage. His spirits were strong and his faith never seemed to sag or fail. " Müller went on to say, that for some inexplicable reason in the fall of 1952, "Roland was forced to leave his 'cushiony' job as a lab assistant in the infirmary where he was doing simple chemical analyses of blood samples and taking the blood pressure of fellow prisoners. Roland was unfortunately forced to work in the coalmine for several months before he was allowed to return to his job in the infirmary."

The letter went on to say that Father had been "demoted" once again sometime in January 1953 and had been forced to work as an attendant in the *banja* or bathhouse where his job consisted of washing his fellow prisoners' dirty clothes, taking care of the clothing storage area in general, as well as overseeing their baths. "Apparently the prison camp authorities perceived him as a dangerous leader, whatever that meant, but then in April, Roland was allowed to return to his former job in the infirmary. I was then released in September 1953."

It was also encouraging to read in Müller's letter, "After Stalin's death in 1953, restrictions on us prisoners started to ease somewhat. We were now allowed to listen to the radio but only to stations from within the Soviet Union. We could also watch a movie about once a month, which made our lives much more bearable."

After reading this, we became hopeful once more that this meant that other restrictions were easing as well, which might ultimately culminate in Father's release.

This was one of many informative letters through which we learned to some degree what Father was doing during his years in captivity. All the writers confirmed that Father was very much alive when they last saw him, which in many cases was no more than a few months ago. Every one of them also underscored how well liked and respected he was and what a shining example he set for his fellow captives.

From Ludwig Born, a former colleague who had been captured by the Soviets in 1944 at the same time as Father, we learned that he was together with my father in Moscow at the Lefortovo Prison in 1945 where they were cellmates for a while. They shared a similar fate in that both were condemned to twenty-five years of hard labor on Christmas Eve 1948. Neither Father nor Born went through a trial but had simply been read their sentences as a *fait accompli*. Born also claimed that this was the fate shared by most of the political or civilian POWs who had the misfortune of ending up in the hands of the Soviets.

Ludwig Born was also together with my father on the transport from Moscow to Vorkuta in January 1949 after they had received their sentences. "Many prisoners died either from the *bitte*r cold weather or starvation on our wearisome and very trying four week-long journey to the Siberian slave labor camp, but Roland survived even though he became very sick with pneumonia and almost died."

When Mother read this account aloud to us, she gave a pitiful yelp, almost choking on her words. "Oh, no! Poor Roland! He almost died! He must have been really ill. That must have been around the same time when that man, who attested to your pappa's death in 1952, had seen him and assumed that he could not possibly have survived the harsh journey north. Your poor pappa!" She was visibly shaken by the image that Born's last words had evoked.

Several minutes passed before she picked up Born's letter that had fallen into her lap. "A year after our arrival in Vorkuta I was transferred to another prison camp while Roland stayed behind in the #40 coal mine shaft with twelve other Germans, all of whom were civilian or political internees. Although I no longer saw Roland after that, I heard from other fellow prisoners that he was still working as a lab assistant in the summer of 1953." The letter then goes on to describe in great detail what Born had experienced in the camp where he was sent after getting separated from Father.

How much Father must have suffered on his journey from Moscow to Vorkuta! Whenever I studied our wall map in the living room, I could see that Vorkuta was located just above the Arctic Circle and not far from the Arctic Ocean, so much further north than Borås in the southern half of Sweden, where I lived. How much colder must the weather in Siberia therefore be where my poor pappa lived, especially without proper food and clothing or warm shelter? The mere thought of how he must be suffering living under such terrible conditions made me shiver. Even today, just hearing or saying the word "Siberia" makes my blood run cold.

Mother always seemed much more upbeat after reading letters like the one from Born. Since we did not hear anything directly from Father, these letters from the *Spätheimkehrer*, German for men who were returning home late from the war, served as mounting proof that Father was very much alive. Now it was just a matter of being patient until he was released as well. That was the hardest part!

Every time such a letter arrived, we read it and reread it and then talked about what Father's life must be like. It certainly helped bring him closer to us, if not in body, then at least in our minds and hearts. It gave us concrete information to hang on to while we waited.

Sometime in May 1954 I found another letter with a German stamp when I came home from school. I had never seen that particular name as sender before and was dying to hear what this Otto Bachmann had to say. The letter was really thick, which added to its allure because it made me think that he must have a lot to tell.

Once supper was over, we all sat down to hear what Bachmann had written. He began by telling us that he had been together with Father from May 1951 to the summer of 1952. Because of his anti-Soviet propaganda and having the audacity to form an opposition party in East Germany after the war, he was condemned to the customary twenty-five years of hard labor in Siberia. He assured Mother that Father was doing quite well because he had some influential friends among the doctors even though they were also prisoners. They had requested that my father be allowed to work in the infirmary since he spoke fluent Russian as well as many other languages and could therefore communicate easily with the other prisoners when they came to the ambulatory infirmary. Bachmann then went on to say that as a result,

> *Roland was assigned to the infirmary as a laboratory assistant, which was a lot easier job than working in the coalmines. His food rations are much lower but his working conditions are much better by far in so many respects...*
>
> *Roland served as the cultural center point for all the Germans, as well as for many of the other nationalities because of his vast knowledge and great intellect. He was always so full of hope and confidence ...*
>
> *Reading books is something else we were able to enjoy. Just before I left the camp, Roland loaned me Goethe's Faust in German that some Russian officer had given him because he couldn't read it anyway. No one who has not been in a Soviet labor camp can possibly understand how much it meant to me and to all the other Germans to be able to read Faust in our own language. Roland helped us do that...*

Mother also heard directly from Anton Mohrmann and Fred Felchner, two of Father's colleagues from the German Legation in Sofia, Bulgaria. They had been captured, along with Father and most of the members of the legation, as they tried to escape into Turkey in September 1944. Both had just recently been released by the Soviets and were able to confirm that Father was very much alive the last they heard. Their letters included a list, published by the Foreign Office, which showed what German Legation staff members had died in captivity. They pointed out that, Roland

Gottlieb's name was not on it.

In his six-page letter, after informing Mother that he had been a next-door cellmate to my father in Lefortovo Prison in Moscow until 1948, Felchner described in greater detail than anybody else what life was like for the prisoners.

We communicated by knocking on the wall between our cells almost on a daily basis using a unique type of code, which involved using the Cyrillic alphabet, divided into five rows with six letters each that formed a kind of grid. Each line was represented by a number of knocks from one to five and each letter within the grouping by a number of knocks from one through six. We had to be very careful not to be caught. The danger of being discovered was very great and none of us wanted to experience the so-called punishment cell in the cold basement of Lefortovo...

We stayed hungry because we never got enough to fill our stomachs, only just enough to keep from starving to death. In the morning, breakfast usually consisted of some tepid water passing for tea, a packet of sugar and a small dark heavy and hard as a rock loaf of barely digestible bread that three people had to share. It could not have weighed more than 400 gm. Then around noon a small bowl of watery soup was pushed through the food slot opening which was followed at night by some sort of unappetizing gruel made of who knows what, but most often based on some rotten cabbage or grains or some other unspeakable substances. Once in a blue moon we might get some salty fish or meat. The food was sufficient although very monotonous and unappetizing...

We also suffered from sleep deprivation during the nights when we were forced to wake up in the middle of the night in order to proceed to an interrogation. And then on the other nights when we were allowed to sleep, we were forced to lie on our backs with our hands always showing above the coverlet. A single glaring light bulb was always kept burning ...

Monotony, together with lack of sleep during the night and sufficient nourishing food during the day, was our biggest enemy...

Both Roland and I received the same sentence of twenty-five years of hard labor. But instead of going to Vorkuta, like Roland, I went to Inta, both of which are located in the Komi Republic around 140 kilometers apart. The climate here is brutal ten months out of the year but especially in the winter when the wind from the Arctic could make the temperature outside feel like - 40° or - 50°F. No one could hope to escape in a climate like this although some tried because when the snow thawed somewhat, we discovered corpses of men who had tried to flee...

In the same letter Felchner also wrote that he had learned that the Soviets always acted quite arbitrarily and without any logical reasoning whatsoever. Proof of that was that he had been released long before his sentence was up. This should give her heart, he wrote, because it could just as easily happen to her husband. Felchner encouraged her to believe that he might already have been released or be on the verge of being released and could already be in transit and on his way home.

That particular letter raised our hopes once again. Perhaps our wait would soon be over.

The correspondence between Mother and Joseph Ortmann, another of Father's former colleagues from his days at the German Embassy in Stockholm from 1939-40, was also quite enlightening. Although Ortmann had not been imprisoned by the Soviets, he was able, through official channels not easily accessible to Mother, to help her in many other ways.

Among other things Mother asked if he could find out something about the number that Father had written as part of the return address on his postcard. He answered that 5110/36 was the number of Father's prison camp, but unfortunately it was known as a *Schweigelager*, which simply meant that the prisoners in that camp were not allowed to write or receive mail. Nobody knew why that was the case. The number was also confirmation that he was definitely in Vorkuta and not somewhere else in the Soviet gulag system.

"Aha! That explains why we didn't hear from your pappa for so many years," Mother said after reading those lines about his camp being a "silent camp."

From the exchange of letters between Ortmann and Mother, it became clear that Ortmann offered to be her spokesperson, her "Johnny on the spot" so to speak, with the Red Cross in Germany since she could not be there in person like he could. This helped tremendously in keeping Father's case before the German Red Cross officials. He apparently also served as her personal courier of information, both to that organization as well as the Foreign Office in Bonn and the Evangelical Help Organization.

On a more personal level, Ortmann even became her strong encourager. In several letters he talked about how strong Father was and how much he had always admired his intellect. He assured her that because of those qualities, he knew that Roland would never give up. Therefore she must not despair either. Their days of happiness would surely come soon and their ordeal finally be behind them. He also indicated that because the Soviets were now releasing their POWs, this should fill her with hope.

He also kept her informed as to what was happening politically between Germany and the Soviet Union. Swedish newspapers hardly reported on the negotiations taking place, and when they did they were not as detailed, mainly because Sweden was not directly affected, not like Germany was.

Ortman went on to explain what made these negotiations between Germany and the Soviet Union particularly complicated. Part of the difficulties stemmed from the Soviet Union claiming that Germany had never officially declared war in 1941. To the Soviets this apparently meant that there could be no peace treaty either. Furthermore, they claimed that because the two countries had officially not been at war, they could not possibly be holding any Germans as POWs. According to Ortmann that was the crux of the matter. The Soviets were either going to have to admit that they were still holding Germans imprisoned or continue to oppose their allies, who insisted that a treaty must be signed between Germany and the Soviet Union in order for Germany to be recognized once more as a sovereign nation. That apparently was a hard pill for the Soviets to swallow.

According to Ortmann most of the world was completely mystified by the Soviets' refusal to acknowledge having any Germans in captivity. If they truly believed what they were claiming, why were they suddenly releasing so many of these so-called non-existent POWs? That was the question everyone was asking. Their action, he said, was incomprehensible to anyone not familiar with the Soviet mindset and agenda.

Politics was not the only subject of conversation in the correspondence between Mother and Ortmann. A passage from a letter dated August 1954 clearly shows how concerned Mother was about my sisters and me.

> *...First and foremost I want to make sure that my daughters do better this coming school year, especially my two oldest girls. They both received very bad report cards. Birgitta's grades also slipped although not as much. Karin, my middle daughter, has to repeat the grade because all her grades were so poor that it made no sense at all for her to go on to the next grade. It is understandable because in the spring we were all so consumed with worry. All three girls just simply had no desire to do their schoolwork. Often they just sat there and stared into thin air. Their thoughts were usually with their father, wondering when he would come home, or what he looks like or whether he is ill, or will he be able to help their mother when he comes home. The biggest question in all our minds is: WHEN WILL HE COME? Therefore I plan to make sure that I help them in any way I can, especially with English, French and literature...*

When I read this, it brought back some very strong memories of Mother constantly fussing with Karin for not working hard enough and warning her that if she didn't do better, she would fail the class and become a repeater. Unfortunately, her dire predictions came true for Karin.

My grades also suffered, which my report cards from that time only prove too clearly, fortunately not to the extent, however, that I wasn't promoted. Because Father was never far from my mind, I could not concentrate at school and was often called down for woolgathering. I wondered what he was like or fantasized what life would be like once he was back home with us. I often neglected my homework and sometimes forgot to study for tests, all of which did not do my grades any good.

"Mamma, do you think Pappa will help me study?" I asked Mother out of the blue sometime that spring when I was sitting at our dining room table with my geography book open in front of me. I was worried about the test next day because I had received a very bad grade on the previous one.

"Of course, he will, Gittan, I am sure that he will be more than happy to help you any way he can. He is so smart, so much smarter than I am. Until that day comes, why don't you just let me help you instead? Hand me your book, and I will ask you some questions. Ok?"

Nodding eagerly, I handed her my book, thrilled to have Mother's full attention for once. She always seemed so preoccupied and busy with writing all those letters to all those returning POWs in Germany as soon as she came home from work. I hated to bother her.

On another occasion I interrupted Mother at her task and asked if she thought Father would love me when he came home. That was something that really concerned me.

"How can you even ask such a silly question, Gittan? Of course, he will love you just as much as I love you." She left her desk, came over to the dining room table where I was doing my homework, and hugged me really hard around my shoulders. This helped dispel my fears somewhat. Not ever having had a father, it was hard for me to imagine what it would be like to be loved by one. I couldn't wait for the chance to find out.

"Do you think he will be stricter than you, Mamma?" That was another worry I had.

"I don't think so, but I haven't been all that strict or have had to discipline you all that much, have I, Gittan?" She patted me on my head and gave me another big hug, adding, "If I were you, I wouldn't worry my pretty little head too much about it."

As I bent down over my math homework again, I could not help but mull over Mother's answer. The more I thought about it, the more I realized that her question back to me about not being all that strict was really up for debate. She never put up with much nonsense from any of us, her three daughters. I knew first hand that it was not wise to disobey her or to talk back disrespectfully to her. The consequences were always swift to follow.

Reflecting about how Mother disciplined us brings back another strong memory from those early years in Borås. One in particular comes readily to mind when she came home from work one day, carrying a bakery box filled with four different kinds of *bakelser*, every slice of cake a favorite of ours. An argument ensued over who should get to choose first. Ingrid argued that because she was the oldest, she should have first choice while I demanded the same right because I was the youngest. Karin loudly put her own two cents worth in. Mother became very upset and angry at our bickering. Before we knew what was happening, she took the box with the cake slices, went out on the balcony, and threw the *bakelser* over the railing, telling us that this would teach us not to argue over who would be first. Imagine our long faces!

When we talked about the incident some years later, Mother claimed that it had been well worth it because it taught us not to argue about food again. A little sheepishly she admitted that she had also learned her lesson. It was never a good idea to offer children a choice if there were only one of each kind. "Besides," she added laughingly, "I regretted throwing the pieces of cake out because I hated wasting my hard earned money."

I also remember how firm and strict she was about bedtime. "Children need their sleep in order to grow up healthy and be able to concentrate at school" was one of her favorite sayings to which I never had a good counter although it was not for lack of trying.

Another one of her maxims was that children must finish all the food on their plate. She did not tolerate our being picky or finicky and always succeeded in making us feel guilty when she said, "There are a lot of children who are starving in Austria and Germany and would love to have all the food you have. Be grateful that you are not starving like they are." Such a statement usually put me to shame, but not enough if fried liver was the main course. I baulked at eating that supposed delicacy.

Mother was also keen on our exhibiting good table manners. Thus, for example, we were not allowed to have our elbows on the table or prop our head up with our hands. If we did, she would tell the offender, "If you are that tired, you may go to bed right now!" Or if one of us happened to keep one hand under the table instead of above, her favorite comment was, "Be grateful you haven't lost an arm in the war!" Obviously, that particular saying was colored by having lived through a war.

All that spring and summer, we waited for another card to arrive but none came. When school was out in June, we spent the summer as usual, either at our cottage in Mollösund or visiting with various relatives.

POW CAMPS, PRISONS AND LABOR CAMPS IN RUSSIA WHERE GERMANS ARE HELD

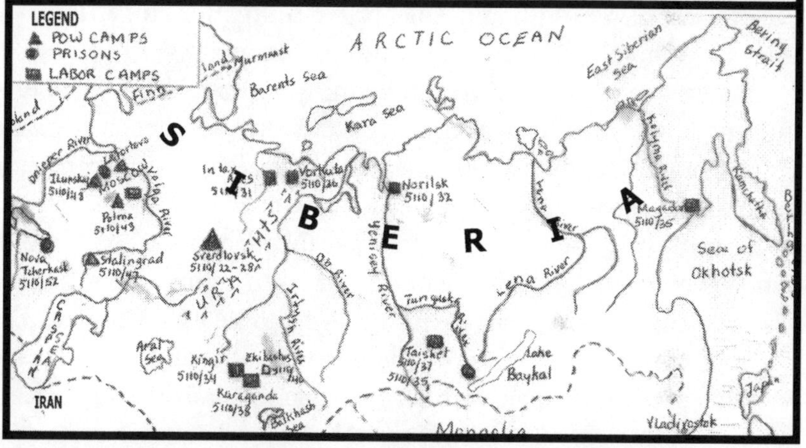

This map is copied from one supplied in 1954 by the Evangelical Help Organization of the Lutheran Church

CHAPTER XX

Hope Renewed

Fall 1954-Spring 1955

After returning from Mollösund at the end of August, I started the fourth grade, Ingrid the last one before her graduation, while Karin stayed in the same one as the previous year. Mother went back to work. We still had not heard anything more directly from Father although all indirect indications were positive.

One evening I was sitting at the dining room table as usual doing my homework and noticed that Mother seemed unusually quiet, even a little depressed. I decided to ask what was bothering her. I hated to see her unhappy.

"I am a little sad today, Gittan, because I had so hoped your pappa would be here to celebrate our 19th anniversary today." Mamma sighed. "Oh, how I wish he were home with us by now."

I had totally forgotten what date it was—September 7—their wedding anniversary. No wonder Mamma was sad. Then I noticed her pulling out a card, not a post card but a kind of index card, and starting to write on it.

"Who are you writing to this time, Mamma?"

"To your pappa, Gittan. I have decided to take matters into my own hands. I can't wait any longer until I receive another card from him. Hopefully this card will reach him even though I am not sending it via the regular channels. Perhaps the Soviets will let it get through somehow." She sighed audibly.

"But Mamma, how do you know where to send it since you don't have another reply card?"

"You are right, Gittan, I don't have a regular reply card, but I have his address because I copied it down from the first card we received, thinking I might need it some day." This is the message she penned that evening.

My darling Katermann! Today is our anniversary! I love you more than ever today. You are our model. I have a lot to learn from you. I am reading all your books that did not interest me as much earlier and which I want to discuss with you. We spent the summer in Mollösund as usual where we have a small cottage since 1950. The children are so happy about this. I only have three weeks vacation but Ingi is always such a great helper and is in charge when I can't be there. The children are very sweet and loving and have good manners, as all my friends assure me. You can be proud of them. Their report cards were not so good this time but that is understandable considering the uncertainty about you. Your card from December 6 got us all so excited and happy. Your mother is still living and Walther, his family and Heinz, all are well. I hug you heartily and remain with you in my heart and thoughts. All our friends send their love. Stay healthy! Love, from your wife Bimbam Ruth.

Another month passed. In early October, Mother received a telegram from Uncle Walther, Father's oldest brother in Austria.

TWO CARDS FROM ROLAND STOP WILL FORWARD IMMEDIATELY STOP LETTER FOLLOWS STOP

We were giddy with happiness and full of curiosity after reading Uncle Walther's short telegram. Imagine! Father has written two more cards! That must mean that he was still alive, but why in the world had he sent the cards to Austria instead of to us in Sweden? Had he not received Mother's reply card? How did he know where Uncle Walther was living since he had moved after Father was captured?

A few days later the letter from Uncle Walther waited for us when my sisters and I came home from school. It felt thicker than usual. Impatiently we waited for Mother to come home, the hour until she finally arrived seeming interminable to us. Two cards with that weird script on their front were tucked inside the envelope that Mother carefully slit open with her letter knife.

One card was dated July 3, 1954, and the other August 7, 1954.

Uncle Walther explained that the cards had arrived at the same time just over a week ago. “This only goes to show,” he wrote, “how unbelievably long it takes the mail to get from the Soviet Union to the outside world.”

Dear Walther!

Today I have finally been allowed to write my second card. Since I have not heard from anyone after writing my first card on December 6, 1953, I am very uncertain and concerned about everyone's wellbeing. I only know that you at least, thank God, are still alive because of a personal package I received recently. Otherwise, thousands of unsolved mysteries plague me daily, such as: Are Lumpi [another one of Mother's nicknames] *and our three girls still alive? What about Mutti and Heinz? What about your loved ones and everybody else? Where and how do they live? Are they healthy? I take comfort and hope from the fact that cards are still arriving daily to others here. Perhaps the answer to the card I wrote to Ruth in care of Montalvo, Varberg will still reach me. Up until now I have received 19 packages from many different places with 9 of them having your address as sender. So no mistake there. I want to emphasize that all packages arrived in great condition. I thank you and all the other donors from the bottom of my heart for your faithfulness and love and for the help that the contents afford my comrades and me. Please send photos of everyone, medicines for high blood pressure, vitamins, toothpaste, soap, gym shoes and a hard cover notebook—I am well! Do not worry about me needlessly. My love for you and my family gives me great strength. My thoughts were with Ingrid (my big girl) on her 18th birthday. Does she still remember Vati? And Karin will soon turn 13 and Birgitta (?) 10. Are they still alive and what are they doing? How are my darling Bimili and Mutti? Be brave and strong. Hugs and kisses from your unchanged Roland*

When Mother read that part about me, I was totally awestruck. Pappa knew that he had a daughter named Birgitta and that I was ten years old!

After Mother finished reading the first postcard, written in

Father's most miniscule handwriting, we urged her to go on and read his second one even though we were still trying to mentally process the first one. This one was directly addressed to her rather than to Uncle Walther.

> *My darling Bimili! I wrote my first card to you on Dec. 6, 1953,in Varberg (Montalvo) and the second one to Walther on July 3. Since to my great sorrow, worry, and consternation I have not heard from you yet, I am sending this third card to Laakirchen* [Walther's address]. *From the packages I have received I only know that he is alive and where he lives. I am now longing and very anxious to finally hear that you, my darling Bimili, our children, Omama, Schnicki* [Heinz' nickname] *and everyone else I hold dear are still alive. Everything about you remains such a great mystery to me. But my constant thoughts of you give me a never-ending strength and hope. Don't worry about me needlessly. I am fine and am as always your faithful Katermann and Vati. I send kisses and hugs to my little Birgitta (?) for her 10th birthday on August 31.*

When Mother read that special greeting to me for my birthday, I cried. I could not help it, but they were happy tears. Not only had he mentioned me by name in the first card, but he had also gone on to wish me a happy birthday in the second one. That was incredible! What a wonderful birthday present, even if it was over a month late! I only wished he could be here right now so that I could give him a great old bear hug as thanks for remembering me. It thrilled me no end to find out for sure that Pappa really knew I existed and when my birthday was.

While I was still in somewhat of a trance, Mother continued reading the rest of the second card. It took a few more minutes before it began to penetrate my brain what else he had written.

I don't know how in the world he managed to say so much in such little space for the card was no larger than 6"x 8". He thanked for the packages, which did not come from us but from the German Red Cross and other organizations in Germany, giving a fairly detailed account from whom and what he had received so far. They arrived on a regular basis, he wrote, which stood in such sharp contrast to any other kind of mail that seemed to take forever, according to his friends who were already receiving mail from home. He warned that personal messages were not permitted in the packages but photos were. He asked for some specific items to be included in any future shipments and thanked everyone for their generosity towards him and his comrades with whom he was sharing because some of them were still not getting any packages from home.

The manner in which he signed the second card, "From your unhappy *Katermann* and *Vati*, son and brother Roland," upset us terribly though. We hated that he should be "unhappy" because he had never received Mother's reply she sent over nine months ago. This must mean that he did not know anything about us and was therefore still living in fear and uncertainty about what might have befallen us during that last year of the war and whether we had even survived it. That had to tear at him and make him terribly unhappy.

When I studied the card more thoroughly a little later, I discovered the question mark behind my name. When I asked Mamma about that, she answered that Pappa couldn't be sure whether she had actually named their baby daughter what they had discussed beforehand.

"Did he also want my middle name to be Gunilla?"

"I am not sure that we ever discussed your middle name, but I think he told me one time that was a name he really liked."

However, that turned out to be completely inaccurate on Mother's part. Since I never cared for my middle name anyway, I had no trouble dropping it after I got married and replacing it with my maiden name "Gottlieb," which just happens to start with the same letter.

Later that evening Mother wrote back, this time using the bottom half provided for that purpose.

My beloved Roland! I thank you from the bottom of my heart for your three cards dated Dec. 6, 1953, July 3 and August 7, 1954. We are overjoyed that you are well and so courageous. We are so proud of you. Just keep it up and be patient. I am living on the third floor in my parents' house even though it is sold after both parents died 1948 and 1951. The children and I are all quite healthy and are doing well. We speak of you all the time and I often dream about my Katermann. I have a good position at the Chamber of Commerce. I have been living in Borås since 1945. All the furniture was saved and the Lumpi-Dudi home is just waiting for the head of its household...

Since Uncle Walther had asked her to leave some room for him to respond, she couldn't say as much as she wanted to. She had to send it to Austria anyway because the mail to Father was supposed to be postmarked either in Germany or Austria rather than in Sweden, the authorities in Germany had informed her. Her card would have a better chance of reaching him that way. It might otherwise lead to problems for him because the Soviets were very suspicious of any kind of mail coming from anywhere else, especially from Sweden, as in his case. We didn't understand why at the time, but after hearing that, Mother surmised that this was the reason he never received her first reply card sent from Sweden.

Word somehow spread quickly that our family had finally received another card from our father. Once again several Swedish national newspapers came knocking on our door asking Mother for interviews. As a direct result of these newspaper articles, canned goods, medicines, warm gloves, caps, and under garments began pouring in from strangers all over Sweden. Their generosity was overwhelming. Mother then forwarded everything to the German Red Cross, one of several organizations that sent care packages to its captive countrymen in Siberia. We know from Father's later cards that these must have reached the prisoners because he was always very careful to thank everyone involved for all the goodies that were making his and his fellow prisoners' life so much more tolerable.

Once we realized that photos were allowed in these packages, we were of course eager to include some of us. Because we didn't own a camera, my sisters and I were going to have our picture taken at a professional photographer's studio in town. I felt very important because I had to leave school early the day of our appointment, bragging to my classmates where I was headed. But what was even more important to me was that finally Father would have a chance to see what his youngest daughter looked like, the one he had never seen before.

Mother was more than happy over this renewed interest. She was convinced that keeping Father's case in the public's eye could only help him, which a comment I overheard her make to a friend proves. "I hope the Soviets will be sufficiently shamed into releasing Roland soon if their ill deeds are written about in the press."

Svenska Dagbladet, a national Swedish daily newspaper, was one of the papers that covered our story extensively. After refreshing their readers about our family's situation, it quoted Mother directly as saying:

> **The Red Cross has taken up my husband's case and a memorandum with complete details has been given to Moscow. In May Jan de Geer delivered a letter written by me in Russian to the Russian delegates who were visiting Sweden at the time. I only wrote that we were alive and were healthy and included some photographs of the children and myself. Apparently Roland never got that letter either because he still didn't know anything about us according to the last two cards I just received from him.**

In the same article, Jan de Geer, the chairman for the international division of the Red Cross in Sweden, stated that it was a given that the Red Cross was following Roland Gottlieb's case.

> **The first step is to get in direct contact with Gottlieb to let him know that his wife and children are well. The second step is to get him repatriated ... The Red Cross has given a memorandum with complete information to my Russian colleague, Nikolai Tschikalenko, and a letter from Mrs. Gottlieb addressed to her husband. I have personally written two reminders in which I emphasized the importance and urgency of this matter. So far we have not had any response from the Russians, although I would like to say that Tschikalenko was very positively disposed during his visit to Sweden. (October 10, 1954)**

When we received Father's fourth card, dated September 22, 1954, also by way of Uncle Walther, the calendar already read November, almost two months later! In it Father repeated what he had said in his first three, that he was once again addressing the card to his brother because he was the only one he knew for sure was still alive, not having heard anything from his Ruth yet. It was totally incomprehensible to us why he had not yet received any of

Mother's replies to him.

Father begged his brother to help his wife and children and that he would be eternally grateful to him if he did. He went on to say that he was sick with worry and close to despair because of not knowing whether we were still alive. The rest of the card continued in the same vein as the previous ones by thanking for all the packages he had received and listing what items were especially needed and helpful. He closed by saying:

I pray to God that you are all alive and doing well. On November 23, my little Karin celebrates her birthday. Perhaps this card will get there in time for that. May she feel my loving arms around her! I send a thousand warm kisses and hugs to all of you, your loving and unchanged Roland.

Then in mid-December we received a fifth card dated October 10, 1954. Once again Father wrote how worried he was that he still had not heard from Mother.

My darling Bimili! Ten months have passed since I sent you my first card (12.6.1953). In the meantime I have written several more cards some addressed to Walther and some to you and still not a word from you. It puts an unbearably heavy burden on my heart that is almost intolerable. I refuse to believe, however, that something could have happened to my Bimili and to our beloved children or that the 10 years of separation could have forced us further apart rather than closer together. Whatever the case may be, please write me honestly how you are. Where and how do you live and how are you managing? How are our girls doing? I am full of hope that the next month or two will bring news of you, which will put an end to all my uncertainties…

I remember how happy Mother was to hear from him again, as were we all. At the same time, however, she was extremely upset and frustrated that he was still living in uncertainty about us because of not having received any of her replies.

She fumed and fussed about it. "I am so mad at the inefficient Soviet postal services that I can hardly see straight. Oh, how I hate that your pappa still doesn't know anything about us. How could my cards not have reached him? I sure hope that he has received them in the meantime!"

The postcard, which had once again been sent to Uncle Walther, continued in the same vein as all the previous ones, thanking for packages, asking for photos, stating what items were most needed, asking for news of the family, hoping everyone was well and alive, and trying to reassure everyone that he was just fine.

Then another card, this one dated November 13, 1954, arrived shortly before Christmas. It took only five weeks to reach us from Siberia. Wonders never cease!

> *When I finally received Walther's letter from September 25 on November 3, I was the happiest man after reading that you were well and living in Borås. It was such a relief finally to find this out after ten years' suffering from the uncertainty of not knowing. My poor sweet Bimili, how much you have had to suffer because of marrying me. I just hope that I will soon be with you again so that I can make it up to you by taking care of you and the children once more and so that you will be able to forget how much you have had to suffer. I was just so sorry to hear that Pappa Albin and Mamma Emmy no longer are living so that I can thank them for all the love they always showed me. I am now just impatiently and eagerly waiting to get your cards and pictures of you. We both know that we are not young any more but our love for each other will have grown that much deeper. And now I want at least to get to know my three darling girls through pictures. I know that you, Ingi, my brave and oldest daughter, are a big help to Mother and Karin, I wish you many happy returns on your birthday on November 23. Surely I will be home for your next birthday and then you, my little Birgitta, (Is that what you are called?) will get to know your father. You will see how wonderful all that will be. Please, my darling Bimili, write me how you live and by what means you live. Is anyone helping you? Are you getting any subsidy from the German government? When Christmas arrives this year I want you all to be happy and look at all the candles in the Christmas tree and believe that Vati* [short form for father in German] *will soon come home*

to you. I will be with you in my thoughts and if pictures have arrived by then I will celebrate Christmas here with you. Stay healthy! Many kisses and hugs from Katermann and Vati

This card was the best Christmas present. We felt a sense of peace descend upon us that Father finally knew that we were alive even though it sounded like his information only came second hand through Uncle Walther and not because he had received Mother's response cards. We talked for days about this latest card and all it said. None of us could understand why it had taken so long before Father found out that we were very much alive.

"That is so cruel of the Russians," I said as I chewed on the end of my pencil. "How can they be so mean? It is simply not fair. Poor pappa, how much he must have suffered, not knowing. I am so glad he knows now, aren't you, Mamma? Don't you wish he could come home in time for Christmas? I do!"

"Of course I do!" Mother exclaimed as she picked up a letter she had just received from Joseph Ortmann in Hamburg. Looking at it once again, she confessed how hopeful she had been that Pappa would be one of the 55 Austrians being sent home from the Soviet Union in time for Christmas, as she had read in a press release that Ortmann had included in an earlier letter.

"When I first read it, I got very excited, but now Herr Ortmann has informed me that those Austrians were actually *Volksdeutsche*, that is, people of German heritage from Yugoslavia and Poland, who claimed Austrian citizenship. Unfortunately, this excludes your father who most definitely is not a *Volksdeutscher.* "

No wonder Mother sounded so depressed and disappointed. Once again her hopes were dashed!

"That is not fair, Mamma," Ingrid exclaimed. "I don't understand why people who are not truly Austrian can come home while those who really are Austrian must stay."

"I agree wholeheartedly with you, Ingrid. It is very difficult to understand how the Soviets reason about such things. But we have been warned that they don't think like we do. We just have to be patient. That isn't easy, I know, but we just have to trust that Pappa's turn will come one day soon." She tried to infuse her voice with as much optimism as possible.

In her third reply card to Father, Mother wrote the following:

We are so happy that you finally know of our existence. All four of us are well and think about you day and night. Our longing for you is tremendous. Hopefully you are healthy! Annicka and Lennart [good friends] *are sending medicines for laryngitis; other good things are sent you from Ingrid Alfrida* [Mother's sister] *Erland and Elisabeth* [the Swedish Chargé d'Affaires from their Bulgaria days] *from Vanio und Lillan* [also friends from Bulgaria]. *As you see, all friends are well and are thinking and praying for you. Our children are healthy and growing up well as you can see in the photographs I sent. You will be proud of them. We are reading* The Odyssey *and like the 22nd chapter in particular because of the parallel I see in it to Katermann-Bimbam. We kiss you and hug you and are hoping for a reunion soon. As always, your Bimili-Ruth.*

And with that we entered a new year—1955. Our one and only wish that New Year's Eve was that the Soviets would let our father come home soon.

We received three more cards that spring. The first one took four months to arrive. It was dated December 2, 1954, and arrived on April 5, 1955. The next card was dated January 20, 1955, and took only three months to reach us, arriving on April 15, 1955. When we received a card, dated March 1, 1955, the calendar read May 16, 1955, which meant it had only taken two months to reach Sweden. To the Soviets perhaps this felt like an improvement, but to us it served as undeniable proof of the unreliability of the Soviet Union's postal service. Not that we needed such proof because we already knew that Father had not received many of Mother's replies.

Every time these cards arrived, we were thrilled and felt a sense of renewed optimism. But it also always raised the question of when it finally would be his turn to leave Russia. After all, at this point the war had been over for ten years! As far as we knew, none of the countries involved in WW II were still holding any POWs. Wasn't it high time for the Soviets to let all their remaining ones go, not just a few at a time? This was the question we asked almost daily.

It was also very trying and nerve-racking when we read in German newspapers that Ortmann sent us in January and then again in April that several more waves of German POWs had returned from the Soviet Union as a result of negotiations between the chancellors of Germany and Austria and the leaders of the Soviet Union. We could simply not understand what was keeping the Soviets from releasing our innocent father.

All we could do was continue to wait and hope.

This is a professional portrait Mamma had made of us to include in a box for Pappa.

CHAPTER XXI

Patience Rewarded

Summer 1955

By the time school was out in early June 1955, we still did not know for sure if or when Father might be released. We were very hopeful, though, when we realized that the camp number listed as part of his address on his last card was different from those of his earlier ones according to a list of prison camp designations that the Lutheran Help Organization had sent to us earlier. While Father's earlier cards either listed 5110/33 or 5110/36 as sender address, which meant he was still in the Vorkuta region when he wrote them, his latest card showed 5110/46 instead. This meant he must now be in a camp in Potma, Mordovia or Mordvinia. When we located it on our wall map, we were very happy to discover that it was a lot further south than Vorkuta and just slightly to the northeast of Moscow. This was definitely a step in the right direction, a positive sign that infused us with renewed hope that it might not be long now.

In the meantime, all we could do was take one day at a time and do what we usually did during summertime, which included going to our beloved cottage in Mollösund in June, visiting relatives in July, and then returning to Mollösund in August.

Although I don't actually remember by what means we travelled to Mollösund this particular summer, a little reddish brown hard covered notebook, which Mother had started as a diary, guestbook, and account book the first summer after buying the cottage, helped prod my memory. On June 11, 1955, Ingrid, who was often the designated keeper of the diary, made the following entry:

Kap Horn has once again been opened up. Mamma Ruth went by boat this time with her two youngest ones, but she returned to Borås the next day leaving Karin and Gittan by themselves. Mamma has to work until Midsummer. According to her, the cottage was in excellent condition. Then on June 14, I arrived and the cottage still looked just fine. On the 16th I started working in the fishery factory and was very tired after the first ten hours on my feet, cleaning herring. But it is a lot of fun...

Apparently Ingrid couldn't come with us to begin with because she and her fellow classmates had a lot of activities planned in connection with their graduation from Borås Flickskola, a secondary school for girls.

This diary certainly makes for some interesting and fun reading today. It puts a smile on my face as it brings back wonderful memories of bygone days that I might otherwise have forgotten. Thus, for example, in an earlier entry, Ingrid made a note about how we travelled to Mollösund in the summer of 1954.

We packed Ella's car full with suitcases, coats, a kerosene hotplate, bags of food and Mother, Ingrid Johnsson, Gittan, Karin and the undersigned. We left Borås at 9:15 for Mollösund. The weather was beautiful, the trip was long, but we arrived at our beloved cottage around noon.

We filled our stomachs with excellent sandwiches we had brought with us. Mother and Ingrid J. left for Borås around 7 pm. [Mother had to return to Borås because she had to be back at work on Monday morning.] *Karin, Gittan and I went to Aja's house for some tea...*

Not only did this diary often relate by what means we went to Mollösund, but it often also served as a place for friends or relatives, who came to visit, to thank us for a wonderful time, good food, and great fellowship. Some of these entries sound quite lyrical or poetic, sometimes filling up a whole page with rambling thoughts and musings. Stuck in between those pages, Ingrid or Mother made comments about the weather, or how cold the ocean water was, or what we had for supper. If Ingrid happened to be the recorder, she often also made a note of having fussed at Karin or me about something or other that she wanted Mother to know about.

Some of the pages even look like those of an accountant. Column after column shows the food or other necessities Ingrid purchased that were needed to take care of the three of us when Mother was not there. It seemed she wanted to account for every *öre* she spent. It is fascinating to see how much, or rather how little, things cost in those days. Of course, salaries were much lower then. For instance, one entry shows that one liter milk cost 45 *öre*, which at today's exchange rate would be the equivalent of around seven cents. Another one shows that Ingrid gave me 25 *öre* with which to buy candy. That entry did not surprise me at all because I can't remember a time when I did not have a weakness for sweets.

An entry that surprised me some showed that Mother had given Ingrid five *kronor* in pocket money, which would roughly translate into one dollar today. When I asked her why she got so much more than I did, she laughingly answered, "Don't you think I deserved it for having to put up with you two all the time, making sure that you didn't go hungry, or keeping you and Karin from killing each other?"

I agreed to some extent. Karin and I fought sometimes, but never physically, only verbally, which is quite normal for sisters I always thought. Karin often fussed at me when I borrowed some of her clothes without asking and then simply put them back without first washing them. And who could blame her? That was pretty thoughtless of me. Or we fussed at each other about whose turn it was to do the dishes or fetch the water from the well. These were ongoing battles while we were growing up.

Although the 1955 entries helped me remember the mundane things that happened during the earlier part of that summer, I certainly don't need that kind of help in recalling the events that occurred toward the end of June.

After Mother returned to Borås on Sunday, Karin and I stayed by ourselves until Ingrid joined us on Tuesday. Being alone was a first for us. After all, we were only ten and thirteen years old, but apparently Mother thought we could be trusted. Ingrid, however, seemed to have had reservations about whether Karin and I were responsible enough to take care of anything without her directing and telling us what to do. This is clearly evident from the way she

heavily underlined the word "still" in her 1955 diary entry.

Although Ingrid only mentioned that she worked in the fishery that summer—probably because she was the one writing in the diary—Karin and I did as well. Both of us were eager to earn some pocket money for movies, goodies and comic magazines, things that usually were not part of Ingrid's stringent budget.

Soon after we arrived in Mollösund, we heard that the fishing season happened to be extremely heavy and bountiful. We asked Signe Berg, our neighbor who worked in one of the fisheries, if she thought the fishery owners would hire the two of us, even as young as we were, to help out in getting the herring ready for the market. "They probably will, if you think you can stand up for several hours cutting off the gills and fins from the herring," Signe answered in her broad Mollösund's dialect.

Karin and I were ecstatic when the fishery down the hill from us let us work several hours a day. Although it meant getting up very early in the morning, I really didn't mind especially because we were so close to summer solstice, the longest day of the year. It made getting up at the wee hours of the morning that much easier.

Besides, it was a lot of fun listening to the local women as they chatted away in their dialect. I simply loved to hear them talk and was able to pick up some of their typical expressions, which I then sprinkled into my own conversation. It made me feel good when they seemed to accept me as one of their own kind and no longer looked at me as one of the "bratty and pesky" summertime kids. For some odd reason, I have always felt this strong need to belong and fit in wherever I happen to live.

For every crate filled with hundreds of slippery herrings I finished cleaning, I earned 68 *öre*, or 10 cents. I don't remember exactly how many such crates I completed, but it must have been quite a few. When I received my first pay at the end of the week, I was proud as a peacock, strutting about with the coins jingling in my pocket for everyone to hear.

I had never earned so much money before or worked so hard. Taking our neighbor's baby out for a stroll in her buggy through the Borås City Park, for example, or running short errands for the hairdresser or the post office clerk from around the corner were child's play in comparison.

When it was time to go home, I reeked to high heaven of smelly fish. To get rid of the smell and the fish scales that clung to my skin, I simply jumped into the salty ocean, after shedding my clothes and scrubbing down with a special saltwater soap. What could be more fun than using the wide-open, albeit very cold, ocean for my very own bathtub?

That year Ingrid's birthday on June 23 happened to fall one day before the Midsummer's Eve celebrations. The day started out as any other birthday with Karin and me serving Ingrid breakfast in bed consisting of toast and orange marmalade, her favorite. We decorated her "birthday" tray with lots of freshly picked wild flowers and lit a candle beside her plate. It was her nineteenth birthday; the eleventh one without Father.

Ingrid had just finished opening her presents from Karin and me when Signe Berg, our neighbor, came running over, shouting that Ingrid should come quickly because Mother was on the phone. This was very scary because we never used our neighbor's phone unless it was an emergency.

Dressed only in her pajamas, Ingrid rushed out the door and followed Signe back to her house while Karin and I looked at each other in perplexed astonishment and trepidation. What could have prompted Mother to call using the Berg's phone? Had Mamma fallen and hurt herself? Was she in the hospital and a neighbor had called? Or was this just a birthday call although that was strictly speaking not an emergency?

Impatiently we waited on our little front porch, watching for Ingrid to return and tell us what Mother said. Finally, although it couldn't have been more than three minutes, we saw her come running toward us, waving her hands back and forth over her head and yelling something we could not understand at first.

"What is she saying, Gittan? What could have happened?" Karin looked as baffled as I felt.

"I have no idea, but it doesn't look like it is something bad. She is smiling."

Once Ingrid came within earshot, we could clearly hear her yelling, "Guess what! Pappa is coming home on Saturday! Mamma is flying down to Wiener Neustadt in Austria to meet him!" Her voice quivered with excitement.

Completely dumb struck, Karin and I just stood there with our mouths gaping. Had we heard her correctly? Had she said what we thought she had?

"Are you sure, Ingrid, that you heard right? Father is actually coming home?" The two of us shouted back when we found our voices again.

It took a while for the most marvelous news in the world to sink in, but once it did Karin and I felt as if we had been given a birthday present as well. The rest of that day we went around in a daze. We wished we could get more details, but there was no easy way to do that. Mother was in town and couldn't let us know anything further without imposing on our next-door neighbor again. Besides, long distance calls were very expensive. It didn't help lessen our anxiety even though we understood these constraints.

For the next few days Pappa was never far from our minds. It was very difficult to remain calm and patient not knowing anything or being able to find out what was happening. We didn't even know whether Mamma actually went to Austria to meet him or what we were supposed to do. If she went, how would she find him at the station? Would they recognize each other after eleven years? What if he wasn't on the train he was supposed to be on? What would she do then? And if he were, where would they stay? What would happen next? How was his health? Was he sick after so many years in Vorkuta? Did he still speak Swedish or had he forgotten it, and if he had, how would we be able to talk with him? This last question only worried Karin and me.

Although the Midsummer festivities helped take our minds off what was happening with Mother's trip and Father's return, we were anxious for more news from Mother. The situation now facing us was so unique and so different from anything we had ever experienced before that it made it very difficult to know what to do. It was one thing to talk and dream about such a possibility but quite another now that it was turning into reality.

Several days passed in this state of complete ignorance and anxiety. We had almost given up hope of hearing from Mother again. But then on June 26th Signe Berg came running over to tell us that Mother was calling from Vienna and that we should hurry.

While Karin and I waited with bated breaths outside the Bergs' house, Ingrid quickly followed Signe inside. No more than two minutes later, Ingrid came rushing down the stairs, grinning from ear to ear.

"Pappa was on the train from the Soviet Union just as we hoped he would be. Mamma said everything went well and that Pappa is very happy to be a free man at last and that he can hardly wait to see us. She also said she would write to us soon, but in the meantime we should to go on with our plans for July. She said that she was staying on in Austria with Pappa for a few more days and that they would be discussing what to do next." By this time, Ingrid was totally out of breath.

We were beside ourselves! Holding hands and running around in a circle, we shouted at the top of our lungs "Pappa is free! Pappa is free! Pappa is coming home! Pappa is coming home!" over and over again for the whole world to hear.

All day long and for several days afterwards we felt giddy with happiness and excitement. The Soviets had at last released our father. What we had hoped for and longed for had at last become reality.

The question now uppermost in my mind was when would we finally be reunited as a family, or rather, when would Father come to Sweden? When would I finally get to meet him? Mother had just briefly mentioned they were going to discuss what to do. For the life of me, I couldn't understand what there was to discuss. Why couldn't he simply come back with Mother when she returned in a few days? What was so complicated about that? Asking us to follow through on our original plans for July sounded to me like it might be another whole month before I would finally see Father. Hadn't I waited long enough? I didn't like this delay one bit, but what could I do? Absolutely nothing!

As planned, my sisters and I left our beloved Kap Horn on June 30th just before the renters came to take possession of it the next day. Together we took the bus to Stenungsund on the mainland before going off in different directions. Ingrid boarded a train north for a leadership camp in Gimo, Karin went south on a train bound for Kullavik to look after the children of Mother's cousin, and *Morbror* Carl Arne picked me up in his car to spend the next two weeks with my cousins in Munkedal. After that I was supposed to visit *Moster* Anne-Marie in Lysekil until it was time to return to Mollösund in August.

I had only been in Munkedal a few days when I received a five page long letter from Mother addressed to Karin and me. Mine was obviously a carbon copy of the original, but I didn't care. I was just happy to finally hear from her. It opened by saying that she didn't really know where to begin. Her reunion with Father still seemed a little unreal after so many years of waiting for him. She then continues:

> *What I have dreamed of for so many years finally became reality. It is difficult for me to express in words what a fantastic and wonderful feeling it was to hold your Vati in my arms again! I can hardly believe that it is true...*
>
> *He is suntanned, not skinny at all, weighs 70 kg* [154 pounds]. *He seems rested and has gray hair at the temples... you will meet a Vati whom you will be proud of in every respect. If you only knew, my dear children, what Vati has been through! The most horrible and unreal things! He had at least twenty different jobs in Vorkuta, everything between heaven and earth, heavy and difficult work. He knows that he was officially declared dead but can't understand how that happened because he didn't know a Siegfried Meyer. But now he is alive and that is all that counts. He is quite unchanged otherwise. He likes to talk about his experiences. It is as if he has a strong need to get it off his chest now that he can talk without risking being shot...*

He is really enjoying his freedom and is so happy, so happy, and has even begun to tease me like he used to do. We are so much in love and soooo happy! It is like our second honeymoon. He is longing to see you...

Further on down Mother also wrote that the mayor of Salzburg had invited the two of them to enjoy a free three-week stay at an Austrian resort. Since she had to get back to her job in Borås, she had asked if Ingrid could take her place instead, which of course was quite acceptable.

You can understand how happy Ingrid will be at such a marvelous opportunity to be together with Vati again. She will meet him in Bonn, where we are going soon, and then the two of them will go on to Pongau in the Alps close to Salzburg...

After reading this last comment, it dawned on me that Ingrid was going down to spend time with Father in an Alpine resort and would meet him long before I did. I couldn't help but think it was a little unfair; jealousy was raising its ugly head. Why wasn't he coming to Sweden immediately so that I could meet him too?

In my frustration and deep disappointment, I threw Mother's letter down. But then chiding myself for my childish behavior, I immediately picked it up again because I was curious to see what else Mother had to say. She went on to explain that it would be good for Ingrid and Father to have this time together because it would help them get reacquainted with each other. Since he did not really know either Karin or me, it might prove easier for him if it were just the two of them to begin with. This might help ease him back into being a father once again. After all, Ingrid had been a little girl of eight when she saw him last, but now she was a fully-grown young woman of nineteen, not an easy gap for a father and daughter to bridge.

Meeting all three of us at the same time might prove a little overwhelming after having been gone for so long. She concluded this particular passage by saying that she realized this arrangement was a big disappointment although she hoped that Karin and I would not be too upset but would understand why they had decided on this course of action.

How well she knew me! Even though her explanation made perfectly good sense, I didn't have to be thrilled about it. But it was not in my happy-go-lucky childish nature to worry about such things for too long. After making up my mind to be happy for Ingrid, I started to count the days instead until it would be my turn to meet Father as well.

Mother's letter went on to describe Father's first visit to a dentist because he had lost six teeth from being malnourished.

He didn't have a toothbrush for eight years. And such horrible meals! But he was never beaten or tortured physically during his time in the Moscow prison, but he suffered so much and had to do such hard work. Vati will probably write a book once he has settled down. He knows the Soviets so well ... Then, tomorrow a doctor will give him a thorough examination including an EKG to determine if there are any problems with his heart even though outwardly he looks healthy...

A day or so after receiving this lengthy letter, I sat down to to write a welcome-home letter to my father. Although I had never written a letter before, I had watched and observed Mother often enough to know exactly what to do. As it so happened, this was the first of many letters that I would write to my parents in the years to come. Being the meticulous and careful person that I got to know over the years, Father stored all my letters from the first to the last in thick filing folders marked "Gittis" in his precise handwriting.

On a torn out piece of school notebook paper, because that was all I could find at my cousins' house, I penciled the following letter in my best cursive handwriting.

Munkedal, July 7, 1955

Dear Vati!

How are you after all 11 years of prison? I really hope you are healthy, dear Vati, so that you won't be sick when you come home. It feels a little strange to write to you because I have never seen you. I am happy that Ingrid is going to travel to Bonn and be with you there. I am not at all jealous but when I received Mamma's letter, I just knew how happy Ingrid would be. It will be so much fun during all the terms when we are in school and you can help us with our homework. I am so happy to have such a kind and good pappa, who can teach us a little so that we will get somewhere in life. Now that I am talking about school I will tell you what grades I made. They were all right. [Here I rattled off all the subjects with their corresponding grades]... *I applied to get into the school for girls but did not have enough points. I had 17½ points but needed 1½ point more. It was really too bad that I did not get in, but I will try harder next year again. Now I cannot write any more, dear Pappa, but we will meet soon. I long for you, Pappa.*

Kisses and hugs from your youngest daughter Birgitta

I was thrilled when I received his reply several weeks later.

Altmünster,

July 26, 1955

Birgitta, my beloved little girl!

To think that at last it is possible to write to my little daughter Birgitta, whom I don't even know yet, but whom I will soon know, and very soon be able to hug really, really hard. Even though I have never seen you, I knew the whole time that you existed because it was the last message I received before I ended up in prison camp...I have held you so dear in my heart and thought so much about my children. That is why I believe that we will not be strangers for a minute when we meet. But I will immediately think that you are a wonderful and sweet girl and that you will soon figure out that you have a father who loves to have fun with his daughters...

The letter continues for another page or so with a lot of Father's thoughts about our future and what kind of father he hoped to be. I cried happy tears after reading it. I didn't understand everything he said, but one thing stood out clearly. Father loved me even though he didn't know me!! I vowed that once we met, I would never let him go again and would work really hard at school so that he would be proud of me. I wasn't the least bit nervous about meeting him. Oh no, not me! Maybe, just perhaps a little! All I could think about was that I finally was going to have a father who would love me just as much as I already loved him. I had no reservations about that whatsoever.

When I asked Karin many years later whether she had written to Father like I had, her response was to send me a copy of her letter that he had saved in her file marked "Karin."

Dear Vati!

Thank you very much for the wonderful present you sent me. I have never had anything like that before. [She doesn't say what it was] *How is it down there in Austria? I am longing for you and Ingrid to come home. I can hardly believe that I have a pappa again. It feels so strange. You have no idea how wonderful it is in Mollösund. It will be so much fun when we are all together there.*

The rest of the letter consists more or less of a weather report. It is almost as if she didn't know what else to say to a father whom she didn't remember.

In another folder marked "Ingrid," I discovered the one my sister had written to him in German on a bigger than normal sized postcard before she even knew that she was going down to Bonn to meet him.

My dear Vati!

Yes, it was long time ago since you received a card from me. But now I am able to write to you again. We were all so happy when Mother called us in Mollösund that we hardly knew which leg to stand on. I am on my way to Gimo where I will participate in a course on politics. When you are back home with us, we will talk about politics, won't we? You are coming soon, aren't you? We will be so happy to have you back with us, and I am sure everything will go well. You are going to become our father again, and we will be so happy to have you as our father. It will seem strange at first but at the same time so wonderful. As you can probably tell, I have forgotten so much of my German, but when you are back with us the two of us will only speak German with each other, I hope. Many kisses and hugs from your daughter Ingi. P.S. Please say hello to everyone.

It wasn't until I was fully-grown and had a family of my own that I started to think about how my sisters had felt when we heard that Father was actually coming home and that Ingrid was going to meet him before Karin and I did. Until then I had simply assumed that the three of us felt the same way. And perhaps, for the most part we did. However, because we are natured differently and were at different stages of our lives, our reactions to Father's homecoming also varied.

Not too long ago when I visited Karin in Rönninge, a suburb of Sweden's capital city Stockholm, we started to reminisce about our childhood as we often do whenever we have a chance to be together. It doesn't happen too often with us living in two different countries and on two different continents. Because Father's return home in 1955 played an enormous role in our lives, it was not long before our conversation turned in that direction.

"Do you remember how you felt after we heard that Pappa was part of that transport from the Soviet Union, Karin? I was too young and self-absorbed at the time to pay attention to how you perceived what was happening. I seem to recall, though, that you didn't seem as upset or jealous about Ingrid getting to meet Pappa before the two of us did. And then when Pappa finally came to Sweden, weren't you a little stand offish towards him or shy in the beginning?"

While waiting for her answer, I continued to sip on the dark brew that Swedes call coffee. If you put a spoon in it, it can almost stand on its own because it is so strong, something I was no longer used to after living in America for so long. Even after using lots of cream and sugar, I was hard put not to make a face. On the other hand, Karin's homemade *kanelbullar*, or cinnamon buns, were absolutely delicious, making it impossible to resist a third and fourth helping.

I have yet to figure out how Karin, who loves to cook and bake as much as I do, manages to keep her slender figure. Perhaps the reason for that is that she was the only one of the three of us sisters who inherited our Swedish ancestors' genes for height, whereas both Ingrid and I have instead taken after our short, stocky Croatian-Austrian ancestors. I have always envied Karin her ability to eat with abandon and without consequence.

"Yes, Gittan, you are partially right," Karin broke into my enjoyment of the cinnamon buns. "I wasn't really upset about Ingrid being allowed to meet Pappa before us. In fact, I think I was even a little bit relieved that the meeting with him was postponed."

"How come? You were as excited about Pappa coming home as the rest of us, weren't you?"

Her two teenage daughters, Anna-Karin and Kristina had joined us on the terrace in the meantime, as had her husband, Göran. All three of them now looked at Karin expectantly.

"Of course, I was happy that Pappa was finally coming home, but to tell you the truth, I was also just a little nervous and scared about the changes that I knew would come and was therefore happy to have our meeting postponed. This gave me more time to adjust to the fact that the father whom I did not remember at all was going to be a father who would be present from now on, a father who would tell me what I could or could not do, a father who would lay down the law, so to speak. I was a typical teenager then, somewhat rebellious, as you will recall, and not always eager to follow grown-up rules. What kind of rules would Pappa now impose upon me, how strict would he be, is what I kept thinking about." She sighed as she sneaked a look at her two daughters to see how they reacted to their mother having been a rebellious teenager.

But neither Anna-Karin nor Kristina acted too surprised for they knew their mother well. Besides, this youthful rebelliousness had not kept her from becoming a very capable and wonderful district nurse and instructor of nurses.

"Do you remember, Gittan," Karin resumed her tale, "that I had some problems with school? Well, that was the main reason I was scared. I was afraid of what Pappa would think or say about that. Actually, I was very torn in my feelings. Of course, I was very happy that Pappa had finally been released from the Soviet prison, but at the same time it made me feel so guilty for being glad about not having to meet him quite yet."

Looking back on those days from an older person's point of view, I can understand why her feelings about Father's homecoming were somewhat ambivalent.

I decided to query Ingrid about the same topic one day when I was over at her house in the mountains of North Carolina. It just so happened that both of us ended up living in the same town because she and her husband Art, a Swiss-born American engineer, retired to Boone in 1975.

Her reaction to Father's homecoming was also slightly different from mine. Of course, she was very pleased that Father wanted to see her alone at first so that they could get reacquainted. She remembered how happy she was when she heard that she was going to Germany and Austria in order to spend time not only with Father, but also with our cousins Dieter and Irmtraud, and Uncle Walther and Uncle Heinz whom she hadn't seen in eleven years. Staying at an Alpine resort was an added bonus. She was very sad, though, that she did not get to see *Omama*, our grandmother; she had died just a few months before Father returned home.

But then Ingrid went on to admit that she had also felt uncertain and perhaps even a little bit afraid.

"You must remember, Gittan, Pappa had missed out on some very important years in our lives. During his absence, I had grown into a very self-sufficient and responsible young adult, whom Mamma was relying on heavily as her right hand and best friend. I helped take care of both you and Karin in Mollösund, for example, when Mamma could not be there with us."

I nodded in agreement. She was always the dependable big sister, albeit somewhat bossy at times, but who could blame her with such a heavy responsibility resting on her shoulders?

"That was why I was wondering what this would do to my position in the family as Mamma's helper. Can you understand how I felt, Gittan?" Ingrid asked.

"I guess so. You must have felt as if you were being usurped from a place that you had held for the last eleven years?"

"That's right. I wondered what role I would play once Father was back home. As far as the trip down to meet him is concerned, being a very practical minded person, I wondered if Pappa would recognize me and I him when he came to meet me at the train station in Bonn? And of course we did! Would we share a room or would we have separate ones? I fretted about that but needn't have for I had a room to myself. Would he like what he saw when he met me? Would we be able to talk to each other? What would I say to him? Would he mind that I smoked? Those were some of the things I worried about on my way down in the train." She sighed deeply, thinking back to that time a long ago.

I also wanted to know what her impressions were after seeing Austria and our relatives after eleven years. As she has traveled the world since then, six continents to be exact, I wasn't sure how well she would remember that one in particular. Did something stand out to her? In response she gave me one of her little diaries. Just like Mother she liked to record important events in small notebooks, which she has saved over the years. She was always a much better saver than either Karin or I, which has given rise to a lot of teasing. She has saved everything, and I mean everything, including notebooks with essays from her high school days. Today I am thankful that she did.

In her notebook she described in great detail, including all the young men she flirted with on the train going down to Bonn, what she ate, how much money she spent on what, and what her reunion with Father was like. One such entry reads as follows:

> *Father welcomed me with a bouquet of red and yellow roses. He just looked and looked at me and I just cried! After the welcome ceremony was over, Vati and I looked at each other some more and talked and talked and then he gave me a gold bracelet … Vati is really spoiling me. He would buy everything I point at if I didn't stop him … everything is wonderful!*

She raved in glowing terms about the rest of the trip from Bonn to Austria where the two of them spent some time with Father's brothers and their families. She enjoyed every minute, especially when she went dancing and drinking with our cousins and their friends and became a little tipsy after drinking too much wine.

When July 1955 came to an end, I was eager and more than ready to return to Mollösund. I had enjoyed visiting *Moster* Anne-Marie in Lysekil but longed to see Mother, whom I hadn't seen since before Midsummer and her reunion with Father. The past month seemed like an eternity to me, especially because so much had happened, and I still didn't know when I was finally going to meet my pappa.

CHAPTER XXII

Reunion

August 1955

When I arrived in Mollösund on the steamship *Bohuslän* from Lysekil the second day of August, Karin met me at the docks to help me with my luggage, both of us very happy to see each other after our month long separation.

"Has Mamma arrived yet?" I asked after we finished hugging.

"Yes, she came yesterday together with me. Uncle Alf drove me to Göteborg where Mamma met me at the station. The two of us then continued on to Mollösund."

"Has Ingrid arrived as well?"

"No, not yet, she will be here in three or four days, I think. I can hardly wait to see her and hear what she has to say about her trip with Pappa. How about you? You got Mamma's letter, didn't you?"

"Yes, sure did. I am looking forward to seeing Ingrid but will be even happier when Pappa finally comes. Has Mamma said anything about when that will be?"

"No, not yet, but she told me that as soon as you arrived from Lysekil, we would talk about it."

Winding our way through the village, I soaked up the welcoming fishy scent that always permeated Mollösund. It only took us about ten minutes to reach our cottage where Mamma waited with open arms. I almost squeezed the life out of her when we kissed and hugged and then kissed and hugged some more. I was trying to make up for the last month and a half of being away from her.

During supper, I never stopped talking. Not only did I have a lot to tell Mamma about what I had done during the past month, but I also had many questions about Father, the most important one of which was: "When is Pappa coming to Sweden?"

Putting her fork down, Mamma answered that at first Pappa and she had planned for him to come directly to Borås where we would greet him after which we would then return to Mollösund for a few more days until school started. “Unfortunately, because of having to take care of so many unexpected things, *Vati* had to postpone his trip to Sweden for at least two weeks. This means that if he doesn’t come here first, he might not get to see Mollösund until next summer. That is why we decided it would be best if he came directly here to begin with.

“But when, Mamma? When is he coming? Why didn’t he come with you now?” Even to my own ears I sounded a little petulant. My patience was wearing thin at what seemed to me to be unnecessary delays.

“I know you want to meet him, Gittan, and I promise it won’t be too long now. The plan is for *Vati* to arrive on August 20th in Göteborg, where we will pick him up and then take the steamship back to Mollösund,” Mamma answered cajolingly as she chucked me under my chin.

“That’s almost three more weeks!” I protested stomping my feet. ”I don’t know how I can possibly wait that long, Mamma. It is taking forever!!! Can’t he come any sooner than that?”

“No, Gittan, he has to go to Germany and stay there for two weeks after Ingrid leaves him.”

“But why, Mamma?” Karin piped up.

“Well, the circumstances are a little complicated. It has to do with the question of citizenship.”

"What do you mean, Mamma? We are Swedish now, aren't we?" I looked questioningly at her, wondering what possible problems she could have now. This issue was resolved over two years ago, when we all became Swedish, wasn't it?

"Yes, Gittan, we are, but this doesn't concern our citizenship but *Vati*'s. The Soviets regarded him as Austrian because he was born in Vienna, and that was why they returned him to Austria rather than to Germany even though he had been captured as a German diplomat."

"But why does that matter?" This was a new twist.

"If Vati wants to reenter the German Foreign Service, he must be a German and not an Austrian citizen. But in order to be considered a German citizen, he must be re-released into Germany, which means that he must spend two weeks at the repatriation camp in Friedland before coming to Sweden. This will then facilitate his becoming a German citizen again just as he was after Austria's annexation in 1938," Mother responded patiently.

"Is that what Pappa wants to do? Become a German diplomat again?" I was still trying hard to understand what this had to do with Pappa's coming to Sweden.

"Yes, Pappa definitely wants to work as a diplomat again. The only question is whether he should do this for Germany or Austria. After consulting with many people in the past few weeks, he has come to the conclusion that it would be more advantageous for him to be reinstated by the German Foreign Service. By doing that he will get credit for the eleven years he spent in captivity as a German diplomat, which Austria cannot give him because he wasn't representing Austria when he was captured. Besides, this will also help *Vati* advance more rapidly, which hopefully will help him make up for lost time."

This was rather a lengthy explanation, but I understood the gist of it. I resigned myself to being patient a little while longer and making the best of the situation. If I had waited this long to meet Pappa, what possible difference would a few more weeks make? After all, I would then have him for the rest of my life! Right?

By now I should have been used to that nothing was ever simple or ordinary with my family. But it was only as I grew older that

I realized the truth of that. As a ten-year-old I was still learning this reality.

The next couple of weeks seemed to move at a snail's pace.

After Ingrid returned from her trip, she kept Karin and me entertained with her tales of adventure with our cousins and all the things she had done with Father. Although I was eager to hear all about her exploits, I was really more interested in what she thought about Father. What was he like? I wanted to know.

"You will both love him because he is very lovable." Ingrid told Karin and me when we were sunbathing on the cliffs below the cottage one afternoon. "He also likes to kid around with you, but at the same time he can be very serious when he is explaining something. When I told him that he didn't look as skinny as I thought he would, he laughingly explained that was because the Russians had fed him really well the last month or two. When I asked him why when they hadn't done that before, he answered that the Russians probably didn't want the rest of the world to think they had starved their prisoners half to death even though they had."

I could not help but still feel just a little bit jealous that she had already spent so much time with him when I hadn't even seen him yet.

Shortly after Ingrid's return, now that we were all together in one place again, we begged Mother to tell us about her reunion with Father, starting with the moment the telegram arrived in June. Until then all we knew was second hand information from reading about it in in the magazines and newspapers.

"When they called me from the telegram office that I had a message from Austria, I did not dare hope that it would be the one I had been waiting for all these long months." Mother began her tale. "I could hardly believe my eyes when I read your uncle Walther's telegram stating that Vati was scheduled to arrive on June 25th according to a Viennese newspaper."

The anguish Mother must have felt clearly comes through in a piece of paper I found years later tucked into one of her little black diaries.

> *How many times during the past eleven years but especially now during the last six weeks have I not answered the phone in the hopes that it would be a message from the*

telegram bureau saying "there is a telegram." But no, they never called. Day after day went by with nothing happening. Nothing came. Two transports arrived but no Roland, no telegram! But then on Wednesday, June 22, the phone rang at 6 pm. This time it was the telegram I had fantasized in my thoughts about receiving but never dared go there completely. Was I ever going to receive it? Was I ever going to receive a telegram that said 'Roland is on his way. Roland is coming to Vienna'?

Some words are blotted out, perhaps from the tears she shed.

"After I stopped crying," Mother went on as we enjoyed the beautiful sun set over the distant skerries,"I wanted to announce the wonderful news to the whole world. Running all the way home to Villagatan 17, I waved the telegram in the air shouting 'Roland is coming home' over and over again. Anyone who saw me must have thought I was some crazed mad woman. But I simply had to share the wonderful news with everyone who saw me. As soon as I got home, I called Ella [Mother's best friend and the mother of my so-called boyfriend, Christer]. My hands trembled and my voice shook but somehow I managed to stammer out the wonderful news."

Of course, Ella was overjoyed at Mother's news and told her that she would have to go to Vienna to meet Father's train. "I didn't know how I could manage that since I didn't have any money for the train ticket and hotel. Ella told me not to worry and that she was going to call all our friends."

It apparently didn't take Ella long before she called back and told Mother that everyone was pitching in to pay for a flight from Stockholm to Vienna, which was the only way to guarantee that she would get there in time. She was not to worry about any other expenses either because everything would be taken care of. "I don't know what I would have done without my wonderful and generous friends."

"But how did the press find out what was happening? Did you call and tell them?" Ingrid wanted to know.

"No, it wasn't me, but Ella. She told me that Sören [Ella's husband, who owned a textile factory in Borås] immediately contacted Christer Jäderlund, who was the reporter from Stockholm

Tidningen who had written about our family earlier in the year. Christer was more than happy to accompany me along with a photographer, so that all of Sweden could get a first-hand, eyewitness report of the happy event everyone hoped was about to take place in Austria. You know, girls, it was also Sören who gave me several new shirts, a new suit, underwear and socks to take to your pappa, which helped make him feel like a new man."

Christer Jäderlund from the Stockholm Tidningen was not the only reporter, however, who accompanied Mother on the plane as the clippings from other newspapers and magazines prove. I don't know how these other reporters heard about what was about to take place in Vienna, but their account of this indescribably happy event in the Gottlieb family's life really helps to round out the picture, as did all the photographs taken at the time. Otherwise we would not have had any pictures whatsoever since neither Mother nor my uncles owned a camera. Although these newspaper articles and the pictures are now yellowed with age and frayed on the edges, they are a veritable treasure trove.

With the help of the many clippings in the worn-out, red album along with my parents' own recollections, I have pieced together what took place on that historic day in June 1955 when they were finally reunited after eleven long and difficult years of being apart from each other.

Everything went according to plan. Mother flew from Stockholm on Friday, June 24. After arriving in Vienna, she immediately made her way to the home of the Rollers in the Schulgasse 90. They were friends from Father's childhood, Mother told us, whom she had not seen since leaving Austria in 1945 but with whom she had continued to stay in contact over the years. That was why she felt free to telegraph them to ask if she could stay with them while she was in Vienna.

What often seemed to be the case with Mother, when she was emotionally tied up in knots, was that she found solace in writing down her feelings. The night before she hoped to meet Father was understandably just such a time. Her rambling and jumbled thoughts, scribbled in an unsteady handwriting in one of her black diaries, clearly show how her mind was racing.

The twelfth year has begun. The twelfth year!!! Years of uncertainty and worries and longing! Many years of waiting that will end soon. Tomorrow, within twenty-four hours, I will come face to face with my beloved husband. How can I dare believe that it will be true? How can I dare give in to such happiness, as our reunion will be? I am so scared, so worried that something will happen in the end that will keep this from happening. Perhaps he has become sick or perhaps the train has met with some kind of mishap. Oh, there is so much that can still go wrong that will cause our reunion to be delayed yet again. How it feels? What thoughts are running through my brain? A brain that is so shaken up that it can hardly think straight. But still, let me try to tell how I feel before this meeting with my beloved after eleven years of separation. It is a feeling of happiness, so big, so mighty that I can hardly bear it. Will our long wait finally be rewarded? I am more convinced than ever that the higher powers that steer our lives are at work here. I have to admit that I have sometimes believed in blind fate but at other times in a predetermined fate as well. But let me leave that thought for now, it is far too difficult to talk about just now.

Very early in the morning of the 25th, she met my two Austrian uncles at the railwaystation when they arrived from Salzburg and Lakirchen respectively. The three of them then went on to Wiener Neustadt, located a very short distance just to the south of Vienna, where Father's train was supposed to arrive at six o'clock in the morning from Stalingrad. Unfortunately, *Omama*, Father's mother had passed away just two months earlier and would therefore never know the joy of holding her beloved son in her arms again although she did know that he was still alive.

After arriving at the station in Wiener Neustadt, my two uncles suggested that Mother should let them meet the train first to make sure that Father was actually on it. Although this did not make her happy, Mother told us that she gave in because she realized this might be for the best. "After all, we had no guarantee that your father would be on that train since all we had to go by was that list of published names from a newspaper."

She then went on to tell us how she waited at the corner of the platform, very close to the station house. From there she could easily see the train come rolling into the station, which was overflowing with people, everyone having come in the hopes of welcoming home a loved one just like she had. It tore at her heart to see so many old men and women holding up photos of lost sons, husbands, daughters and mothers or placards with names written on them in large letters.

Finally, the green Soviet train rolled into the station and ground to a stop. "It was very difficult to see individual faces because of so many men and women waving their arms frenetically and trying to push their heads through the compartment windows, all eager to catch a first glimpse of someone welcoming them home after so many years. It was an unbelievable sight! I was about to despair when I could not discover your father's beloved face right away." Mother paused as if lost in thought.

Impatiently we waited for her to tell us what happened next. "Suddenly I heard Heinz and Walther shouting at the top of their lungs and gesticulating for me to come forward. Pressing and elbowing my way through the crowd, I finally made it to where they were standing just below one of the many compartment windows of the train."

And then she saw him! This was a moment that would stay with her for the rest of her life, as I often heard her tell people when they asked her what it had been like. "There he was, waving just like everyone else, tears coursing down his cheeks. His mouth was split into a wide grin, very closely resembling a grimace. But it was Roland, my beloved Roland! It was true! He had come back to me!"

To another reporter who was not present at the reunion she said, "I can hardly talk about this breathtaking happiness that I felt. There simply are no words with which to describe the feelings I had inside me. I can only say that it was fantastically wonderful. Just fantastic! It is so difficult to describe!" (*Kuriren*, August 10, 1955)

A photograph portrays it all very vividly, this extraordinary first moment of recognition. It shows uncles Walther and Heinz hoisting Mother up on their shoulders so that she could grab hold of Father's hands. Another photograph shows them kissing with

Father stretching as far as he could reach out of the window. An amazing moment captured for all eternity!

Whenever Father talked about this moment in time his voice was always heavily charged emotionally. "When I pulled on her hands as hard as I could so that our mouths could finally meet for our first kiss in eleven years, it felt unreal somehow. Was I dreaming? No, it was very real, an indescribable moment, a moment I had dreamed about for eleven long years!"

Just thinking and writing about this scene fifty years later brings tears to my eyes, goose bumps on my skin, and shivers down my spine. Looking at the pictures makes it all come to life again. It took the Soviet officials at least fifteen more minutes before they finally opened the doors to allow their former prisoners to detrain. According to Father, in typical Soviet fashion, the lists with all the names had to be checked and rechecked before anyone could be released.

When telling about what stepping off the train was like, I often heard Father describe his feelings this way: "At last the moment arrived when I was able to get out and shed the yoke of my involuntary and unjust serfdom to the inhumane Soviet regime. I was finally a free man. For the first time in eleven years I would be able to hug and kiss my wife as much and as often as I wanted to, something I had often dreamed about but feared might never become a reality. It was almost too much for me, but not more than I could handle." At that point he usually winked at Mother and blew her a kiss.

Father was also often asked what he thought when he saw his wife for the first time after so many years. His answer seldom varied. "When I saw my Bimbam the last time, she was a thirty-three-year old happily pregnant young mother and wife. What I saw eleven years later was a beautiful woman with short curly gray hair and blue eyes full of happy tears. She was smiling up at me and grinning from ear to ear. She was also wearing the black onyx earrings I gave her when we got engaged. [Incidentally, those earrings are now in my possession!] Whenever she wore those dangling earrings, it always made me think of the sound that church bells make—Bim! Bam! I could hardly take my eyes off my beloved Bimbam."

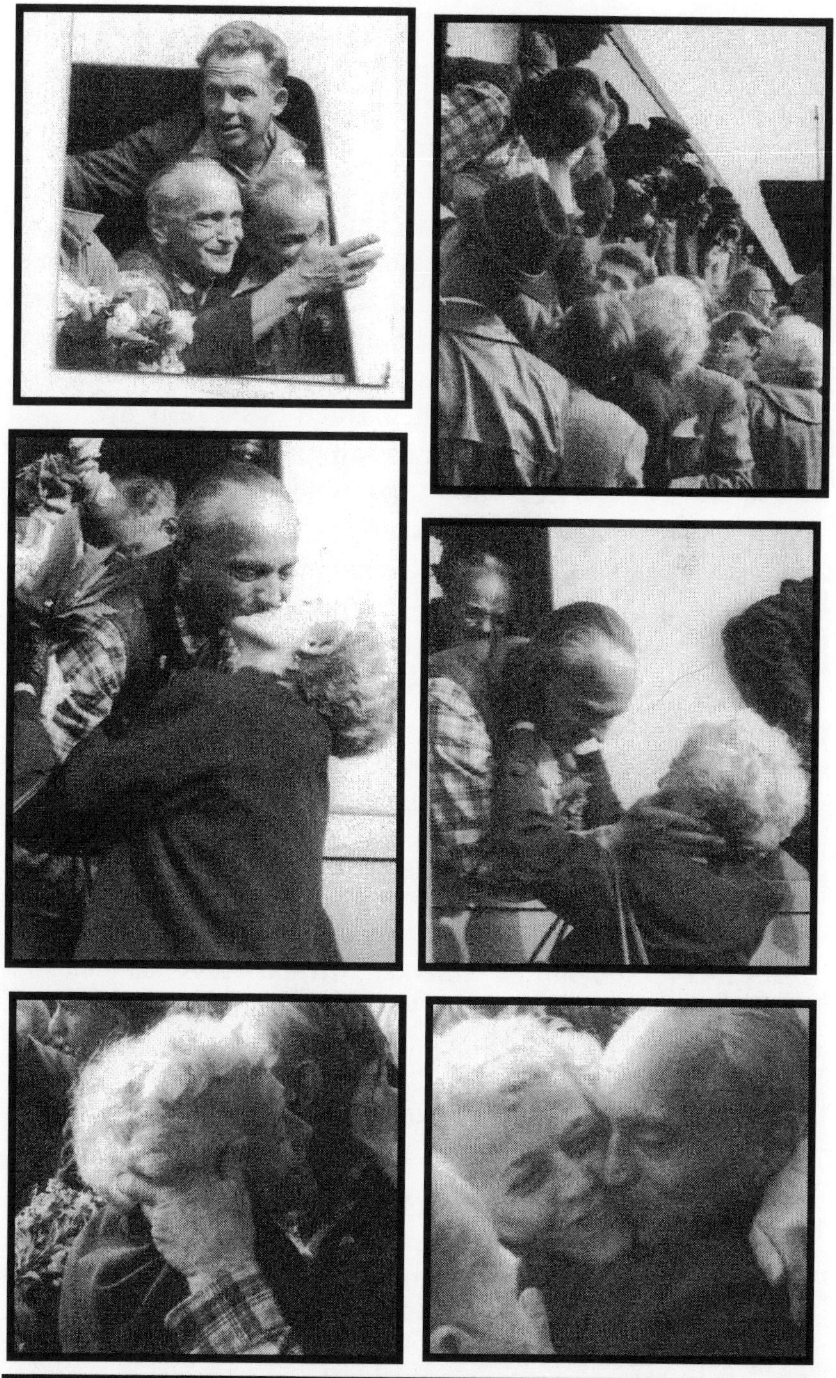

Photos of the reunion from a journalist's contact sheet

When Mother was asked the same question, she described her feelings this way: "After eleven years of wondering, waiting, hoping, sorrowing and hoping again, I saw a much thinner and older Katermann-husband, dressed in a blue-checkered flannel shirt. His hair was gray, his face was tanned with many deep wrinkles, and his hands were work-worn and full of calluses. But his mouth was stretched from side to side as far as it would go in a grin that told me how happy he was to be back home. His brown eyes were just as warm and smiling and completely unchanged. I felt like I could drown in them forever, just like I had when we were newlyweds. It was love at first sight then, and it was love all over again now, a love that has only deepened with the years."

One of the reporters, who witnessed their reunion, stated that there were not many words spoken at first between the two.

> **The two just stood there with their arms wrapped around each other, not ready to let go of each other, as if not yet fully being able to believe that they were actually in each other's arms once again. Several minutes passed in this way. No one else existed for them in those first few moments of kissing and hugging. They totally shut out the rest of the world. It was clear to everyone that no one and nothing else existed for them during these first few moments of being together once again after eleven long years apart. It was a well-deserved moment of deep felt happiness and joy...(*Stockholm Tidningen,* June 26, 1955.)**

When we were discussing that particular quote after I had already met Father, Mother remarked that she was actually the first one to speak when she handed him the gold ring with a small diamond in the middle of the wide band and said, "Roland, here is your ring back that I gave you when we got engaged."

I clearly remember Father's response. "My hands trembled and shook when I tried putting the ring on my finger. It wouldn't fit because my hands and fingers were so gnarled and calloused from years of hard labor in the bitter cold weather in the Siberian tundra. Of course, I immediately recognized it as the same ring that I had secretly entrusted to Erland Uddgren, the Swedish *Chargé d'Affaires* in Bulgaria, just before the Soviets surrounded us at the train station in Sofia so many years ago. In order to avoid the Soviet guards from noticing what I was up to, I whispered to Erland to please make sure that Ruth got the ring in case something happened to me. Obviously, she got it, and I am very thankful to my old friend!"

Smiling at the memory of how hard Father had to work at putting the ring back on his finger, Mother explained that this was a symbolic moment for both of them. It was as if they had gotten engaged all over again with a promise of happier times ahead, a future to look forward to, a future that was now going to be theirs forever and ever. "I will never forget how surprised I was when he showed me how he had kept his wedding ring hidden inside a necklace amulet made of some kind of hard plastic."

"Yes, it is hard to believe that the Soviets never detected it, but they never did, thank God!" Father blew a kiss across the table to Mother, an endearing gesture I often saw him do in the years to come.

That was not the first or the last time the subject of my parents' reunion or what Father had experienced in the Soviet Union came up in the years that followed his homecoming. Luckily, he was never reluctant to talk about it, always enthralling his listeners with what he shared about his eleven years in captivity, but none more than me.

In one article I read the following statement Father made about how hard it was to see all those people at the station, some whose relatives did not return from Russia.

> **All around us old men and women were crying as they stuck a picture of a loved one in front of my face and asked me if I recognized the person or had seen him. Some of the pictures even looked as if they had been taken before World War I. That was how old and yellowed with age they looked. I could hardly believe that it was possible that some of these old people had waited for a loved one to return home for that long. It was a pitiful sight to behold. To my deep regret, I had to shake my head repeatedly since I did not recognize any of the faces. Göteborgs Expressen, July, 1955.)**

Several similar interviews with Father appeared in many different Swedish newspapers before I even met him. I devoured them, reading them over and over. While this allowed me to gain a little insight into what he had experienced and suffered in the years he was separated from us, it also brought him closer to me and let me get to know him just a little bit before I actually met him.

CHAPTER XXIII

The Big Day!

August 20,1955

Shortly after Ingrid's arrival in Mollösund, Mother went back to Borås. She wanted to save her remaining vacation days for later when Father would finally join us in Sweden. Ingrid, eager to earn some money, started working in the fishery again while Karin and I made the time pass by going swimming and playing with our friends.

Finally, the BIG DAY arrived! The calendar on the kitchen wall read August 20th. This was the day I had waited for almost eleven years. It was my D-Day. I was finally going to meet my father for the first time.

It is not surprising therefore that it was very easy for me to get up at four o'clock on this special day in order to catch the five o'clock bus to Stenungsund. I had hardly slept a wink the night before anyway. Besides the sun was already up, promising a day full of sunshine, which would have a hard time outshining my feelings of happy expectations.

After quickly putting on my best dress, the same blue one I had worn on *Examensdagen*, the last day of school, my patent white leather shoes and socks, I was ready to go. I really wanted to make a good first impression on Father and thought that by wearing my best clothes it would help make that happen. Because my stomach was in a jumble of nerves, churning with hundreds of butterflies, I decided to skip breakfast. Even though I was very excited, I was also just a bit apprehensive. Ingrid and Karin must have felt the same way because neither one ate any breakfast either. After all, this was a BIG day for all of us.

Once on the bus, I was constantly jumping up and down, pes-

A rather formal "press' portrait of the family the day I finally met Pappa

tering the driver about how much further it was as if I had never gone this route before. I must have driven him crazy, but I was simply too giddy with excitement to sit still. The bus journey seemed interminably long. After arriving in Stenungsund, we continued by train to Göteborg, where Mother, who was also coming by train but from Borås, was going to meet us at the station.

Since Father's train from Germany wasn't due to arrive until one o'clock, we had several hours to kill. We spent the better part of the morning having our hair washed and getting a haircut at a nearby beauty shop, which was a rare treat. For one thing we had only been able to wash our hair in cold salt water in Mollösund, and for another I had never even been to a hairdresser before because Ingrid had always cut my hair.

In an interview with a newspaper, this is how Mother described what we did until it was time to return to the station.

> **We had a lot to do in Göteborg and I don't know if I can describe exactly how those last few hours felt before his train arrived. But now afterwards, I can only laugh. We were just like the kind of whimsical women you read about who want to have time for so many things at the same time. We were running in so many different directions all at once. I had booked a private room for our lunch at the Hotel Eggers [situated a block from the station]… and little Gittan got her first pair of white gloves ever. (*Husmodern*, September 1955).**

It is true. Those were my very first pair of dress-up gloves, which added tremendously to the importance of this day and made me feel very grown up and proud.

A few hours later as we were on our way back to the station, Mother happened to see a flower stand where she purchased three small bouquets of summer flowers, one for each of us with which to welcome Father. When I noticed that she bought ten red roses instead of twelve for herself, I asked her why.

"Each rose represents a year your pappa and I didn't hear from each other, Gittan." I did some quick arithmetic in my head because I thought the number should have been eleven instead of ten and I told her so.

"I am counting from 1944 to 1954 when I received his first post card," Mother explained, which of course made good sense. But could it also have been because ten roses cost less than twelve, I have sometimes wondered knowing how strapped for cash Mother always was.

Finally, it was time to get back to the station. When Father's train slowly came chugging in, we waited just where the tracks ended. Because Göteborg is a terminus station, all trains have to back out when leaving, or they would ram right into the stationhouse. As soon as the train came to a stop, hundreds of passengers poured out onto the platform, which made it more difficult to discover Father immediately. Stomping impatiently from one foot to the other, I craned my neck trying to see over the throng of people.

Suddenly I heard Ingrid yell out: "There he is!"

I looked to see where she was pointing. Before anyone could stop me, I broke away and heedlessly pushed my way through the crowd, never even stopping to say "excuse me" even though I must

This photo is a much truer picture of how I adored my pappa.

have banged into a few people in my headlong dash. All I could think of was that I had to be first in reaching Father.

When he saw me come rushing towards him, he dropped his two suitcases and held his arms wide open. That was the only invitation I needed. I threw myself at him, clasped my arms around his neck, wound my legs around his body, gave him a big kiss, and clung fiercely to him as if my life depended on it. At long last I had found my pappa. I wasn't about to let him get away from me ever again!!

Even after the rest of the family joined us, I would hardly let go of him. For the next few days, I stuck like a leach to his side, afraid to let him out of my sight, sat on his knees at every opportunity or held tightly on to his hand whenever we were out walking.

Wherever he went, there I went also. When he spoke, I listened. I was like an insatiable sponge trying to soak up everything he said, never straying far from his side.

For me it was love at first sight, so to speak. I was in seventh heaven! Pappa had finally come home. From that first moment of jumping into his arms, a very special bond existed between us. Although distance would often separate us in the future, we always remained very close.

As he later pointed out in an article, I was in the most malleable and formative stage of life. He was absolutely right about this perception because from that day on, I was like clay in his hands, which he helped shape into who I became. Eager to please him, I always listened and tried to follow his advice. He was like the shining beacon guiding my steps.

An example of what I am talking about occurred two years later, just after we had moved to Toronto, Canada. Obviously, my English was still far from fluent. Therefore I was petrified when my English teacher told the class we had to give a speech. To help me out, I decided to memorize my text. But just in case I should forget it, I also wrote everything down on small index cards. When I asked Pappa to listen to me, he was horrified. He said I sounded like a robot and told me to throw those cards away and speak from my heart instead, especially since my topic was, "The day I met my father for the first time." Reluctantly, I did as he suggested. I must admit that he was right and have never regretted following his sage advice. It has stood me in good stead throughout my life.

After the initial welcome that long ago August day, we all walked over to Hotel Eggers where Mother had ordered lunch to be served in a private dining room. Our table looked so festive with its two blue and yellow Swedish flags in the center of the white-clad table and a beautiful bouquet of Swedish summer flowers on each side. Mother had ordered traditional Swedish fish dishes for both the first and second courses because Father had not eaten these since leaving Sweden in 1940.

Our first meal together as a family of five instead of only four was a memorable occasion indeed with lots of laughter and even tears, tears of happiness, that is.

At long last we were a family united instead of a family divided.

Although journalists and photographers asked if they could be present, Mother refused to let them interrupt this very special time in our family's life. This was to be our time and only us five in that dining room, she told them, but promised that they could join us later as we walked down to the boat that would take us back to Mollösund. They probably weren't too happy about Mother's decision but nonetheless honored her request.

As we were walking towards the harbor to catch the steamboat *Allebrektsund*, I was surprised to hear Father say: "This is the last time I am going let my wife pay for a dinner. And this is also the last week of the old regime, and therefore we must appoint a new chief of police for the new regime. Gittan will take up the post of minister of police and her duty will be to ensure that everything is in order in our home."

I had no earthly idea what he meant by this comment, but it made me feel very proud somehow to have been appointed to such an important sounding post in the family. In looking back on that remark today, however, I think that it may very well reflect Father's mindset at the time. After all, he had just left a totalitarian prison regime behind where everything was under strict supervision, and conditions had been extremely harsh. He probably had not had enough time to cast off the yoke of the gulag, which he had carried on his shoulders for over a decade.

Prison camp aside, during the rest of my growing up years, I learned that orderliness was very much part of my father's intrinsic nature, which he demanded of his children as well. He always set great store in doing everything in an orderly fashion, being careful and thorough, thinking things through logically, and being reasonable, all very positive characteristics that I tried to emulate as I was growing up.

A prime example of his attitude occurred shortly after his return and while we were still in Mollösund. Listening to Karin and me squabble over whose turn it was to set the table or wash the dishes, Father decided to cure us of this unpleasant but for us very normal sibling behavior. He posted a weekly schedule on the kitchen cabinet door, showing a rotation schedule of when each of us was to do the dishes, sweep the floors, set the table, clear the table, or fetch the drinking water from the well. It worked at first because we were both anxious to please him, but before long we returned to squabbling, as sisters are prone to do.

Shortly after our return to Mollösund I witnessed another example of Father's high expectations. My particular task that morning was to sweep the floor. After stooping down to check if I had done a good job, he discovered that I had simply pushed the crumbs and dust around instead of picking them up with the dust pan. In a stern voice, he then proceeded to point out to me that it was very inappropriate for me as chief of police to do such sloppy work. I must always set a good example by doing a job properly

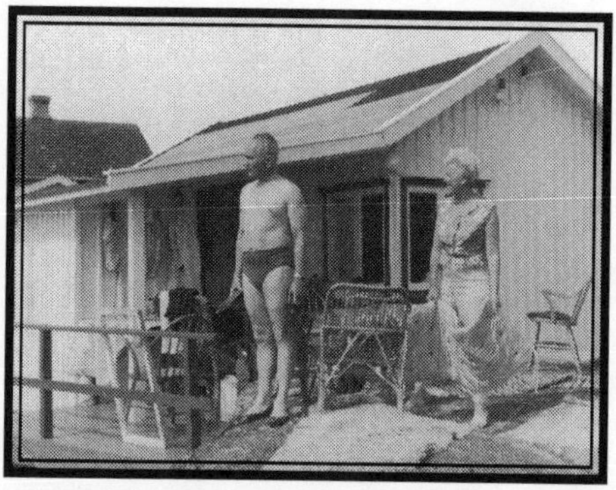

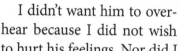

Cleaning out Kap Horn
in a later year

the first time. Chagrinned and somewhat shamefaced, I picked up the broom and carefully went back over the floor. I was very happy when it passed his next inspection with flying colors. Right afterwards I whispered softly into my mother's ear, "He is really nitpicky, isn't he, Mamma?"

I didn't want him to overhear because I did not wish to hurt his feelings. Nor did I want him to be mad at me for thinking this way about him.

I also discovered that Father had a great sense of humor, albeit a kind of humor I didn't always understand at first. One of my favorite foods was tiny shrimp, boiled directly in the seawater on the high ocean and salted down for the journey back to port. One evening not long after his return, I was just getting ready to chomp down on my toasted piece of bread stacked high with the succulent but hard and tedious to peel shrimp when I suddenly heard Father say, "How sweet of you, Gittan, to make that sandwich for me."

With the sandwich half way to my mouth, I looked at him in surprise before I quickly wolfed it down. Afterwards, shamefaced at my action, I sneaked a look at him to see if he was upset at my hasty and selfish action. Somewhat nonplussed to see him grinning from ear to ear, it dawned on me that he must have been joking.

In the years that followed I was going to learn many things from my father. My life was tremendously enriched because of his return. I discovered firsthand what a father's love for his child means, which he showed in hundreds of ways. He helped me in my studies, taught me to be organized and thorough in everything I did, listened to me, and guided me when I had to make a difficult choice. I could always count on his support and wise counsel. Knowing a father's love was something I had only been able to dream about until then. Now it was finally a reality!

CHAPTER XXIV

Interviews

Mollösund, 1955

We spent the last days of August in a heavenly bliss of togetherness as a family, eating, talking, swimming, and getting to know Father. We were at last united.

However, reporters, eager to follow up on the story about one Swedish family's happy reunion, often interrupted our days. Fortunately for them, and for me, Father was always very agreeable and didn't mind all their questions; he was more than willing to share his experiences in the Soviet Union. Perhaps in some way this telling acted as a catharsis.

Naturally, I always tried to sit right beside him whenever these reporters, often unannounced, arrived at our vacation retreat. I loved listening to him talk. It was as if I were trying to make up for the eleven years that he had been absent from my life.

One afternoon as we were sitting on the terrace below the cottage drinking coffee and munching on store-bought but very delicious cookies, a reporter asked him whether or not he had ever been in danger from any of the other prisoners.

Taking a deep breath before answering, Father stated quite calmly. "Yes, I almost got killed by one of the *blatnois,* who are thieves and murderers. A seventeen-year old young man, who had murdered his mother at the age of twelve, tried to do me in. He came at me with his two fingers at a V-angle, aiming for my eyes." He demonstrated with his fingers what he meant. "But luckily I was able to dodge him. He ended up in the *bur*, a prison within the prison."

I gasped, as did all his listeners, realizing how close he had come to being killed. Because he could tell how shocked we were,

he quickly began to explain about *blatnois.*

"They are a special kind of Russian criminal that band together like a gang and whom the Bolsheviks wanted to get rid of by sending them to slave labor camps. But they refuse to work and wage bloody battles with each other if any one dares break their internal rules of not working or of doing as little as humanly possible. The rest of us were understandably afraid of them and always tried to steer clear."

"Did you ever have any more run-ins with them, Pappa?" I asked.

"Yes and no, but never to the point where I was in any more danger from them once I learned to recognize who and what they were. They were people who had often been mistreated in early life because of the deplorable conditions in the Soviet Union and its totalitarian system of government. That is why I must emphasize that I certainly don't hate the Russian people and neither must you, Gittan." He paused slightly before continuing to tell us about some other experiences to prove his point.

"Just as these *blatnois* were bad, I found equally many if not more 'good' Russians, like the young female doctor, who took pity on me when I was in the punishment camp after the Vorkuta Revolt in 1953, where writing was strictly prohibited. She smuggled a postcard to me so that I could write home. She could have been severely punished if she had been caught. If it hadn't been for her kindness, you would never have received that first postcard from me. Then, how long would it have been before you heard that I was still alive?" He looked pointedly at Mother and us three girls, who all nodded to show that we understood what he meant.

Remembering that first postcard, I, for one, resolved never to hate the Russians for keeping my father from me for so long but to find out as much as I could about Russia, its people and its history. What happened to him left me with this burning desire to understand the Russian mindset. As time went on, I began to read books set in Russia hoping this would give me insight into why things happened the way they did.

"Encountering human kindness such as that became the highlights of my otherwise dreary existence." Father turned back to everyone sitting on the crowded terrace. He had our full attention. "I have many more such instances. Take the Ukrainian doctor, for example, who was a prisoner himself. He saved my life when I first arrived in Vorkuta by making sure that I was assigned to work in the infirmary instead of in the coalmines. I was still so weak from the pneumonia and from losing so much weight—I only weighed about 45 kilos [100 pounds]—that if it weren't for his intervention on my behalf, I would more than likely have perished. Many other fellow Russian prisoners also supported me when I was suffering from pneumonia on the journey to Siberia and could hardly put one foot in front of the other marching through the sub-zero temperatures of the tundra. If it weren't for people like that, life in Siberia would have been much, much worse. Living under these harsh and almost inhumane conditions, a person either gives up or becomes somewhat of a philosopher or a stoic, while just trying to get through each day. I chose the latter.

"No, I certainly don't blame the Russian people for what happened to me. Instead, I squarely put the blame on the Soviet Communist regime who thinks nothing of condemning their own people, as well as people from other countries, to long prison terms in slave labor camps, while more often than not basing their charges on minor or trumped up infractions, all without any due process. There are probably more than twenty and perhaps even as many as forty million people illegally imprisoned and condemned in Soviet slave labor camps," he concluded.

That was a very long answer. No one even tried to interrupt. In fact, no one spoke for a long time after he finished his monologue. How could we? We were aghast at the horrors Father must have lived through.

Many of the newspaper articles that appeared after these interviews also commented on how remarkable it was that Father's Swedish was so fluent and accent free considering that he was not a native Swede but Austrian by birth. They quoted him as saying that he gave lessons in Swedish to his fellow prisoners because they had to have something to occupy them in order not to deteriorate mentally. He also stated that he always made a point of thinking in complete sentences, alternating the languages in which he thought. Some days it was German, and on other days it was Swedish or English, or even French. Sometimes he held imaginary conversations with different people in different languages, such as talking with his mother and brothers in German and with his wife and children in Swedish. He even wrote imaginary letters to each of them. This exercise helped him keep his sanity, he claimed. That was the only way he knew not to forget anybody or anything. During his long years in captivity he also became fluent in Russian.

Interestingly enough, Father continued to promote this habit of keeping each language alive and separate once we began to move from one country to another. He didn't like it if any of us inadvertently mixed our languages, that is used an English or German word while speaking Swedish for example, because it was easier or quicker than to think of the appropriate expression. This was sheer laziness on our part, he said. If such a slip-up happened, the culprit sometimes had to deposit some coins in a family piggy bank as penance depending on where it happened. We also used to alternate languages during mealtime, Swedish one day followed by German or English the next time. This probably explains why everyone back home in Europe is always astonished at how fluent I still am in both Swedish and German even though I have been living in the U.S. since 1969.

Of special interest to the Swedish press was whether or not Father knew anything about Raoul Wallenberg, the Swedish diplomat, who disappeared during World War Two in Budapest. Sweden still believes that the Soviets captured him as he was helping thousands of Jews escape deportation to concentration camps, but so far the Soviets have disclaimed having any knowledge of him and his whereabouts. Therefore, all negotiations for his immediate release were completely stalled.

"Did you ever meet Mr. Wallenberg?" a reporter asked one day.

"No, not personally. But I can tell you that while I was still in Lefortovo Prison, back in 1947 or '48, I heard through the system of knocks on the cell wall, which we prisoners developed as a secret way of communicating with each other, that a Swedish diplomat was being held in a few cells away from mine. His name was Raoul Wallenberg. Since everyone in neighboring cells knew by now that I was married to a Swedish woman, they thought this might be of particular interest to me."

He then went on to say he had heard that Wallenberg had been arrested in Budapest while driving around in a car flying the Swedish flag. He had been there on behalf of the Swedish Red Cross trying to save as many Jews as possible. In spite of claiming diplomatic immunity, Wallenberg had been arrested and taken to Lefortovo Prison in Moscow, the same prison where he himself had been held for six years. This had not been relayed to him all at once but over time because the prisoners had to be very careful not to be caught communicating in this way. "It certainly helped pass the time though, which always weighed heavily on our hands."

"Have you heard what happened to him since?" The same reporter asked.

"I only heard about him one more time in one of the transit camps on my way back home, but I am sorry to say that I don't recall exactly what I heard. Maybe it will come back to me later. If he is alive, he is probably in Vladimir, east of Moscow, which is a prison for diplomats. Or he could be in Sverdlovsk, another place where diplomatic prisoners are held," I heard Father answer.

Over fifty years have passed since that particular interview with my father took place. What happened to Raoul Wallenberg is still a mystery that the Wallenberg family and the Swedish government continues to investigate. To this day the Russians continue to deny

Min döde man lever. V.

För Husmodern av Rut Gottlieb återberättat av Sonja Magnusson

Så blev det sant

Min Roland, barnens älskade Vati, är hemma. Det är så underbart att jag ännu ibland frågar mig om jag inte snart ska vakna och finna allt som förut, all ängslan, hopp, förtvivlan. Men Roland finns här hos oss och jag behöver bara sträcka ut handen så rör jag vid honom. Efter nästan tolv år får vi åter leva tillsammans. Den blev sann, drömmen om hemkomsten, som jag tröstat mig med alla dessa år.

Han kom till Sverige lördagen den tjugonde augusti. Ingi, vår nittonåriga dotter som varit nere i Österrike hos honom, hade kommit hem (Forts. på nästa sida)

having any knowledge of the Swedish diplomat wrongfully taken prisoner in 1944.

Another frequently asked question during those early days after his return was whether or not the Soviets ever tortured him. His response seldom varied. "In the beginning, I was subjected to nightly interrogations. They were pure torture both psychologically as well physically even though I was never actually beaten.

My biggest problem was that I was never allowed to sleep longer than an hour or two at a time and then always with a bare light bulb shining down in my face. On those nights when I wasn't interrogated, I had a hard time adjusting because I never knew when to expect to be taken back to the interrogation room. As a result I was never able to relax into the deep sleep phase that is so essential to all human beings to function properly. A severe fatigue began to set in, which was underscored by too little nourishing food, certainly something I can no longer complain about." Father grinned as he glanced at the table filled with all kinds of pastries and cookies.

Surreptitiously, I squeezed his hand and whispered softly in his ear, "Aren't you glad, Pappa, that you have all the food you want now?"

He smiled down at me and nodded before he continued to tell his attentive audience what his life in prison had been like. "As the months turned into years, I grew less and less alert for lack of sleep and food. What was worse for me was that it also became harder to discern what the interrogators wanted of me or what they would infer from my answers and whether these answers might ultimately hurt me."

"Do you think your answers in the end made a difference?" the reporter wanted to know.

"Perhaps. For instance, the fact that I had learned Swedish as a child when I was sent to Sweden after World War One probably factored into the sentence I was eventually given."

"What do you mean? How could that possibly have played a role?"

His audience, me included, waited with bated breath for his answer.

"For one thing, I was sentenced to twenty-five years of hard labor for espionage. Their claim was that I had been trained from a very young age to speak foreign languages, such as Swedish. That of course was far from the truth. The only reason I spoke Swedish was because a Swedish family had kindly invited me to spend the summer with them right after World War One was over. Besides, I was not the only Austrian child treated in this generous and kind fashion." He paused and looked around at his listeners, who were fascinated by what he was telling.

"Part of the Soviet methodology was deprivation, whether in the form of food, sleep, exercise or cleanliness," he then continued. "As far as the food was concerned, it was awful and never sufficient or rich enough with vitamins and protein to keep any of us prisoners from being undernourished. Gnawing hunger pangs were my constant companions. I was just barely given enough food to keep me from total starvation and death, which in essence amounted to physical torture. That was why I was just a walking skeleton by the time I arrived in Siberia."

How could anyone have survived under those conditions? It was incomprehensible to me! I had certainly never known any real hunger and don't know how I would have reacted if I had. And yet here was Father sitting in front of us, alive and well, telling us how he had almost starved to death. Amazing!

Another reporter finally broke the awed silence. "What about exercise? Were you ever able to go outside while you were still at the Lefortovo Prison in Moscow?"

"No, not really, not unless one can call the occasional ten minute solitary walk in a minuscule enclosed prison yard exercise where I could hardly even tell that I was in the open air. The few feet of open sky above was the only daylight I saw and then only about every five days. Otherwise my light consisted of the eternally burning bare electric light bulb dangling from a wire high up in my windowless cell. That infrequent walk into the exercise yard, the walks to and from the interrogation rooms, and pacing around my seven by nine feet cell were the only forms of physical activity for six years."

"What else did you do to make the time pass?" the reporter wanted to know next.

"I was able to read many books, which helped me forget my virtual non-existence in that dreary, dank, and tiny prison cell. It became a source of true escapism for me. Thankfully, Lefortovo apparently had access to an extensive collection of books in several different languages, which were made available to us on a 'request for' only basis. We couldn't go to the library, of course, but had to tell the guards what we wanted to read. I learned Russian, by the way, by asking for books I had already read in English or German. Knowing what the books said in those languages, and having studied some Russian at the university already, helped me learn it that much more quickly and easily. Having also spent three years in Bulgaria, where the same Cyrillic alphabet is used, didn't hurt either."

Just as I was on my way to go for a dip in the ocean during one of our few remaining days in Mollösund, I happened to see a stranger coming through our neighbor's gate. That must be a reporter I thought, dressed like he was in his white shirt, sports jacket and tie, much too formal for a visit to a fishing village. When he asked me if this was where Roland Gottlieb lived, I nodded eagerly and showed him the way to our cottage. Of course, I didn't get my swim in that day because I didn't want to miss any of Father's answers to the man's questions. I still had so much to learn about his time in Siberia.

This time I found out that one of Father's more pleasant pastimes in Vorkuta was to reflect upon the happier days before all his troubles began. He said that he had always been a deep thinker and philosophizer. What really peaked my curiosity was when I heard Mother's say, "I can attest to that" and saw a secret kind of wink pass between them. I did not understand it at the time, but nonetheless, it was there for all to see.

It was not until many years later that I understood what that wink actually meant. I could hardly believe how philosophical rather than romantic Father sounded in the letters he wrote to Mother during their five year long engagement period in the early 1930s. He filled page after page with talking about his philosophy of life and his view of the world affairs and what he hoped to accomplish in life. All that was not bad in and of itself, but I didn't think it was exactly topics for love letters either.

"Ruth is absolutely right!" I now heard Father respond to Mother. "That is why it was quite natural for me to try to figure out how it was possible to have ended up in such a miserable hellhole when all I had ever wanted in life was to live harmoniously with my beloved Ruth and to bring up our children to become happy, healthy,

and well-educated persons. I tried to picture what my children might look like now, especially little Birgitta, whom I had never seen. I am so happy that I now know! I always wondered whom she favored, her mother or me. When I finally received a photo of my three girls in 1955, I could immediately see that she looked just like her mother, which gladdened my heart." Father looked directly at me, grinning from ear to ear.

I was very happy that I had stayed home that afternoon instead of going swimming. His words warmed my heart and gave me a fuzzy feeling all over.

He then went on to say that what bothered him the most was that he didn't know what had become of us. He constantly worried about whether we had survived the war and if so, where we were. Had we managed to get back to Sweden? It also worried him not knowing whether his friend, Erland Uddgren in Sofia, had been able to get word to his Ruth about what had happened to him. Did we even know that he was still alive and where he was? "A thousand questions plagued me day and night, consuming me with constant worry. You have no idea what torture that was for me!"

A hush fell after this last statement. How he must have suffered!

But Father wasn't done yet. "What was worse than all the interrogations was that for two years after the initial two with constant nightly ones, I was left completely alone. No one came for me anymore. Total silence! I thought I had been completely forgotten and forsaken. I couldn't help but wonder if I was simply going to rot away in prison just like the Count of Monte Cristo in the adventure novel by the French author, Alexandre Dumas. I felt a great affinity with this particular hero, who was also tossed into prison for no reason whatsoever and nearly died there.

"At first I was relieved when no one came for me in the middle of the night, but after a while I almost began to long for those times to return. I had no idea why I was still being held, especially once I heard in 1946 that the war was over. Thank goodness I had cellmates even though they came and went."

The reporter followed this lengthy answer with another question. "Did you like having different cellmates?"

"Yes, I did because it helped relieve some of the boredom and monotony. New cellmates always served as new sources of information, which gave rise to different topics of conversations. Some of my cellmates were not always as nice or friendly as others, just like in real life. All the same, it added some variety to my otherwise very dull and dreary existence. I would have gone absolutely crazy from loneliness if it hadn't been for those cellmates."

Everyone, who listened to him talk about his years as a POW, could not help but wonder how anyone could possibly live through such conditions. Happily for us he survived to tell about it although not all at once but over time.

Leaving the subject of the past, the reporter now turned to the present. He wanted to know what Father's plans were for the future.

"Before coming to Sweden, I was in contact with the German Foreign Office in Bonn. After examining my personnel file, which by some miracle was not lost during the war, I am going to be reinstated and will be given one year's paid leave of absence to allow me to recover from my ordeal of the past eleven years. Besides going to Bad Neuenahr for a paid three-week long health cure, I plan to spend the rest of the time with my family in Borås. I want to help my wife all I can, ease the burden she has carried for so many years, and spend time with my three wonderful daughters. We have a lot of catching up to do."

Father was absolutely right about that. We smiled and nodded in unison although I also saw Mother surreptitiously wiping away a tear.

CHAPTER XXV

Fulfilled

1955—

When the eventful summer of 1955 came to an end, we all returned to our city life in Borås where a new school year started for Karin and me. Mother went back to her job at the Chamber of Commerce while Father began a round of speaking engagements in various Swedish cities, which kept him very busy. Apparently, in the eyes of the Swedish people, his story was so extraordinary that they were eager to hear firsthand about it and not just through the newspapers and magazines. As a result he was very much in demand and was sometimes even gone overnight.

A week after our return to the city, Ingrid, having graduated that spring, packed her bags to depart for Stockholm. She was going to take care of my summer friend Birran and her younger brother Anders while their parents went to the United States for a month, partly on business and partly for pleasure. Ingrid would thus gain the necessary practical experience outside the home required for entry to the Kindergarten Teacher Training Program although she ended up going to nursing school instead.

Father's return home brought many changes. Although the major ones did not occur until almost a year later, many minor ones manifested themselves almost immediately. For one thing, when I returned home from school I often found him preparing supper in the kitchen or vacuum cleaning and dusting. It was strange at first to see him perform these household duties that Mother or Ingrid had always done before. I often heard him laughingly refer to himself as the new household *factotum*, but we soon got used to this new way of operating. Mother seemed happy and thankful that Father didn't mind doing these mundane but necessary chores. That must have been what he meant when he told the reporter that he wanted to ease the burden on Mother.

I also became aware that money no longer seemed to be as much of an issue now that Father was receiving a monthly salary from the Foreign Office. This was brought home to me when he took me to a fancy dress shop one day, something Mother had never been able to afford. While I reveled in trying on one outfit after the other, he sat contentedly watching me and smiling in approval at my prancing about and modeling for him. I was in seventh heaven when he told me I could choose any two outfits I wanted. As a teenager I found that it was always great to have Father along because I always ended up getting more than originally planned. He was generous to a fault.

Another big change was seeing Father sitting at the desk writing letters instead of Mother if he wasn't cooking dinner or doing some other household chore. When I asked him why he was writing so many letters, he replied that these letters were to his comrades from Vorkuta. "We went through so much together. Therefore, I want to hear how they are doing now that they are back home again just like they want to know the same thing about me."

"You must have a lot of friends, Pappa?"

"I sure do, Gittan. These are some of the best and bravest men I have ever known. We shared many hardships during those long years in the Soviet Union. Some of these people I am writing to, though, don't know me or I them because they are the relatives of comrades who haven't returned from Siberia yet and begged me to contact their families as soon as I could if I was released before they were."

"But isn't it hard to write to people you don't even know, Pappa?"

"Yes, it is, but I am doing it anyway because I think it will help them to hear about their sons and fathers, just like it helped your mamma to hear about me from those POWs who returned home before I did."

Sitting quietly by Father's side while he continued to fill page after page with his beautiful handwriting, I mulled over his answer. Yes, had it not been for all those letters Mother received from complete strangers, we would never have heard anything about him at all. Mother would have remarried and I would now be living in Stockholm with a stepfather instead of my real father. I was glad that Father was writing all those letters.

Pappa got together with fellow POWs from Siberia every year until he died. This was taken at their first reunion in 1956.

A few days later when I saw him busily writing away at the desk again, I asked if he was writing to another one of those friends from Vorkuta.

"No, Gittan, this time it is a letter to the German Foreign Office. I am writing about our change in citizenship status. This does not only involve my becoming German again but also the rest of you, except for Ingrid, of course. It is a very slow process that involves a lot of writing and filling in forms on my part."

"Why is Ingrid not going to become German?" I wanted to know. This was news to me.

"Because she is staying in Sweden to begin nursing school next fall," Father replied patiently. "It wouldn't be practical for her to change her citizenship."

One of the more important changes, as far as I was concerned, was that Father was usually waiting for me nowadays when I came home from school at three o'clock. When he greeted me with a hug and a kiss, I felt very secure and very much loved.

I was no longer alone in the apartment. This was a totally new experience because Mother never came home from work until after five o'clock and my sisters always arrived long after I did.

I also discovered that I even enjoyed doing homework because I could have Pappa's undivided attention. In the past, I had often been careless and shirked it, either claiming I had none when

Mother asked or telling her I had already completed it. These days I usually got right down to it because I wanted to stay close to Pappa. I really looked up to him and thought he was the smartest person in the world. He just knew everything, and I wanted to grow up to be just like him.

Sometimes, however, he could become a little too painstakingly slow and thorough in his explanations, which had a tendency to frustrate not only me but also Karin. He could go on ad infinitum to our exasperation. Eventually this led to a saying in our family: *Warum es einfach machen wenn man es kompliziert machen kann?* Why do something in a simple way if you can make it complicated?" Over time, I learned how to navigate around such tricky situations. If I had other plans for the rest of the day, I avoided going to him for help when sensing it might lead to lengthy discussions or explanations.

Our lives also became much more hectic, fun and interesting. The public's interest in our family did not die down immediately after Father came to Sweden. On the contrary! Reporters continued to drop by in the evenings if my parents weren't out gallivanting around eating dinner with friends or having dinner parties at home, all of which kept them very busy.

Every time another article appeared in the paper, I enjoyed moments of fame at school. It really upset my nemesis Ann-Margaret that I was the center of attention with everyone vying for my friendship rather than paying attention to her. I loved every minute of it. Who wouldn't have? Basking in the limelight, I took every opportunity to rub her nose in it. Perhaps it was not right to be so gleeful, but I considered it payback for all the taunts I had suffered at her hands throughout the years.

When November arrived, I was unhappy to see Father pack his suitcase and leave for Bad Neuenahr as planned. Only the knowledge that this would help make him healthier and that he would soon return made it easier to wave goodbye at the railway station. The house felt suddenly very empty. I really missed him.

Before leaving, he extracted a promise from me that I would write to him and let him know how I was doing at school. Faithfully, as promised, I wrote detailed letters at least once a week, which turned into a lifelong habit whenever we were apart. Today I am thankful because all these lengthy letters—I am my father's daughter after all—serve as the diary I never managed to keep but always planned to. What is also fascinating to observe are the changes that took place in my thinking as I grew from a pre-teen to an adolescent, from a university student to a wife and mother.

Shortly before Christmas Father finally returned to Borås from Germany. I almost fell backwards in my surprise when I saw all his many newly acquired suitcases. He had left with only two but returned with six! He must have bought everything that was on my long wish list, I thought, and hoped that one of them also contained the guitar I had ardently wished for. Judging by the size of the suitcases, it was doubtful somehow.

From then until Christmas Eve I pestered Father about the guitar. He just grinned and pretended that he did not know that I had asked for one. One evening while he was gone to a dinner party with Mother, I decided to sneak into his room. Heaps of wrapped presents lay piled high on the bed. Wanting to see which ones were for me, I discovered to my great chagrin that all the packages were labeled in Russian and that none were big enough to hold a guitar. I fervently hoped he had hidden it somewhere. I was still holding out that hope when I opened my last present on Christmas Eve. When a small plastic toy guitar was inside the package instead, I completely lost it. Bursting into tears, I cried out in anguish, "That is not what I asked for, Pappa. I wanted a REAL guitar, not a toy guitar! Didn't you understand that?"

In my utter and complete desolation, I did not notice that Father was giving Karin a wink and a nod to go into his room. Suddenly Karin was standing in front of me holding a real guitar in her hands. In the blink of an eye my tears were replaced by shouts of happiness as I grabbed my precious new guitar from her hands. When I heard everyone laughing, it dawned on me that Father had played one of his small practical jokes on me. Because the joke was on me, I did not think it was a bit funny.

In retrospect, I am not so sure that playing such a joke was the wisest thing for Father to do this early on in our newfound relationship. I absolutely worshiped the ground he walked on and thought he could do no wrong. It was simply too much for my young and fragile psyche to handle and understand such a joke. By the time I joined some of my friends for a first guitar lesson in the New Year, I had forgiven him his little faux pas although obviously it made an indelible impression on me.

In May of 1956 Father became restless and was eager to get back to work. When I asked him why he was leaving so soon, he told me that he felt it was necessary in order to catch up on all the time he had lost during the last eleven years. "Besides, I need to find an apartment for us so that you, Mamma and Karin can join me in Bonn. The sooner I get down there the better. I have been warned that the wait for an apartment can be very long, perhaps as long as up to six months."

He went on to explain in his by now very familiar long-winded fashion. "You have to understand that because Berlin is a divided city today, The Federal Republic of Germany did not think it wise to have its capital in an area surrounded by the Soviet sector. Instead, it chose Bonn, a sleepy little university town. This has resulted in a great influx of government employees all needing a place to live. But erecting so many new apartment houses takes time and the queues for an apartment are long. By going down now, maybe we will get one sooner rather than later. I also have to look at all the schools to determine which one will be best for you and Karin."

Although I was excited about moving to Germany and finally being able to learn to speak German, something I had wanted to do for a very long time, I was not quite ready to let Father go by himself and leave us behind.

The night before he was leaving, I whispered as I snuggled up close to him, "Pappa, I wish they would hurry up and build our apartment so that we can move to Germany with you. I really don't want you to go without us. Please wait for us to go with you, Pappa," I pleaded. "Won't you miss us? I know I will miss you terribly."

"I know you will, Gittan, and I will miss you too! In the meantime, promise me that you will work hard at school so that you will get a good report card. Before you know it, we will be back together again. I promise!" He kissed me tenderly and hugged me hard.

The retirement home in Mollösund built on the site where the old cottage once stood

I clung to that promise until we joined him in Germany when school started in the fall of 1956 and our new apartment on Lahnweg 34 was finally ready for us to move into.

At first, I was very sad leaving Sweden and my friends, but the prospect of a life full of adventure, seeing the world, and learning new languages filled me with great excitement and anticipation. We only stayed in Bonn for little over a year, during which time I became a German citizen for the second time, learned to speak German, and attended a Gymnasium, which is not intended for sports, but rather is the name for secondary schools that entitle the graduate, after nine years of study, to continue at a university.

Just before Christmas 1957, Father was transferred to the German Consulate in Toronto, Canada, where I learned to speak English and French. When he was transferred back to Germany in 1963, I wanted to stay on in Canada. However, the long and the short of it is that I returned with my parents to Bonn instead, where I completed my Gymnasium education two years later before returning to Sweden to attend the University of Stockholm.

All in all it took fifteen years before I could fulfill my dream of attending the University of Stockholm, not because I was stupid or had failed classes. No, several moves from country to country, changing schools and instructional languages were the reason behind the delay. But once again I proved to be my father's daughter because I never gave up on my dream.

Before retiring to our beloved Mollösund in 1975, Father also served six years as the German Consul General in Atlanta, Georgia, where his jurisdiction stretched over six southern states. After graduating from the university in 1969, I decided to join my parents in Georgia, where I began my teaching career.

When my parents left Georgia, I stayed in America, eventually becoming an American citizen after falling in love and marrying an American. My husband Bill and I now live in North Carolina where we raised our son.

In the meantime, Ingrid completed her nurse's training and married a Swiss American a few years later. His work took them all over the world before they decided to retire to North Carolina. Karin, on the other hand, after a three-year stay with us in Toronto, moved back to Sweden, where she also trained as a nurse before marrying a Swede.

Mother became a very happy stay at home wife and mother, who loved nothing better than to help her diplomat husband entertain. She also wrote a book about entertaining; *Help for the Helpless Hostess*, held classes on the subject, and did a six-part series on it on PBS in Georgia in 1974. In 1977 she passed away from breast cancer while Father lived on twelve more years missing Mother every day.

Mamma & Pappa in 1976

Glossary

Key: (S)=Swedish (G) =German (R)=Russian
(F)=French (B)=Bulgarian (L)=Latin

Annelundsskogen (S): the Annelunds Forest
Auswärtiges Amt (G): The Foreign Office or State Department
Året Runt(S): The Year Round (weekly magazine)
ångbåten (S): the steamboat or steamship
badhuset (S): public indoor swimming pool
bakelse (S): slice of cake
banitsas (B): flaky cheese and meat-filled pastries
banja (R): bath house
bitte (G): please
blatnois (R): a very dangerous Russian criminal
bollebygdssoffa (S): a type of wooden bed sofa
bokmärke (S): bookmark
bur (R): a prison within the prison.
Chargé d'Affaires (F): the second man in charge at a minor embassy
Dagens Nyheter (S): The Daily News
dansbrygga(n) (S): dancing platform
dasset (S): outhouse
demokrate(n) (S): a democrat
deutscher (G): German
diplomkaufmann (G): equivalent to a an MBA degree in Economics
doppet i grytan (S): literally it means "dip in the pot" and is part of the Christmas traditions in Sweden
examensdagen (S): last day of school
Expressen (S): The Express (name of a newspaper)
einfach (G): simple
evaspegeln (S): Eve's Mirror (Mother's name for the decorated mirror she made)

fait accompli(F): established fact, something already done
falukorv (S): a type of Swedish bologna
fängelse (S): prison
fångenskap (S): prison camp
flickrummet (S): the girls' room
flickskolan (S): a secondary school for girls which does not qualify for university studies
Gasthaus (G): inn/hotel
Gasthof (G): inn /hotel
Gastwirtin (G): hotel hostess
Gemütlichkeit (G): cosyness
Gittan or Gittis(S): common abbreviated nicknames for Birgitta
Grenzpolizei (G): border police
gymnasiet (S): highschool
Handelskammaren (S): Chamber of Commerce
havreflarn (S): oatmeal cookies
Husmodern (S): The Housewife, (name of a weekly women's magazine)
ja må hon leva (S): yes, may she live… (Swedish birthday song)
joie de vivre (F): joy of life or enjoying life
jul (S): Christmas
julafton (S): Christmas Eve
julgransplundring (S): plundering or taking down the Christmas tree
julklappar(S): Christmas gifts
jultomten (S): Santa Claus
kanelbullar (S): cinnamon buns
Karusellen (S): the Carousell
Kaugummi (G): chewing gum
Kopfbahnhof (G): a station from where trains have to back out in order to continue
kåldolmar (S): stuffed cabbage rolls
knäckebröd (S): hard tack bread
krona(S): Swedish unit of money where 100 öre = 1crown
kyrkan (S): church
Liebling (G): darling
läroverket (S): secondary school that leads to university studies

lutfisk (S): ling fish that is dried to be soaked in a lye solution in preparation for the traditional Swedish Christmas meal
morbror(S): mother's brother= uncle
morfar (S): mother's father= grandfather
mormor (S): mother's mother= grandmother
moster(S): mother's sister = aunt
Mutti (G): endearing form for Mother, e.g. Mummy
Niemandsland (G): No man's land
Oma or Omama (G): grandmother
Onkel (G): uncle
Ökensandkakor (S): desert sand cookies
Öre (S): Swedish smallest unit of money, where 100 Öre=1 krona
pepparkakor (S): gingersnap cookies
persona non grata (L): unwelcome person or unacceptable diplomat
puff (S): a light puff of air
Ramnakyrkan (S): Ramna Church
Ramnaparken (S): Ramna Park
Ramnasjön (S): Ramna Lake
Reichsmark (G): unit of money in Germany before and during World War II
roliga timmen (S): the fun hour at school
ryggskottsterassen (S): "back pain" terrace
saft (S): juice or soda
secretaire (F): a type of desk
sjöbod (S): boat house
skolan (S): the school
smörgåsbord (S): a Swedish buffet
Spätheimkehrer (G): men who returned home from prison camps many years after the war was over
Svenska Dagbladet (S): The Swedish Daily (a newspaper)
tête à tête (F): intimate conversation
Unghögern (S): young conservatives
Untermensch (G): subhuman
unabkömmlich(G): indispensible
valborgsmässoafton (S): Walpurgis night celebrated on April 30th

Vati (G): endearing form for Father, e.g. daddy
värdshus(S): restaurant
vielen dank (G): many thanks or thank you very much
vitsippor (S): white wood anemone flower
Volksdeutsche (G): people of German heritage from Yugoslavia and Poland, who claimed Austrian or German citizenship.
Wienerschnitzel (G): breaded veal cutlette that origininated in Vienna

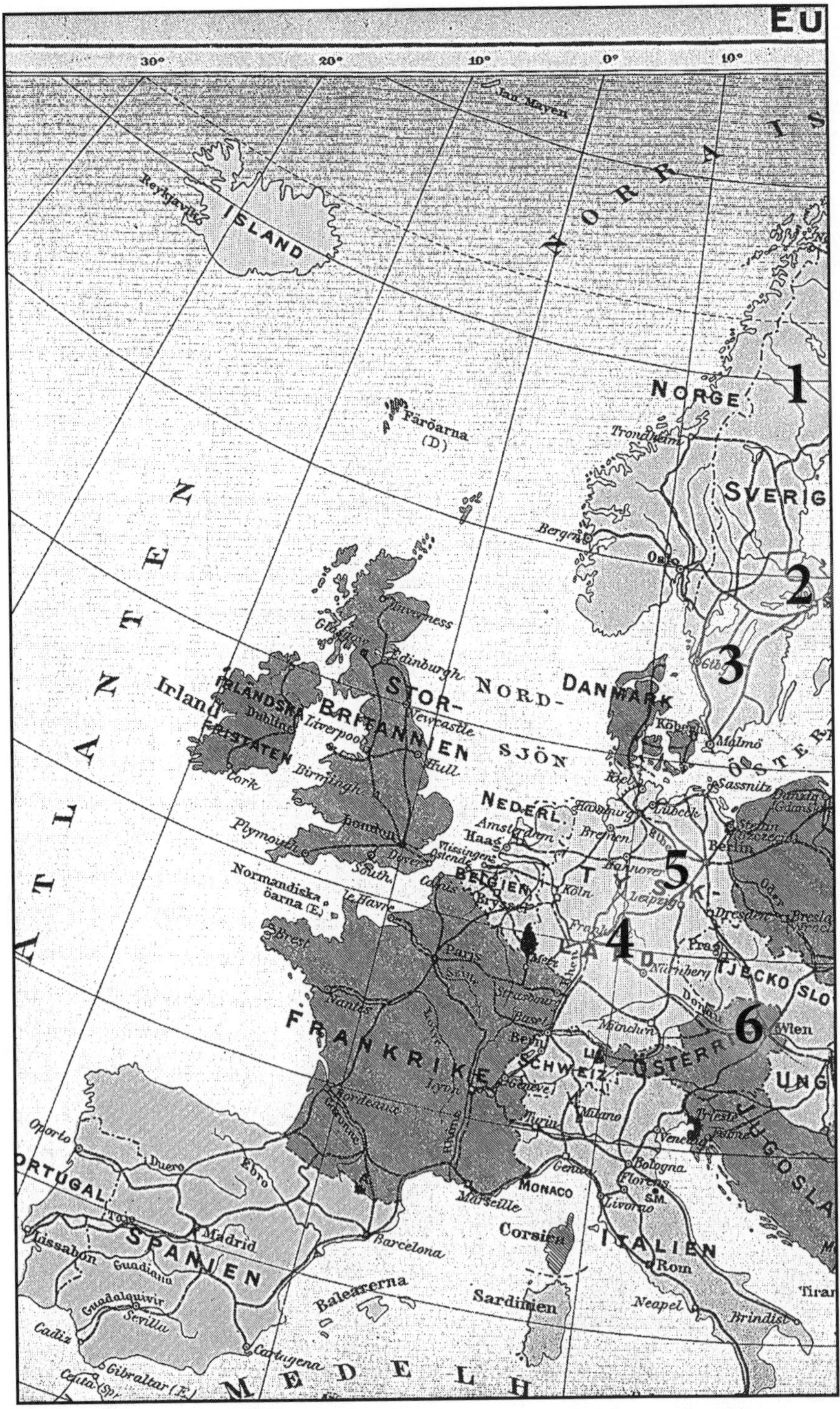
EU
30°
20°
10°
0°
10°
Jan Mayen
NORRA IS
Reykjavik
ISLAND
NORGE
1
Trondheim
Färöarna (D)
SVERIG
Bergen
Oslo
2
3
ATLANTEN
Inverness
Edinburgh
NORD-
DANMARK
Irland
IRLÄNDSKA FRISTATEN
Dublin
STOR-BRITANNIEN
Newcastle
Liverpool
SJÖN
Köbenh
Malmö
Hull
Birmingh
Cork
Kiel
Sassnitz
NEDERL.
Hamburg
Lübeck
Amsterdam
Bremen
Haag
London
Berlin
Plymouth
Dover
Vlissingen
Ostende
5
Hannover
Normandiska öarna (E)
South.
Calais
BELGIEN
Bryssel
Köln
Leipzig
Le Havre
Dresden
Brest
4
Paris
Metz
Prag
Seine
Nürnberg
TJECKO
Strasburg
Nantes
Basel
Donau
6
Wien
FRANKRIKE
Bern
München
SCHWEIZ
ÖSTERR
UNG
Loire
Genève
Lyon
Bordeaux
Trieste
Fiume
Turin
Milano
Oporto
Venedig
JUGOSLA
Duero
Rhône
Ebro
Genua
Bologna
PORTUGAL
MONACO
Florens
S.M.
Marseille
Livorno
Tajo
Madrid
Corsica
SPANIEN
Lissabon
Barcelona
ITALIEN
Guadiana
Rom
Balearerna
Sardinien
Neapel
Brindisi
Guadalquivir
Sevilla
Cadiz
Cartagena
Gibraltar (E.)
MEDELH

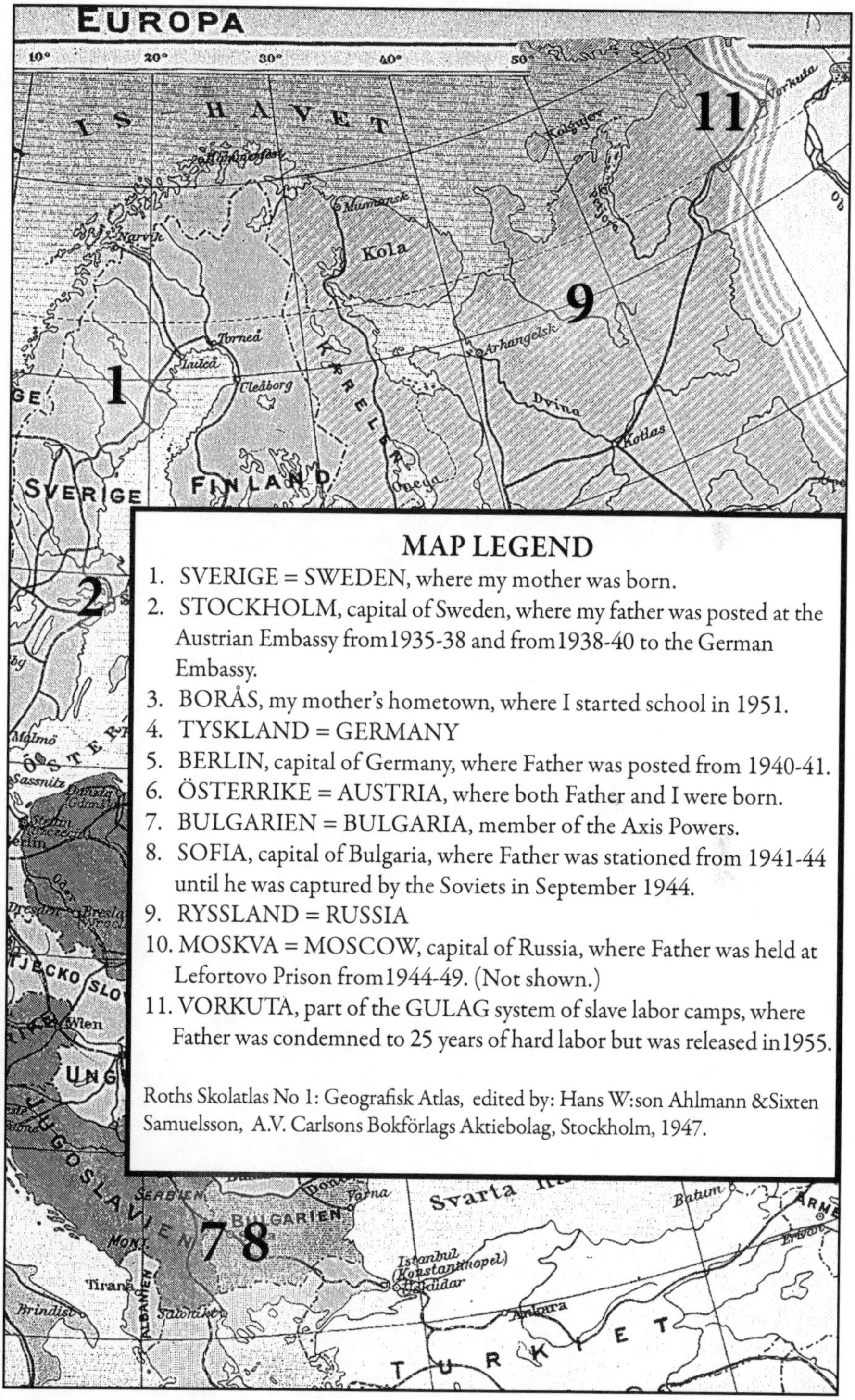

MAP LEGEND

1. SVERIGE = SWEDEN, where my mother was born.
2. STOCKHOLM, capital of Sweden, where my father was posted at the Austrian Embassy from1935-38 and from1938-40 to the German Embassy.
3. BORÅS, my mother's hometown, where I started school in 1951.
4. TYSKLAND = GERMANY
5. BERLIN, capital of Germany, where Father was posted from 1940-41.
6. ÖSTERRIKE = AUSTRIA, where both Father and I were born.
7. BULGARIEN = BULGARIA, member of the Axis Powers.
8. SOFIA, capital of Bulgaria, where Father was stationed from 1941-44 until he was captured by the Soviets in September 1944.
9. RYSSLAND = RUSSIA
10. MOSKVA = MOSCOW, capital of Russia, where Father was held at Lefortovo Prison from1944-49. (Not shown.)
11. VORKUTA, part of the GULAG system of slave labor camps, where Father was condemned to 25 years of hard labor but was released in1955.

Roths Skolatlas No 1: Geografisk Atlas, edited by: Hans W:son Ahlmann &Sixten Samuelsson, A.V. Carlsons Bokförlags Aktiebolag, Stockholm, 1947.

Munkedal den 12/4 55

Kära Vati!

Hur mår du nu efter alla 11 fängelse
åren, jag hoppas verkligen att du är
frisk kära Vati så att du inte behöver
bli sjuk nu när du kommer hem.
Det känns lite konstigt att skriva till
dig eftersom jag aldrig sett dig. Jag
gläder mig åt att Ingrid få åka med
till Bonn och få vara där nere, jag
är inte alls avundsjuk, men när jag
fick Muttis brev kände jag hur lycklig
Ingrid skulle bli. Vad roligt det ska på
alla terminer medan vi går i skolan och när
du hjälper oss med läxor jag är glad att
jag har en så snäll och duktig pappa

This is my first letter to Father that I translated beginning on page 207. The next page was only translated until I started rattling off the grades I made.

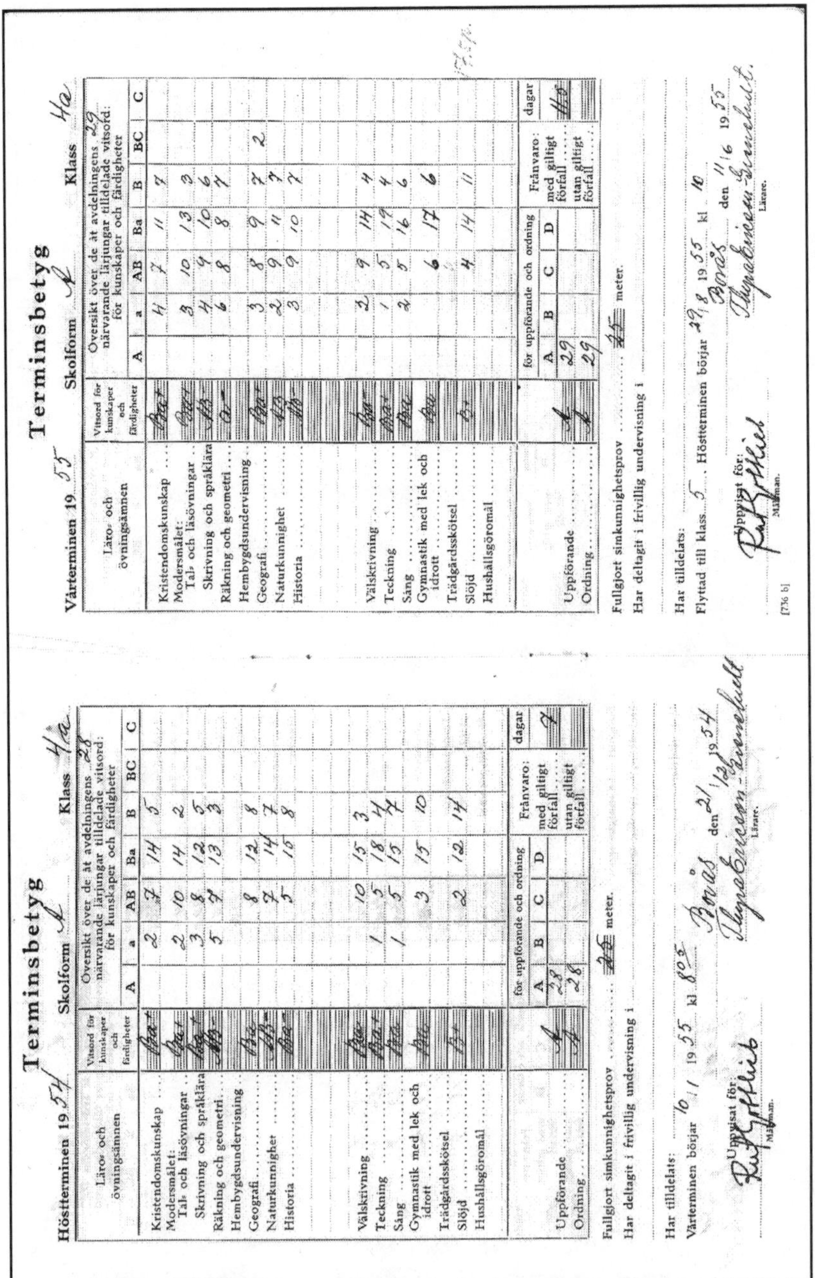

This is my 4th grade report card where "A" is the highest and "BC" means a failing grade. The first column shows what I made and the next columns indicate how many students in the class made a particular grade. Notice that no one received any "A" and only very few a "a".

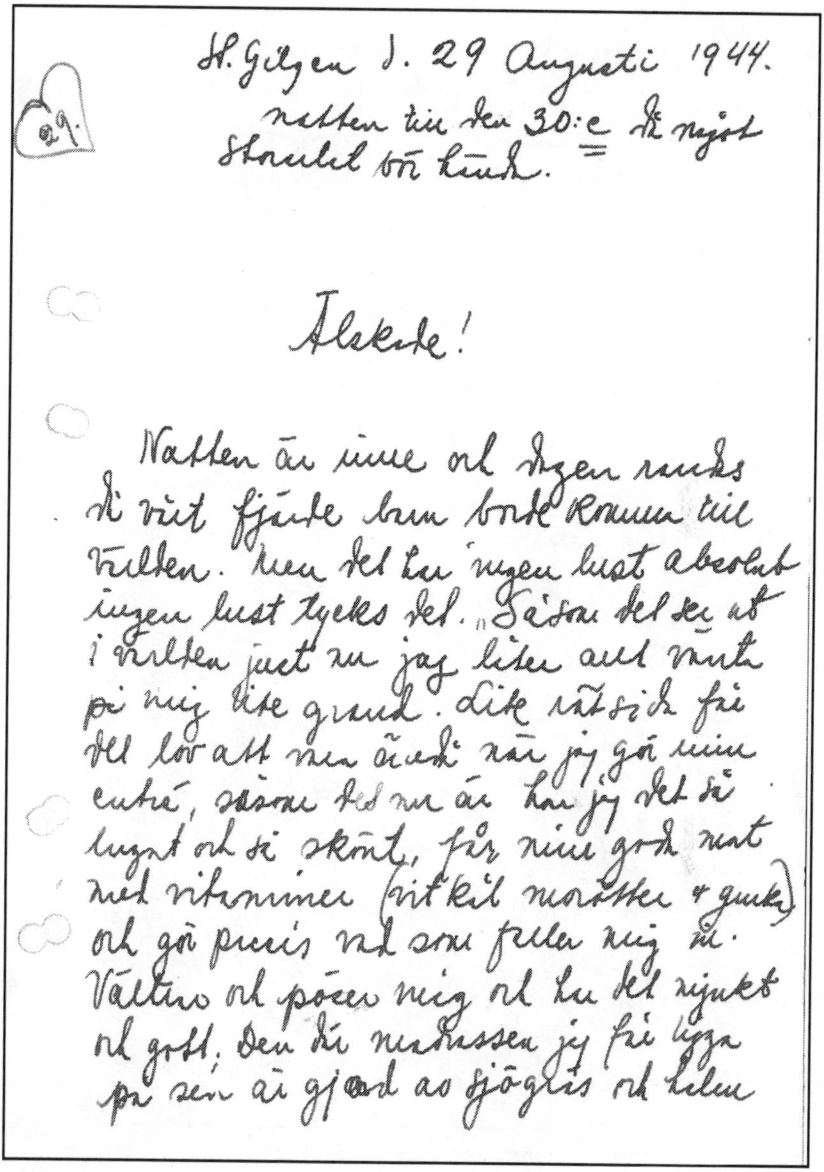

St. Gilgen d. 29 Augusti 1944.
natten till den 30:e då något
skrivet var känd.

Älskade!

Natten är inne och dagen randas
då vårt fjärde barn borde kommen till
världen. Men det har ingen lust absolut
ingen lust tycks det. "Såsom det ser ut
i världen just nu jag låter allt vänta
på mig lite grand. Lite rätt sig får
det lov att min ärende när jag gör min
entré, såsom det nu är har jag det så
lugnt och så skönt, får nice god mat
med vitaminer (vitkål morötter & gurka)
och gör precis vad som faller mig in.
Vältrar och pösar mig och har det mjukt
och gott; Den där madrassen jag får ligga
på sen är gjord av sjögräs och helen

This is the letter Mother wrote to Father the night before I was born
in which she speculates what her unborn child might be thinking and feeling.
I refer to it on page 78.

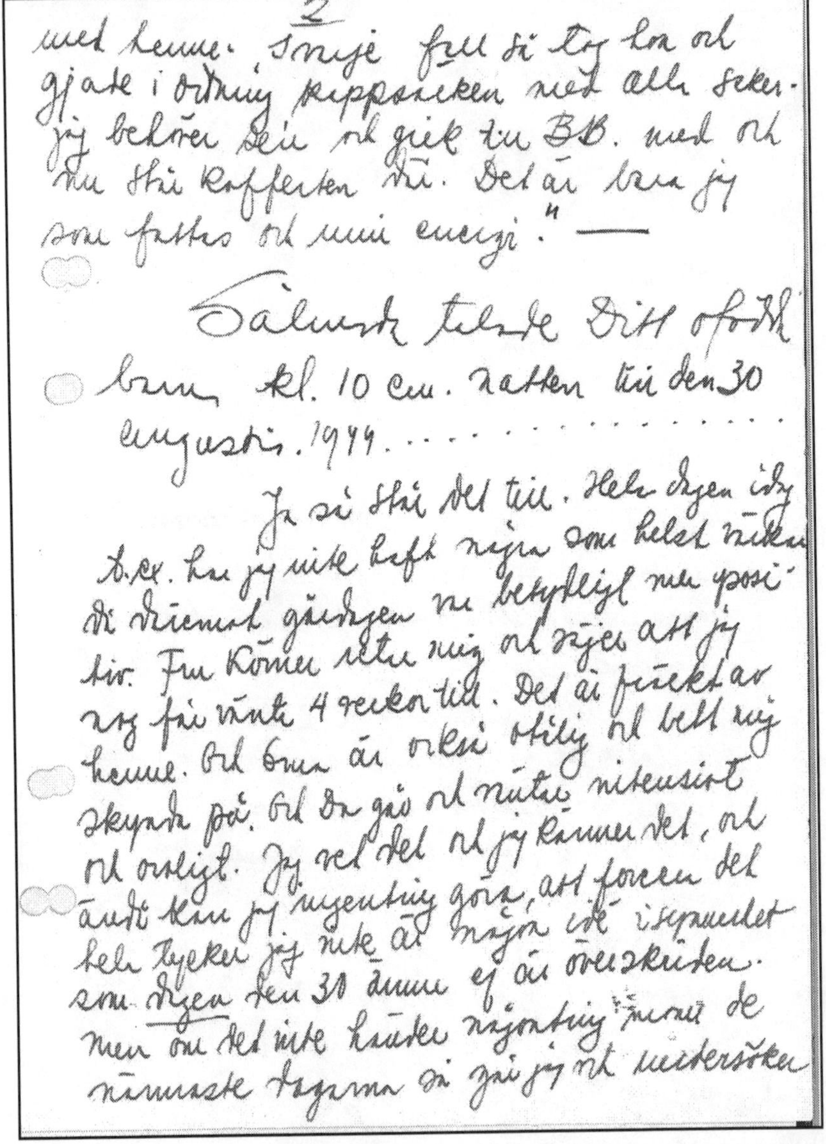
2

med henne. "Sonja fick då tag [illegible] och
gjorde i ordning kappsäcken med alla saker
jag behöver där och gick till BB. med och
nu står kofferten där. Det är bara jag
som fattas och min energi." —

Sålunda talade Ditt ofödda
barn kl. 10 em. natten till den 30
augusti. 1944 ....

Ja så står det till. Hela dagen idag
t.ex. har jag inte haft några som helst värkar
[illegible] gårdagen var betydligt mer posi-
tiv. Fru Kömer [illegible] mig och säger att jag
nog får vänta 4 veckor till. Det är [illegible]
hemma. Och barnet är också otålig och bett mig
skynda på. Och Du går och väntar intensivt
och oroligt. Jag vet det och jag känner det, och
ändå kan jag ingenting göra, att forcera det
hela tycker jag inte är någon idé i synnerhet
som dagen den 30 ännu ej är överskriden.
Men om det inte händer någonting inom de
närmaste dagarna så går jag och undersöker

Here Mother finished the letter telling my father that she had just received a letter from him, which he wrote on August 18, and that it had taken 11 days to arrive. She must not have sent this letter to him probably because I started making my entry into this world shortly afterwards. Had she sent it to him, it would not have been saved since he was trying to escape from Sofia at the time.

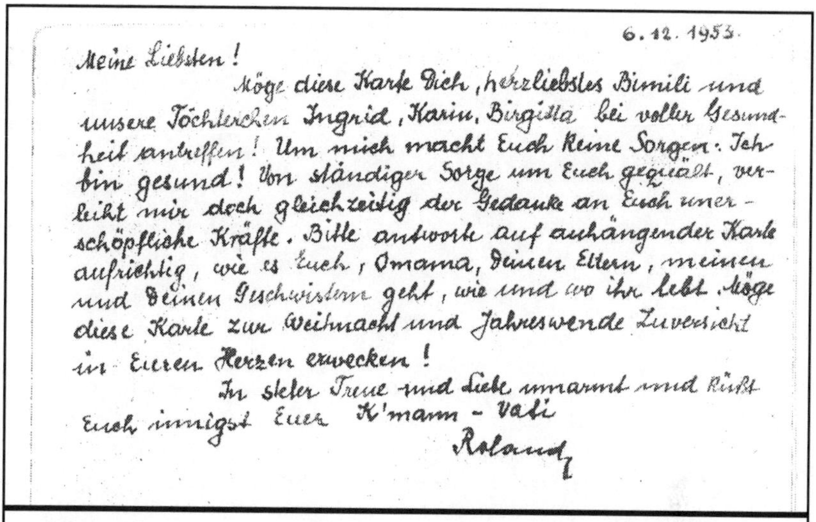
6.12.1953.

Meine Liebsten!
Möge diese Karte Dich, herzliebstes Bimili und unsere Töchterchen Ingrid, Karin, Birgitta bei voller Gesundheit antreffen! Um mich macht Euch keine Sorgen. Ich bin gesund! Von ständiger Sorge um Euch gequält, verleiht mir doch gleichzeitig der Gedanke an Euch unerschöpfliche Kräfte. Bitte antworte auf anhängender Karte aufrichtig, wie es Euch, Omama, Deinen Eltern, meinen und Deinen Geschwistern geht, wie und wo ihr lebt. Möge diese Karte zur Weihnacht und Jahreswende Zuversicht in Euren Herzen erwecken!
In steter Treue und Liebe umarmt und küßt Euch innigst Euer K'mann - Vati
Roland

This was Father's first attempt to contact us written on December 6, 1953, which is the one Mother received on her way back from Germany (also reproduced on page 157), where she had gone to interview some returning POWs about what they knew about Father, especially since he had been officially declared dead a year earlier.

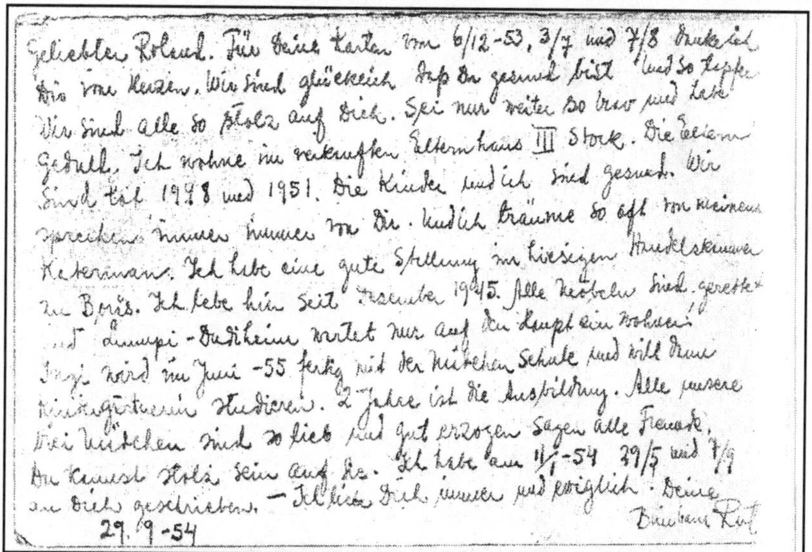
Geliebter Roland. Für Deine Karten vom 6/12-53, 3/7 und 7/8 danke ich Dir vom Herzen. Wir sind glücklich daß Du gesund bist und so tapfer. Wir sind alle so stolz auf Dich. Sei nur weiter so brav und habe Geduld. Ich wohne im verkauften Elternhaus III Stock. Die Eltern sind tot 1948 und 1951. Die Kinder und ich sind gesund. Wir sprechen immer immer von Dir. Endlich träume so oft von meinem Katerman. Ich habe eine gute Stellung im hiesigen Kunstkammer in Borås. Ich lebe hier seit Dezember 1945. Alle Möbeln sind gerettet und Lumpi-Dackelchen wartet nur auf den Hauptein wohnen! Ingi wird im Juni -55 fertig mit der Mädchen Schule und will dann Kindergärtnerin studieren. 2 Jahre ist die Ausbildung. Alle unsere drei Mädchen sind so lieb und gut erzogen sagen alle Freunde. Du kannst stolz sein auf sie. Ich habe am 1/1-54 29/5 und 7/9 an Dich geschrieben. — Ich liebe Dich immer und ewiglich. Deine Bimbam Ruf
29.9-54

This is the response to the 3rd of Father's cards, the one he wrote on August 8, 1954 and that arrived at the end of September. He never received her first responses.

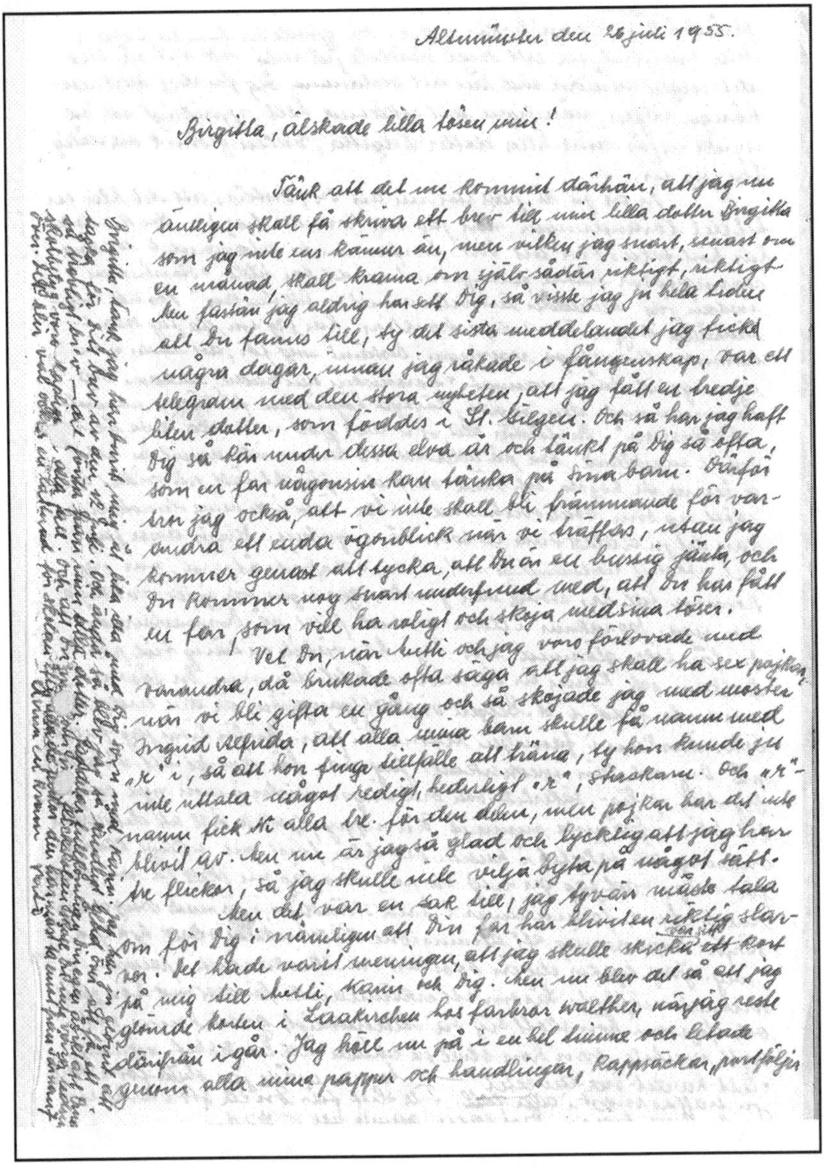

Altmünster den 26 juli 1955.

Birgitta, älskade lilla tösen min!

Tänk att det nu kommit därhän, att jag nu äntligen skall få skriva ett brev till min lilla dotter Birgitta som jag inte ens känner än, men vilken jag snart, senast om en månad, skall krama om själv sådär riktigt, riktigt. Men fastän jag aldrig har sett Dig, så visste jag ju hela tiden att Du fanns till, ty det sista meddelandet jag fick några dagar, innan jag råkade i fångenskap, var ett telegram med den stora nyheten, att jag fått en tredje liten dotter, som föddes i St. Gilgen. Och så har jag haft Dig så kär under dessa elva år och tänkt på Dig så ofta, som en far någonsin kan tänka på sina barn. Därför tror jag också, att vi inte skall bli främmande för varandra ett enda ögonblick när vi träffas, utan jag kommer genast att tycka, att Du är en bussig jänta, och Du kommer nog snart underfund med, att Du har fått en far, som vill ha roligt och skoja med sina töser.

Vet Du, när Netti och jag voro förlovade med varandra, då brukade ofta säga att jag skall ha sex pojkar när vi bli gifta en gång och så skojade jag med moster Ingrid Alfrida, att alla mina barn skulle få namn med „R" i, så att hon finge tillfälle att träna, ty hon kunde ju inte uttala något redigt, hederligt „r", Skrakarn. Och „r"-namn fick Ni alla tre. För den delen, men pojkar har det inte blivit av. Men nu är jag så glad och lycklig att jag har tre flickor, så jag skulle inte vilja byta på något sätt.

Men det var en sak till, jag tyvärr måste tala om för Dig i nämligen att Din far har blivit en riktig slarver. Det hade varit meningen, att jag skulle skicka ett kort på mig till Netti, Karin och Dig. Men nu blev det så att jag glömde korten i Laakirchen hos farbror Walther, när jag reste därifrån i går. Jag höll nu på i en hel timme och letade genom alla mina papper och handlingar, Rappsäckar, portföljer

This is the first letter Father wrote to me before I had even met him. It is written in Swedish since he knew I didn't speak German yet.
It is translated in part on page 208.

Kullavik 17.7.1955

Kära Vati!

Tack så hemskt mycket för den fina presenten. En sådan har jag gått och önskat mig länge. Hur är det där nere i Österrike? Jag längtar tills Vati och Ingrid skall komma hem så. Jag tror knappast att det är sant, att jag har fått en egen pappa igen. Det känns så konstigt.

Vati kan inte ana vad det är härligt på Mollösund. Det skall bli jätteroligt när vi alla kommer att få vara där igen. Hur är det med vädret hos [illegible] Här har det varit fint, så det(d) går knappast med ord att beskriva. Nu när jag sitter här (tro) och skriver så är det inget vidare. Det börjar mullra. Vati får ursäkta mig men jag kan inte skriva brev. Jag kastar meningarna hit och dit så att det blir en farlig röra. Nu kan jag inte skriva mera. Det är säkert. Hälsa Ingrid så hemskt mycket ifrån mig.

Hjärtliga hälsningar från Vatis mellersta dotter Karin

My sister Karin's first letter to Father written on July 17, 1955.
It is translated on page 209.

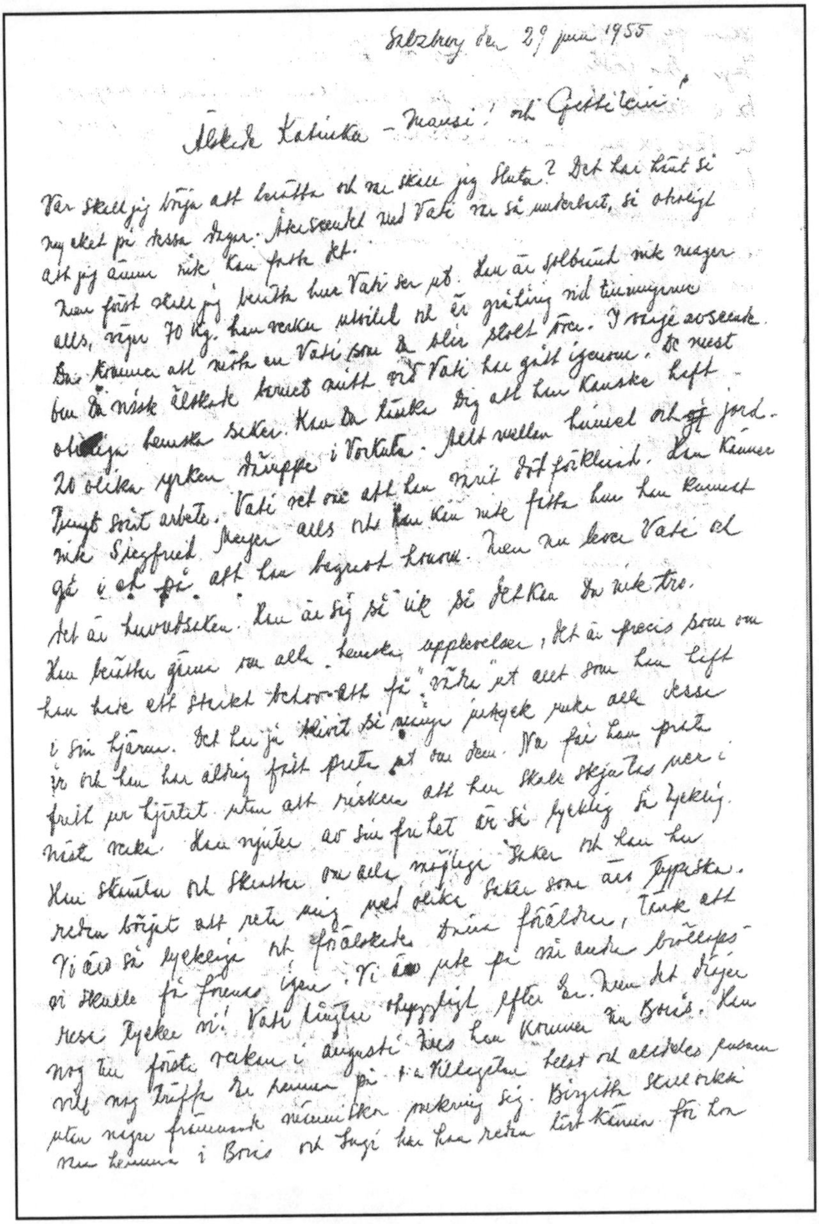

Salzburg den 29 juni 1955

Älskade Katinka-Mausi! och Gittilein!

Var skall jag börja att berätta och var skall jag sluta? Det har hänt så mycket på dessa dagar. Återseendet med Vati var så underbart, så otroligt att jag ännu inte kan fatta det.

Men först skall jag berätta hur Vati ser ut. Han är solbränd inte mager alls, väger 70 kg. han verkar utvilad och är gråhårig vid tinningarna. I övrigt avseende Du kommer att möta en Vati som du blir stolt över. Det mest [illegible] älskade trots allt vad Vati har gått igenom. Kanske haft otroliga hemska saker. Kan du tänka dig att han [illegible] 20 olika yrken [illegible] i Vorkuta. Allt mellan himmel och jord. Han känner [illegible] tungt svårt arbete. Vati vet nu att han [illegible] förklarat. [illegible] inte Siegfried Meyer alls och han kan inte fatta hur han kunnat gå i och på att han begripit honom. Men nu kan Vati och [illegible]

Det är huvudsaken. Han är sig så lik så det kan du inte tro. Han berättar gärna om alla hemska upplevelser, det är precis som om han hade ett starkt behov att få "vädra" ut allt som han haft i sitt hjärta. Det har ju blivit så mycket [illegible] alla dessa år och han har aldrig fått prata ut om dem. Nu får han prata fritt ur hjärtat utan att riskera att han skall skjutas ner i nästa vecka. Han njuter av sin frihet är så lycklig så lycklig. Han skämtar och skrattar om alla möjliga saker och han har redan börjat att reta mig med olika saker som är typiska. Tänk att vi är så lyckliga och förälskade [illegible] föräldrar, Tänk att vi skulle få fira igen. Vi är ute på vår andra bröllopsresa. Tycker ni! Vati längtar ohyggligt efter er. Men det dröjer nog till första veckan i augusti innan han kommer till Boris. Han vill nog träffa er hemma på [illegible] fullt och alldeles ensam utan några främmande människor omkring sig. Birgitta skall också [illegible] i Boris och Ingi har han redan lärt känna för han [illegible]

This is Mother's letter addressed to both Karin = Katinka-Mausi, just another of many nicknames for her and to me, Gittilein, one of my German nicknames. She wrote it from Salzburg on June 29, 1955, just a few days after my parents' reunion. It is partially translated on page 205.

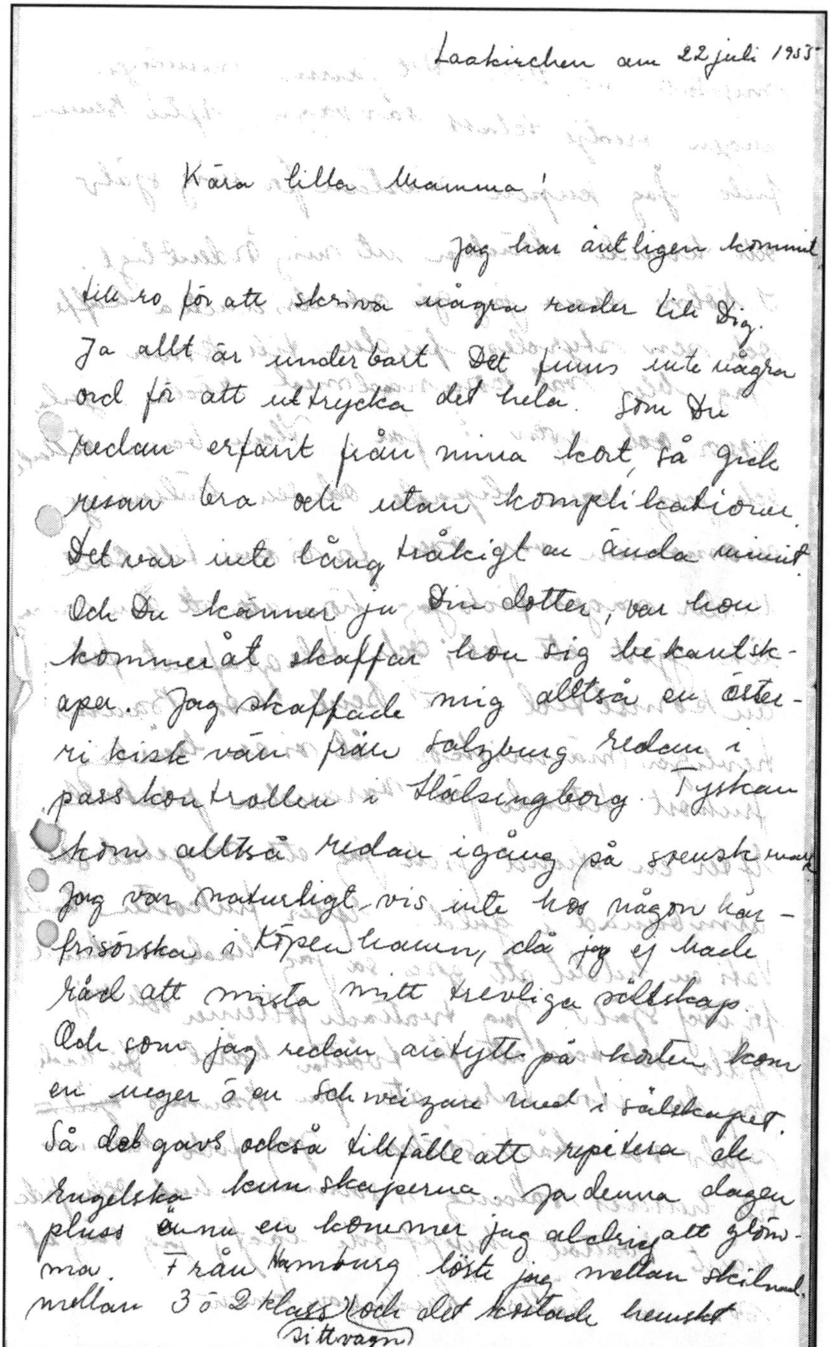

Laakirchen am 22 juli 1955

Kära lilla Mamma!

Jag har äntligen kommit till ro för att skriva några rader till Dig. Ja allt är underbart. Det finns inte några ord för att uttrycka det hela. Som Du redan erfarit från mina kort, så gick resan bra och utan komplikationer. Det var inte långtråkigt en ända minut. Och Du känner ju Din dotter, var hon kommer åt skaffar hon sig bekantskaper. Jag skaffade mig alltså en österrikisk vän från Salzburg redan i passkontrollen i Hälsingborg. Tyskan kom alltså redan igång på svensk mark. Jag var naturligtvis inte hos någon hårfrisörska i Köpenhamn, då jag ej hade råd att mista mitt trevliga sällskap. Och som jag redan antytt på korten, kom en neger o en Schweizare med i sällskapet. Så det gavs också tillfälle att repetera de engelska kunskaperna. Ja denna dagen plus ännu en kommer jag aldrig att glömma. Från Hamburg löste jag mellanskilnad mellan 3 o 2 klass sittvagn och det kostade hemskt

Ingrid's letter to Mother written while she was traveling around with Father for three weeks in order to get to know him again. It was written from Laakirchen, Austria on July 22, 1955.

28240670R00163

Made in the USA
Charleston, SC
05 April 2014